# Acclaim for
## *Who Controls the Internet?:*
## *Illusions of a Borderless World*

"It is time that America learn an important lesson about the Internet—that however cyber the space is, it is also real, and subject to real space governments. This is the very best work to make this fundamental point. Goldsmith and Wu have made understandable and accessible an argument political culture should have realized a decade ago."—Lawrence Lessig, author of *Code* and *Free Culture*

"Jack Goldsmith and Tim Wu are among the most creative and provocative legal scholars of their generation. In this surprising, unsentimental, and ultimately optimistic book, they reject romantic abstractions about the globalizing and transformative power of the Internet. National laws, traditions, and customs are just as important in controlling cyber-space as they are in real space, they argue. And that's a good thing because decentralized control can encourage freedom, diversity, and self-determination. Combining realism with idealism, *Who Controls the Internet?* offers an adult manifesto for the future of freedom in an interconnected world."—Jeffrey Rosen, author of *The Naked Crowd*

"A major contribution to literature about the Internet. . . . an excellent addition to academic law libraries as well as other academic, firm, or large county libraries with collections that emphasize cyber law, intellectual property, digital copyright, and international law."—*Law Library Journal*

"Goldsmith and Wu have written a concise, compact, and highly readable book canvassing more than their basic question of 'who controls the Internet.' It is a sweeping review of all of the key concerns of Internet history, lore and law over the last 20 years."—*Melbourne University Law Review*

"Jack Goldsmith and Tim Wu have written an informative, engaging and provocative book that will undoubtedly challenge most people's preconceptions of the Internet. This is the most important book about the politics of the Internet since Lawrence Lessig's *Code*."—Daniel W. Drezner, University of Chicago and *danieldrezner.com*

# Who Controls the Internet?

*Illusions of a Borderless World*

JACK GOLDSMITH AND TIM WU

OXFORD
UNIVERSITY PRESS

# OXFORD
UNIVERSITY PRESS

Oxford University Press, Inc., publishes works that
further Oxford University's objective of excellence
in research, scholarship, and education.

Oxford  New York
Auckland   Cape Town   Dar es Salaam   Hong Kong   Karachi
Kuala Lumpur   Madrid   Melbourne   Mexico City   Nairobi
New Delhi   Shanghai   Taipei   Toronto

With offices in
Argentina   Austria   Brazil   Chile   Czech Republic   France   Greece
Guatemala   Hungary   Italy   Japan   Poland   Portugal   Singapore
South Korea   Switzerland   Thailand   Turkey   Ukraine   Vietnam

First published by Oxford University Press, Inc., 2006
198 Madison Avenue, New York, NY 10016

www.oup.com

First issued as an Oxford University Press paperback, 2008

Oxford is a registered trademark of Oxford University Press

Library of Congress Cataloging-in-Publication Data
Goldsmith, Jack L.
Who controls the internet? : illusions of a borderless world /
Jack Goldsmith and Tim Wu.
p. cm.
ISBN 978-0-19-534064-8 (pbk.)
1. Internet—Social aspects.
2. Internet—Government policy.
3. Internet—Law and legislation.
I. Wu, Tim.
II. Title.
HM851.G65 2006    303.48'33—dc22    2005027404

9 8 7 6 5 4 3 2 1
Printed in the United States of America
on acid-free paper

*To our friend Larry Lessig*

# Preface to the Paperback Edition

Since we published *Who Controls the Internet?* in 2006, enough has happened in the fight to control the Internet to fill another volume. If anything, the tensions between State power and the challenges posed by the Internet have become more interesting.

Since 2006 the "net neutrality" movement has been a dominant Internet story in the United States, illustrating an important theme of the book: the paradox of government power being used to prevent Internet regulation and censorship. The net neutrality movement, with some similarities to the environmental movement, asks the U.S. government to protect the original, unpredictable, and uncontrolled nature of the Internet. The contrast is clear: in the 1990s, activists were saying that it was impossible for the government to control the Internet. Now in the 2000s, many (including one of us) have demanded that the government act to protect the Internet from perceived threats—whether from telecom firms or foreign governments. That attitude toward government confirms the difference a decade has made. It also shows a deep split between different brands of Internet libertarianism: one that distrusts government and one that mistrusts private gatekeepers such as Bell and cable companies.

In the summer of 2007 one of us (Wu) went to visit Google's Beijing offices, in the northern part of the city. Its sizeable offices are the mark of a surprising change. In the early 2000s, it was rival Yahoo that tried to take on the Chinese market and in the process found itself trying to juggle the contradictory sovereign commands of the United States and China. That venture was a failure, and under pressure from Congress, bad publicity in the United States, and a U.S. lawsuit challenging its China practices, Yahoo retreated from China, selling its China business to a local company in which Yahoo owns a 40 percent stake.

Since then, Google has in most ways taken Yahoo's place as the lead American Internet firm in China. Google is determined not to repeat Yahoo's mistakes—but whether it can do so is another story. Google entered China in 2006 with a censored version of its search product that was in obvious tension with the whole idea of Google as a way to find information. The capitulation to state power was obvious. As Google freely admits, it cannot run a business in China without being physically in China. "It really is a choice between boycott or mak[ing] ugly compromises," said Andrew McLaughlin, Google's senior policy counsel. If Google doesn't operate in China, "then you're not advancing the goal of providing more information to more people."[1] As Google continued to comply with China's censorship restrictions, it found itself lobbying another sovereign—the U.S. government—to include prohibitions on China-like Internet censorship in U.S. free trade agreements.[2] Like the net neutrality movement, Google finds itself seeking State support to preserve freedom of information on the Internet.

Of course it is not just China that regulates content on the Net. An important study of State-controlled Internet filtering by scholars at Harvard, Cambridge, Oxford, and Toronto universities was published in the summer of 2007.[3] It concluded that there is a global trend of enhanced government filtering of the Net: in the number of countries engaging in filtering; in the variety of sites and activities limited by them; and in the level of sophistication that governments are willing to deploy to effect their blocks. Twenty-six countries of forty exhaustively tested around the world were found to filter citizens' Internet access in 2005 and 2006. The filters were frequently implemented for political reasons distinct to each country: South Korea filters pro–North Korean sites; China filters material on Tibet, Taiwan, and Tiananmen, as well as mundane mistakes by local officials; Saudi Arabia, Tunisia, Iran, and Yemen filter material deemed socially offensive or destabilizing to local norms, including information about drugs, Christianity, and sexually transmitted diseases.

Meanwhile the United States continues to take a comparatively hands-off posture toward the Net, but with an increasing number of exceptions. In 2006 the United States passed a strong new law to fight Internet gambling, called the Unlawful Internet Gambling Enforcement Act of 2006. The effect on the industry was immediate and immense—most sites stopped accepting American customers immediately. One industry insider wrote: "This law is the equivalent of the 1929 stock market crash in terms of its impact on the game, its people, and associated business."[4]

In the name of national security, the United States has continued to force search engines and Internet Service providers to turn over information needed for law enforcement, about using credit card intermediaries to regulate banned Internet transactions, and about employing spyware and related technologies to monitor illegal Net activities. All of these top-down pressures continue the trend toward a balkanized Internet.

In the copyright world, the Napster wars largely subsided with, as we suggested, iTunes and other legalized online music sites as the compromise. Naturally, pirate sites persist, and at a much higher level than, say, in 1995, but they do not threaten to become the dominant means of distribution. Meanwhile, in Web video, a different story has played out, as media companies try to figure out whether widespread "piracy" of their shows on YouTube is actually good or bad for them. At the time of writing, companies were mixed: firms like NBC were voluntarily handing over content, and others, like Viacom, were trying to sue YouTube out of existence. More broadly, media firms seem to have loosened their "zero tolerance" policies toward casual and noncommercial use of content on the web. In this area, law enforcement has abated in many areas, but State-enforced copyright remains the fundamental baseline, as we explained in the hardcover edition.

ICANN's effective control by the U.S. government continues to be controversial, especially after ICANN nixed an "xxx" top-level domain for porn, allegedly under pressure from the U.S. government. In fall 2006 the United States and ICANN agreed to a new three-year contract. As it did at ICANN's formation in 1998, the U.S. government once again promised eventually to transition ICANN to full private control, and this time many seem to believe it. But we strongly suspect that the need for security for the naming and numbering system will leave ICANN under some form of state control, although the United States might well continue its moves to share this control with other governments.

Partially in response to the State's making its presence known on the Net, private parties have continued to employ filtering and geo-location technology for legal compliance purposes. Firms like www.blockacountry.com have made it easier for Webmasters to configure Web sites to block access by country. Placing geographical restrictions on content has spread to poker and gambling sites, which seek to exclude U.S. players; to iTunes, MTV online, and other U.S. broadcast networks, which seek to control the geographical spread of copyrighted materials; and to newspapers, which seek to avoid publication in places where they might run afoul of local laws. These geo-identification technologies remain imperfect but, of course, need not be perfect to be useful. Meanwhile, however, geographic circumvention technologies like Psiphon and Tor/ Blossom have also improved. It remains unclear how the arms race between geography-specifying and geography-defeating technologies will play out.

The close cooperation between private Internet firms and the State to control unwanted activities on the Net also grew since the hardcover edition. eBay now has 2,000 people working worldwide to tackle fraud and scams on its service,[5] and it works more aggressively than ever with law enforcement officials. The relationship is so close, in fact, that in many places eBay is training law enforcement officials how to monitor Internet fraud.[6]

These developments largely confirm the main themes of the hardcover edition: the importance of governmental coercion to Internet activities; the trend toward geographical bordering of the Internet as a result of top-down government coercion and bottom-up consumer demand; and the many virtues, and undeniable vices, of a bordered Net. The next decade will teach us still more about the interactions between State power and communications networks; we hope that *Who Controls the Internet?* will remain a guide to what happened when law and the Internet first met.

# Preface

The new technologies will bring "every individual . . . into immediate and effortless communication with every other," "practically obliterate" political geography, and make free trade universal. Thanks to technological advance, "there [are] no longer any foreigners," and we can look forward to "the gradual adoption of a common language."[1]

The invention of the telegraph inspired these words. One hundred years later, another technological revolution inspired their resurrection. In the 1990s, academics, corporate executives, and pundits of all stripes viewed the Internet as the leading edge of a new globalization that was eroding the authority and relevance of national governments. The Internet's arrival seemed to herald a new way of ordering human affairs that would free us forever from the tyranny of territorial rule.

This book depicts the fate of these ideas. It tells the story of the Internet's challenge to nation-state rule in the 1990s, and the ensuing battles by national governments to assert control over the great borderless medium. It is the story of the death of the dream of self-governing cyber-communities that would escape geography forever. It is also the story of the birth and early years of a new kind of Internet—a bordered network where territorial law, government power, and international relations matter as much as technological invention.

By the mid-2000s, where our story ends, the network had undergone profound changes. The American-dominated English-language Internet of the 1990s had grown to reflect the different values, languages, and interests of hundreds of millions of new users around the globe. The Internet's architecture had been shaped by the whims and obsessions of powerful governments in the United States, China, and Europe. And questions of Internet governance had come to be characterized by clashes among the great powers and their network ideologies.

Three themes emerge from this narrative. The first is that even for the most revolutionary global communication technologies, geography and governmental coercion retain fundamental importance. In the 1990s, many believed that nations could not control the local effects of unwanted Internet communications that originated outside their borders, and thus could not enforce national laws related to speech, crime, copyright, and much more. But the last ten years have shown that national governments have an array of techniques for controlling offshore Internet communications, and thus enforcing their laws, by exercising coercion within their borders.

Our second theme is that the Internet is splitting apart and becoming bordered. Far from flattening the world, the Internet—its language, its content, its norms—is conforming to local conditions. The result is an Internet that differs among nations and regions that are increasingly separated by walls of bandwidth, language, and filters. This bordered Internet reflects top-down pressures from governments that are imposing national laws on the Internet within their borders. It also reflects bottom-up pressures from individuals in different places who demand an Internet that corresponds to local preferences, and from the web page operators and other content providers who shape the Internet experience to satisfy these demands.

Many lament the death of the borderless Internet. Our third theme is that, contrary to what many expect, the geographically bordered Internet has many underappreciated virtues. Citizens want their government to prevent them from harming one another on the Internet and to block Internet harms from abroad. Companies need a legal environment that guarantees stability in the network and permits Internet commerce to flourish. The bordered Internet accommodates real and important differences among peoples in different places, and makes the Internet a more effective and useful communication tool as a result.

There are downsides to the bordered Internet. As governments increase their control, they replicate their vices on the Internet. Authoritarian China has used the network as a device of political control and economic self-aggrandizement. Even in democratic societies, government interventions on the Net can reflect the corruptions and imperfections of the political process. We do not discount these and other vices. But we do think that the death of the 1990s vision of an anarchic Internet should be mourned only a little, for on the whole decentralized rule by nation-states reflects what most people want. Something has been lost, but much has been gained.

The Internet age is characterized by the incessant search for the newest "new thing." Our story, by contrast, is about old things—the enduring relevance of territory and physical coercion, and ancient principles governing law and politics within nations, and cooperation and conflict between them. Territorial government is a persistent fact of human history that accommodates humanity in its diversity and allows it to flourish. Behind the mists and magic of the Internet lies an older and stronger order whose relevance remains inescapable.

# Contents

# one 1

## *Introduction*
Yahoo!

Marc Knobel is a French Jew who has devoted his life to fighting neo-Nazism, a fight that has taken him repeatedly to the Internet and American websites. In February 2000, Knobel was sitting in Paris, searching the Web for Nazi memorabilia. He went to the auction site of yahoo.com, where to his horror he saw page after page of swastika arm bands, SS daggers, concentration camp photos, and even replicas of the Zyklon B gas canisters. He had found a vast collection of Nazi mementos, for sale and easily available in France but hosted on a computer in the United States by the Internet giant Yahoo.[1]

Two years earlier, Knobel had discovered Nazi hate sites on America Online and threatened a public relations war. AOL closed the sites, and Knobel assumed that a similar threat against Yahoo would have a similar effect. He was wrong. AOL, it turned out, was atypical. Located in the Washington, D.C. suburbs, AOL had always been sensitive to public relations, politics, and the realities of government power. It was more careful than most Internet companies about keeping offensive information off its sites.

Yahoo, in contrast, was a product of Silicon Valley's 1990s bubble culture. From its origins as the hobby of Stanford graduate students Jerry Yang and David Filo, Yahoo by 2000 had grown to be the mighty "Lord of the Portals." At the time, Yahoo was the Internet entrance point for more users than any other website, with a stock price, as 2000 began, of $475 per share.[2] Yang, Yahoo's billionaire leader, was confident and brash—he "liked the general definition of a yahoo: 'rude,

1

unsophisticated, uncouth.'"[3] Obsessed with expanding market share, he thought government dumb, and speech restrictions dumber still. Confronted by an obscure activist complaining about hate speech and invoking French law, Yang's company shrugged its high-tech shoulders.

Mark Knobel was not impressed. On April 11, 2000, he sued Yahoo in a French court on behalf of the International League against Racism and Anti-Semitism and others. Yahoo's auctions, he charged, violated a French law banning trafficking in Nazi goods in France. "In the United States [these auctions] might not be illegal," said Knobel, "but as soon as you cross the French border, it's absolutely illegal"[4] Ronald Katz, a lawyer representing the French groups, added, "There is this naïve idea that the Internet changes everything. It doesn't change everything. It doesn't change the laws in France."[5]

Yahoo received a summons from Le Tribunal de Grande Instance de Paris, Judge Jean-Jacques Gomez presiding. "The French tribunal wants to impose a judgment in an area over which it has no control," reacted Jerry Yang.[6] Yang's public relations team warned of the terrible consequences of allowing national governments to control content on the Internet. If French laws applied to a website in America, then presumably so would German and Japanese regulations, not to mention Saudi and Chinese law. "It is very difficult to do business if you have to wake up every day and say 'OK, whose laws do I follow?'" said Heather Killen, a Yahoo vice president. "We have many countries and many laws and just one Internet."[7]

Jerry Yang embraced 1990s conventional wisdom in thinking that Judge Gomez could legitimately exercise power only in France, and could not control what Yahoo put on its servers in California. French officials, he thought, simply had no authority over a computer in the United States.

Yahoo's Nazi web pages also seemed hard for French officials to stop at the French border. "The volume of electronic communications crossing territorial boundaries is just too great in relation to the resources available to government authorities," wrote David Post and David Johnson, two proponents of a "sovereign" Internet.[8] Even if French officials identified and blocked the offending offshore website, the same information could be posted on mirror sites outside France.

Moreover, the Internet's decentralized routing system was designed to carry messages from point to point even if intermediate communication exchanges are blocked, damaged, or destroyed. "The net interprets censorship as damage, and routes around it," John Gilmore famously declared.[9] To keep out the Nazi pages France would need to shut down every single Internet access point within its borders—seemingly an impossible task. And even this wouldn't have worked, because determined users in France could access the Net by a telephone call to an Internet access provider in another country.

For these reasons, the Internet seemed in the 1990s to have shattered the historical congruence between individual conduct and government power. Some, like Jerry Yang, were sanguine about this development. But many were alarmed. In the midst of the Yahoo trial, Paul Krugman wrote a *New York Times* column about the Net's threat to traditional copyright and tax laws. Internet technology is "erasing boundaries" and undermining government power, he warned. "Something serious, and troubling, is happening—and I haven't heard any good ideas about what to do about it."[10] In the late 1990s, there was broad agreement that the Internet's challenge to government's authority would diminish the nation-state's relevance. "It's not that laws aren't relevant, it's that the nation-state is not relevant," argued Nicholas Negroponte, the co-founder and director of MIT's Media Lab. "The Internet," he concluded, "cannot be regulated."[11]

Yahoo's fearlessness before Judge Gomez thus seemed justified. By the standards of the day, Knobel's effort to stop Yahoo from violating French law seemed dated, ridiculous, and destined to fail.

Paris's Tribunal de Grande Instance is on the Ile de la Cité, the cradle of Parisian civilization, just a few blocks from the Notre Dame Cathedral. It is housed in the beautiful but haunting Palais de Justice, where Marie Antoinette and thousands of others were incarcerated before being guillotined during a different revolution. It was in this ancient building that Yahoo's lawyers would defend the Internet's conventional wisdom against the tradition and glory of the French State.

In Judge Gomez's courtroom, it became clear that the irrelevance of the nation-state would not go uncontested. Knobel's lawyers asserted that France had the sovereign right to defend itself from the sale of illegal Nazi merchandise from the United States, and asked

Palais de Justice, where the Yahoo case was litigated (Martial Colomb/Getty Images)

Yahoo to explain why it ought be exempt from French law. As one anti-Nazi lawyer put it, "French law does not permit racism in writing, on television or on the radio, and I see no reason to have an exception for the Internet."[12]

This simple argument threw Yahoo on its heels. If Yahoo caused harm in France, why should it be any more immune from regulations in different nations than "real-space" multinational firms? The Ford Motor Company must obey the varying safety and environmental laws of the many countries in which it sells cars. Why should Yahoo be exempt from laws in the countries where it does business?

Yahoo responded with an "impossibility" defense. If Ford found French environmental regulations too costly, it could stop selling cars in France without suffering harm in other markets. But Yahoo claimed that its situation was different. It maintained a French-language website (yahoo.fr) that complied with French law. But it also had a U.S. website that the French could visit. And unlike Ford, Yahoo argued, it had no power to identify where in the world its "customers" were from and thus no control over where in the world its digital products go. Were Yahoo forced to comply with French law, it would need to remove the Nazi items from its U.S. server, thereby depriving Yahoo users everywhere from buying them, and making French law the effective rule for the world.

On May 22, 2000, Judge Gomez issued a decision that, on a preliminary basis, rejected Yahoo's arguments. He ruled that Yahoo's U.S. websites violated French law, and he ordered Yahoo "to take all necessary measures to dissuade and make impossible" visits by French web surfers to the illegal Yahoo Nazi auction sites on yahoo.com.[13]

But Yahoo remained defiant. "We are not going to change the content of our sites in the United States just because someone in France is asking us to do so," reacted Jerry Yang.[14] The trial wasn't

Jerry Yang (Robyn Beck/AFP/Getty Images)

over yet, and the ability of Yahoo to filter its users by geography would be the key issue. And on this issue, Yahoo felt confident. Said Yang, "Asking us to filter access to our sites according to the nationality of web surfers is very naïve."[15]

Yahoo's "impossibility" argument reflected turn-of-century assumptions about the architecture of the Internet. The Net was not built with physical geography in mind. Neither Internet Protocol Addresses (each computer's Internet ID), nor Internet domain names (such as mcdonalds.com or cnn.com), nor e-mail addresses, were designed to dependably indicate the geographical location of computers on the Net. Even domain names and e-mail addresses with geographical clues—such as toystore.co.fr, or tonyblair@gov.uk—were unreliable. The toy store web page might be located on a computer in Germany (and the data might be cached in dozens of nations), or might be sold or re-assigned to an entity outside France. Prime Minister Blair, meanwhile, could have been reading his e-mail on vacation in Italy, or while visiting the United States.

These architectural "facts" meant that users of 1990s Internet technology could not know where in the world their e-mail messages and web pages were being viewed, and thus what laws in which nations they might be violating. "In Cyberspace, physical borders no longer function as signposts informing individuals of the obligations assumed by entering a new, legally significant, place," said Johnson and Post in 1997.[16] One reason why it seemed unfair for France to apply its laws to Yahoo was that Yahoo didn't know where particular users were, and thus didn't know which laws it should be complying with.

France's attempt to govern Yahoo seemed unfair for another reason. Internet firms and users confronted with a bevy of conflicting national laws could reasonably be expected to comply with the strictest among them in order to avoid legal jeopardy. The ultimate effect of territorial control of the Net thus seemed to be a tyranny of unreasonable governments. "We now risk a race to the bottom," said Alan Davidson of the Center for Democracy and Technology about the *Yahoo* case. "The most restrictive rules about Internet content—influenced by any country — could have an impact on people around the world." [17]

There's an old European joke that captures the problem. In heaven, the joke goes, you find French cooks, English government, Swiss trains, and Italian lovers. In Hell, by contrast, you find French government, Italian trains, English chefs, and Swiss lovers. Territorial control of the Internet seemed to promise a parallel version of legal hell: a world of Singaporean free speech, American tort law, Russian commercial regulation, and Chinese civil rights.

Judge Gomez gave Yahoo two months to figure out how to block French surfers. During this recess, Cyril Houri, the founder of a fledgling American firm called Infosplit, contacted the plaintiff's lawyer, Stephane Lilti, and told him that he had developed a new technology that could identify and screen Internet content on the basis of its geographical source. Houri flew to Paris and demonstrated his technology on Lilti's computer. The men blinked and peered into the screen, astonished. Yahoo's servers, which the firm had claimed were protected by the U.S. First Amendment to the U.S. Constitution, were actually located on a website in Stockholm! Yahoo had placed a constantly updated "mirror" copy of its U.S. site in Sweden to make access to the site in Europe faster.[18]

When the trial resumed on July 24, Yahoo lawyers again asserted that it was technically impossible to identify and filter out French visitors to the firm's U.S.-based websites. Lilti responded by discussing Houri's geo-location technology in the courtroom. Yahoo auctions in France, he argued, were not in fact coming from servers in the United States. The assumption that every web page was equally accessible to every computer user everywhere in the world, Lilti claimed, was simply wrong. If Yahoo could target French users from Swedish servers, it could potentially identify users by geography and, if it liked, screen them out.

Judge Gomez responded cautiously to this seemingly audacious claim and appointed three Internet experts—Vinton Cerf, the "father" of the Internet, Ben Laurie, a British Internet expert, and Francois Wallon, a French technologist—to assess the extent to which Yahoo could block transmissions into France. The experts' report was devastating. It relied on the state of technology in late 2000—namely Houri's IP-identification technology, and self-reporting about nationality—and concluded Yahoo could effectively screen out 90 percent of French users.[19]

Based on this report, Judge Gomez issued a landmark final decision on November 20, 2000, that reaffirmed that Yahoo had violated

French law by allowing Nazi goods to appear for sale on web pages there.[20] The judge determined that the French court had power over Yahoo and its servers because the company had taken conscious steps to direct the prohibited Nazi auction pages into France. He pointed out that Yahoo greeted French visitors to its U.S. website with French-language advertisements. This showed both that Yahoo was tailoring content for France, and that it could to some extent identify and screen users by geography.[21] The court acknowledged that 100 percent blocking was impossible, and ordered Yahoo to make a reasonable "best effort" to block French users.[22]

Yahoo remained indignant. It announced that it would ignore Judge Gomez's decision unless a U.S. court made it do otherwise.[23] A month after the decision, it filed a counter-lawsuit in the United States meant to block the French judgment. "We hope that a U.S. judge will confirm that a non-U.S. court does not have the authority to tell a U.S. company how to operate," said Yahoo France's managing director Philippe Guillanton.[24]

But the company had a problem. While Yahoo thought it would be impossible for a French court to exercise power in the United States, Yahoo also had assets in France, including income from a sizeable French subsidiary, at risk of seizure.[25] Judge Gomez warned the firm that it had until February 2001 to comply before facing fines of 100,000 francs (about $13,000) per day.[26] Yahoo executives, who make frequent trips to Europe and who would be subject to legal process there, began to think things through.

On January 2, 2001, Yahoo abruptly surrendered. It pulled all Nazi materials from its auction sites, announcing that it "will no longer allow items that are associated with groups which promote or glorify hatred and violence, to be listed on any of Yahoo's commerce properties."[27] It weakly asserted that it was motivated by bad publicity from the Nazi auctions, and not the French ruling. "Society as a whole has rejected such groups," said a Yahoo spokesperson.[28] But the timing and threat of French sanctions suggest otherwise—that Yahoo's will had broken.

Soon after Judge Gomez's decision, Yahoo's resistance to geographical screening began to wane. In June 2001, Yahoo announced a deal with Akamai, a content delivery company, to use the firm's geographical identification technology to deliver geographically targeted advertising, in order to "increase advertising relevance."[29] One of Yahoo's lawyers, Mary Wirth, had the unenviable job of explaining the firm's contradictions on geo-ID. "We argued that . . . it's not a 100 percent accurate solution for the French court order because we would have to identify (French citizens) with 100 percent accuracy, and that's not possible. [However,] the technology is perfectly appropriate for ad targeting purposes."[30]

And then Yahoo took the next step. In 1999, it had established a new venture in a new place: the People's Republic of China. When Yahoo first entered the Chinese market, it announced that Yahoo China would "give Internet users in China easy access to a range of Yahoo's popular services tailored to meet the needs of this audience."[31] But the Chinese government had its own ideas about what its citizens needed. As a condition of market access, it eventually demanded that Yahoo filter materials that might be harmful or threatening to Party rule. The Chinese government, in effect, asked Yahoo to serve as Internet censor for the Communist party.

We do not know if there was a long internal debate at Yahoo, or whether the company searched its libertarian soul before deciding to go forward. But we do know that in 2002, Yahoo was not the brash and confident firm it had been just a few years earlier. By end of the summer of 2002, Yahoo shares, valued at $475 in 2000, were now trading at $9.71.[32] A new and better search engine, Google, whose motto was "don't be evil," had become the new darling of Internet information retrieval. Yahoo had to do something, and the Chinese market looked to be the future.

In the summer of 2002, Yahoo quietly agreed to China's demands. It signed a document called the *Public Pledge on Self-Discipline for the Chinese Internet Industry* in which it promised to "inspect and monitor the information on domestic and foreign Websites" and "refuse access to those Websites that disseminate harmful information to protect the Internet users of China from the adverse influences of the information"[33] Ken Roth, the executive director of Human Rights Watch, criticized Yahoo for promising "to identify and prevent the transmission of virtually any information that Chinese authorities or companies deem objectionable."[34]

By 2005 Yahoo had come full circle. The darling of the Internet free speech movement had become an agent of thought control for the Chinese government. Yahoo today provides Chinese citizens with a full suite of censored products. Its Chinese search engines do not return full results, but block sites deemed threatening to the public order. Yahoo's popular chat rooms feature software filters designed to catch banned phrases like "multi-party elections" or "Taiwanese independence." It also employs human and software censors to monitor chat room conversations. All this led the group Reporters without Borders in 2004 to label Yahoo a "Chinese police auxiliary."[35]

In the fall of 2005, Chinese Journalist Shi Tao sent an e-mail to a democracy website in the United States. He attached to the e-mail a memorandum recording a Communist party meeting that discussed ways to deal with the anniversary of Tiananmen Square. But Shi Tao made a serious mistake—he used his Yahoo e-mail account to send the document. When Chinese authorities discovered it on the website in the United States, they asked Yahoo to help identify its sender. Yahoo complied, and Tao was thrown in prison for ten years. How did Jerry Yang, the one-time champion of Internet freedom, explain his company's new role? "To be doing business in China, or anywhere else in the world, we have to comply with local law," explained Yang. "I do not like the outcome of what happens with these things," Yang added. "But we have to follow the law."[36]

The Yahoo story encapsulates the Internet's transformation from a technology that resists territorial law to one that facilitates its enforcement. But the Internet's challenge to the nation-state was much more profound than the Yahoo story suggests, and the nation-state's response has been much more complex and, at times, tentative. To understand the transformations of the past decade, we must begin by examining why so many people believed that the Internet might transcend territorial law and render the nation-state obsolete. This is the task of part 1.

*Part 1*

# The Internet Revolution

# 2

two

## Visions of a Post–
## Territorial Order

A decade before the *Yahoo* case, two men in different parts of America began to use the Internet for the first time. One was Julian Dibbell, a New Yorker and pop music writer who covered technology issues for the *Village Voice*. The other was John Perry Barlow of Wyoming, a libertarian, lyricist, and cattle rancher who looked the years he had spent traveling with the Grateful Dead. Dibbell and Barlow were very different people. Dibbell, born in the 1960s, was a member of what people in the '90s called Generation X. Barlow was writing rock-and-roll songs when Dibbell was born, and he never lost the passion or political purpose of the 1960s. But the two had this in common: neither were native computer geeks, and both were lucid, even lyrical writers who wanted to communicate the Internet experience to regular people. In popular magazines like *Wired* and the *Village Voice*, they did just this.

Dibbell and Barlow became the great explorers of the cyberspace age. Like Henry Stanley, the Welsh-American journalist who famously recounted his expeditions in Africa, Dibbell and Barlow had discovered an exotic place and wanted to tell others about it. As with any explorers, the tales they brought back reflected their own experience and assumptions more than objective reality. Nonetheless, these stories articulated a powerful vision: a new frontier, where people lived in peace, under their own rules, liberated from the constraints of an oppressive society and free from government meddling.

Through the writings and actions of Dibbell, Barlow, and others, this chapter and the next depict the era when it was widely believed that cyberspace might challenge the authority of nation-states and move the world to a new, post-territorial system. Today, notions of a self-governing cyberspace are largely discredited. But the historical significance of these ideas cannot be ignored. They had an enormous impact on Internet writers and thinkers, firms, and even the U.S. Supreme Court—an influence that is still with us today. To understand the reality and forgotten virtues of territorial government, we must first understand the possibilities and attractions of a place once called cyberspace.

## Confronting Mr. Bungle

In 1993, back when "Information Superhighway" was still a popular term, Julian Dibbell wrote "A Rape in Cyberspace." It was a story of how "an Evil Clown, a Haitian Trickster Spirit, Two Wizards, and a Cast of Dozens Turned a Database Into a Society."[1] The story's central premise—that the Internet can evolve its own systems of government superior to those of "real-space"—has had a lasting impact. As the influential Internet scholar Lawrence Lessig would say years later, "Dibbell's story is why I teach cyberlaw."[2]

Dibbell taught about Net self-governance through the experiences of the virtual, interactive worlds called "multiple user dungeons," or MUDs. MUDs, the predecessors of today's hugely popular online games (like *EverQuest* or *Sims Online*), were text-based worlds accessible through the Internet. This was the era of the immersive Net, the true age of cyberspace, when people logged on to build online identities and virtual homes, and more importantly, to meet and hang out with others. Though you couldn't actually see or touch anything (other than a keyboard and screen), MUDs worked on something more powerful: collective imagination. Users sometimes called MUDs a "shared hallucination."[3]

"A Rape in Cyberspace" was a true story—the history of a real and rather famous MUD called LambdaMOO. Physically, LambdaMOO ran on a server near Stanford in Xerox's famous Palo Alto Research Center (PARC). But virtually, LambaMOO was set up as a giant home, open to all, located in cyberspace. Dibbell described it as "a very large and very busy rustic mansion built entirely of words."[4] It was here that a thousand or so regulars, logging in from all corners of the earth, became a virtual community. They all had made-up personalities, but their lives in the MUD, though virtual, were vividly real. Dibbell-the-observer soon began to love LambdaMOO and relish his life there.

Dibbell's story was about LambdaMOO's first real social crisis. It revolved around "Mr. Bungle," a "fat, oleaginous, Bisquick-faced clown," whose habit was to humiliate and even "rape" other users.[5] His tool was a tiny "voodoo doll" that allowed him to take control of people and make them do disgusting things. One victim was legba, "a Haitian trickster spirit of indeterminate gender, brown-skinned and wearing an expensive pearl gray suit, top hat, and dark glasses." Another was Starsinger, "a rather pointedly nondescript female character, tall, stout, and brown-haired." Under the control of his voodoo doll, legba was made to eat pubic hair while Starsinger violated herself with a steak knife. Bungle's acts, while not physical rapes, were very painful nonetheless.

The antics and abuses of Mr. Bungle made MUD participants realize that their ungoverned world wasn't working. Bungle was single-handedly wrecking what made LambdaMOO fun by bringing in the abuse and shame from which a MUD was meant to be an escape. Bungle was like the kid who won't play by the rules and ruins everything for everyone else. As legba wrote on the message board, "I tend to think that restrictive measures around here cause more trouble than they prevent. But I also think that Mr. Bungle was being a vicious, vile fuckhead, and I . . . want his sorry ass scattered from #17 to the Cinder Pile."

While the community argued about what to do, a senior MUD administrator, known as a Wizard, took unilateral action. One day, he destroyed, or "toaded," the wanton Mr. Bungle, permanently eliminating the character from the community. But the Bungle experience led to a kind of political awakening on LambdaMOO. Users scattered around the globe began to realize they needed rules to govern their virtual community. Slowly, hesitantly, but with increasing deliberation and self-consciousness, they created a nascent political community untied to physical space but with basic rules of voting, conduct, and dispute resolution. Dibbell's assessment was optimistic. We should, he said, "look without illusion upon the present possibilities for building, in the on-line spaces of this world, societies more decent and free than those mapped onto dirt and concrete and capital."[6]

This parable of cyberjustice captured two important ideas. The first was an influential and charismatic metaphor, that of the Internet as a "place." This metaphor, which still pervades discussions of Internet governance, originated in the early days of the Net when it did genuinely feel separate from the real world. In those days (the late 1980s and early 1990s) the Internet really was more like cyberspace. People in those days didn't use the Net to buy books or make airplane reservations. They used it to participate in communities of people who rarely met face-to-face but who got to know one another intimately. Whether it was participating in a MUD, playing online computer games, posting to "bulletin boards," or talking in early "chat" programs, the experience was self-contained. Whatever the consequences "there," from swapping programming ideas or arguing about the causes of World War I, there would be no consequences "here," in what they called "meatspace." This autonomous and often vibrant communal experience naturally led to the belief that this place could, and should, be governed by the users that constituted it.

Dibbell's parable was also the beginning of a constructive vision of governance liberated from physical and national identity—that is, from our actual bodies and their physical location. These ideas may seem a bit abstract, even nutty. But for many early Internet users and thinkers, they marked the deepest promise of the Internet revolution.

Everyone has a physical appearance, and everyone is born somewhere; these are two facts over which we have little control. Even in the most open real-space societies, where we are born and what we look like influence our life paths and prospects—the kind of opportunities we get, how we are treated by others, the extent to which those around us share our values and commitments. A liberal view of the good society says that individuals should be able to shape their lives as they wish, provided that such choices respect the dignity of others. Just as you choose your mate, your job, and your favorite brand of soda-pop, you should be free to minimize the relevance of how you look and where you live.

This is very hard to do in real space, within the traditional system of territorial governance. For most people, physical traits are difficult to alter, and moving to a different and more congenial geographical community—assuming one exists—is too expensive or psychologically difficult. But as the MUD experience showed, the Internet can render these morally irrelevant physical qualities *actually* irrelevant. Bodily appearance and geographical location were meaningless in LambdaMOO. You could alter nearly every aspect of your identity: you could be a man or a woman, young or old, bald or bearded, whatever. With complete control over their identities, people could cluster with congenial souls to create virtual communities. This vision foresaw communities fully liberated from physical space and the constraints of physical identity—the first truly liberated communities in human history.

## The Education of John Perry Barlow

John Perry Barlow has been called many things—a cyberlibertarian, a visionary, a crazy man. In the 1990s, he was the best-known and most controversial exponent of a separate legal regime for cyberspace. He styled himself the Jefferson of his age, and for many, the description fit.

Barlow, like Dibbell, was not a natural-born computer geek. He didn't write code. He wrote lyrics for the Grateful Dead. And instead of spending time in engineering school, he raised cattle on his parents' farm in Wyoming. His first experiences with the online world came in 1987 when, in search of a Dead Head community, he tried out the early online bulletin board Whole Earth 'Lectric Link. As he spent time with people who lived on the Internet, he began to think of the Internet as more than a computer network. He began to think of it as a kind of a place—what he called an "electronic frontier."[7] It reminded him of the American West: unspoiled, self-governing, and best left to inhabitants to run as they pleased.

In the 1990s, Barlow wrote a series of columns in *Wired* magazine and other publications to explain the wonder of the Internet to regular people in regular language. These writings—and especially the notion of a cyberspace with its own rules—would become enormously influential. They also made the Internet, once strictly the preserve of nerds, seem cool, exciting, and intriguing.

Barlow frequently wrote in language that echoed Henry Stanley's African diary. "Imagine" he said, "discovering a continent so vast that it may have no end to its dimensions. Imagine a new world with more resources than all our future greed might exhaust, more opportunities than there will ever be entrepreneurs enough to exploit, and a peculiar kind of real estate that expands with development." And "imagine a place were trespassers leave no footprints, where goods can be stolen an infinite number of times and yet remain in the possession of their original owners, where businesses you never heard of can own the history of your personal affairs, where only children feel completely at home, where the physics is that of thought rather than things, and where everyone is as virtual as the shadows in Plato's cave."[8]

The frontier theme was pervasive. Barlow encouraged young Americans to make their homes in cyberspace: "Jack in. Go to Cyberspace, and go with all the adrenaline and goofy optimism which ought to accompany frontier enterprise."[9] Barlow cautioned that the Electronic Frontier was threatened by territorial government, the "last ditch efforts of the old Industrial Age powers to colonize and subdue Cyberspace."[10] He argued that the "The American Occupation Army of Cyberspace" (by which he meant the National Security Agency) "meticulously observes almost every activity undertaken [in cyberspace], and continuously prevents most who inhabit its domain from drawing any blinds against such observation."[11]

Just as important as Barlow's provocations to explore and defend the new frontier were the institutions he founded to protect this vision. The charismatic Barlow recruited two wealthy technological libertarians who

shared his ideals, Mitch Kapor, the founder of Lotus 1-2-3, and John Gilmore, the first programmer at Sun Microsystems. Together they founded the Electronic Frontier Foundation (EFF), an organization that—through political participation, litigation, education, seminars, and campaigns of various sorts—was devoted to developing the legal conception of cyberspace as a separate place and to defending it from the intrusion of territorial government. As Kapor and Barlow wrote in announcing the establishment of the EFF on July 10, 1990, the EFF was designed to mediate

John Perry Barlow (Declan McCullagh)

the "inevitable conflicts [that] have begun to occur on the border between Cyberspace and the physical world."[12] Barlow later wrote that the EFF would also "help the folks who pass much of their lives there to find practical means for ordering their own affairs."[13]

With the EFF, Barlow hit a nerve and succeeded in attracting some of the Silicon Valley elite who also happened to be some of the wealthiest political libertarians in the country. Early supporters included Bill Joy, the co-founder of Sun Microsystems, Doug Carlson, onetime CEO of Broderbund software, Rob Glaser, former vice-president of Microsoft, and Rockport Shoes magnate Bruce Katz. All were board members, donors, or both. In time, EFF also attracted major corporate donors, emerging as a lobbying voice for libertarian technologists on Capitol Hill. (It later abandoned its lobbying role as too corrupting of its original vision.) Companies like Microsoft, Hewlett-Packard and others became major EFF donors. All were trying to build a legal wall that would separate and protect the Internet from territorial government, and especially from the U.S. government.

The idea of a generalized cyberspace immunity sounded, to legal ears at least, a bit crazy at first. But the EFF had a very important law on its side. The First Amendment to the U.S. Constitution limits the government's ability to regulate speech, and on a communications network like the Internet, *everything* is potentially "speech." A website, e-mail, and even a MUD are all arguably expressive and thus potentially protected by the First Amendment. In the 1990s the EFF managed to fuse together the territorial U.S. First Amendment and the idea of an independent, sovereign cyberspace.

The year 1996 brought what Barlow and others saw as the first great attack on cyberspace. It came clothed as an "indecency regulation" that was known as the "Communications Decency Act" (CDA). The CDA punished all transmission of "indecent" sexual communications or images on the Internet "in a manner available to a person under 18 years of age."[14]

Why was this law viewed as an attack on cyberspace? In 1997 the architecture of the Internet was open without discrimination to children and adults alike. As UCLA law professor Eugene Volokh said at the time, because "there's no way to check readers' ages, short of the expensive (and imperfect) proxy of demanding and verifying their credit card numbers," the CDA "would have essentially banned [all indecent] material . . . from all parts of the Internet except those that charge people for access using credit cards."[15] This seemed like a very broad constraint because most of the Internet at the time was free, and free access was widely viewed as one of the Internet's great strengths.[16] The CDA's constraints seemed much more severe when one considered how its vague definition of "indecency" might chill a great deal of important speech that was unrelated to the protection of minors. Someone communicating on the Internet might, for example, think that the CDA banned discussion of birth control practices, homosexuality, or the consequences of prison rape.[17]

To Barlow, the CDA's incursion on liberty was as offensive as the Stamp Act or the Boston Massacre. On the day after President Clinton signed the act into law, Barlow wrote an angry e-mail to EFF members: "Well, fuck them. Or more to the point, let us now take our leave of them. They have declared war on cyberspace. Let us show them how cunning, baffling, and powerful we can be in our own defense."[18]

Barlow then wrote and distributed his famous sixteen-paragraph *Declaration of Cyberspace Independence*.[19] Modeled after the American Declaration of Independence, it immodestly addressed the "Governments of the Industrial World, you weary giants of flesh and steel." It proclaimed: "I come from Cyberspace, the new home of Mind. On behalf of the future, I ask you of the past to leave us alone. You are not welcome among us. You have no sovereignty where we gather." The declaration recognized that cyberspace had "real conflicts" and "wrongs," but insisted, "We will identify and address them by our means. We are forming our own Social Contract."

Echoing Dibbell, Barlow argued that the cyberspace legal order would reflect ethical deliberation instead of the coercive power that characterized real-space governance. "Our identities have no bodies, so, unlike you, we cannot obtain order by physical coercion. We believe that from ethics, enlightened self-interest, and the commonweal, our governance will emerge." Barlow's goals were not modest: "We will create a civilization of the Mind in Cyberspace. May it be more humane and fair than the world your governments have made before."[20]

Barlow had issued the call for action. The EEF at the time had a two-person legal staff, including an attorney named Mike Godwin who was EEF's first staff attorney. Mitch Kapor had hired Godwin directly out of law school in 1990, when he noticed him posting interesting messages on Internet forums.[21] The EFF, with Godwin and Shari Steele as counsel, joined forces with the American Civil Liberties Union to challenge the CDA as a violation of the First Amendment. The case, styled *ACLU v. Reno*, quickly ascended to the United States Supreme Court. As Godwin later wrote, "Suddenly, the very legal status of Cyberspace itself . . . was put to the test in a genuine constitutional battle."[22]

The litigation in *Reno* gave birth to a new creature—the geek-activist—and a new political community—the Internet libertarians. Dozens of groups and academics wrote separately to support the lawsuit in a giant, collaborative effort. In addition, more than twenty groups, ranging from the American Library Association to the National Writers Union and the Safer Sex Page joined the case. As Godwin wrote, "we included publishers, service providers, and individuals and organizations whose speech, while often provocative, was clearly central to the American public dialogue."[23]

On June 26, 1997, the Supreme Court announced its decision. By a vote of 7 to 2, it declared the CDA to be an unconstitutional violation of the First Amendment. The Court agreed with the ACLU and EFF that the law was too vague and therefore unnecessarily "chilled" protected speech. Of more lasting import, however, was the Court's embrace of the concept of cyberspace and its apparent conferral of a special legal status for cyberspace communications.

The author of the opinion, Justice John Paul Stevens, was born before the advent of radio stations and television, let alone the Internet. But the then seventy-seven-year-old nonetheless seized upon the Internet phenomenon with enthusiasm. He wrote for the Court that the Internet "constitute[s] a unique medium—known to its users as 'cyberspace'—located in no particular geographical location but available to anyone, anywhere in the world."[24] Stevens characterized cyberspace as containing "vast democratic fora," that have not "been subject to the type of government supervision and regulation that has attended the broadcast industry."[25] He added that "no single organization controls any membership in the Web, nor is there any centralized point from which individual Websites or services can be blocked from the Web."[26]

The implication of *Reno* was that anything related to the Internet would be afforded the strongest possible First Amendment protection.

As Justice Stevens concluded: "The growth of the Internet has been and continues to be phenomenal. As a matter of constitutional tradition, in the absence of evidence to the contrary, we presume that governmental regulation of the content of speech is more likely to interfere with the free exchange of ideas than to encourage it."[27] Justice Sandra Day O'Connor (like Barlow a former rancher) seemed to confirm this interpretation in a separate opinion. "The electronic world" she concluded, "is fundamentally different."[28]

With *Reno*, the idea of an unregulated and post-territorial Internet seemed to many to have migrated from kooky obscurity to the law of the United States as announced by America's highest court. Some even interpreted the Supreme Court to have erected a barrier to *all* U.S. laws that might affect the Internet. "There is very little room for further regulation of the Internet," declared the Electronic Privacy Information Center attorney David Sobel. "[The Court] clearly came down on the side of this being a new medium, that it is inappropriate to graft old broadcast laws onto the Internet."[29] Barlow appeared to have found a way to border off cyberspace from real space, with assistance from a real-world authority. Not only was his *Declaration of Independence* vindicated; suddenly, it had become the supreme law of the land. As Mike Godwin said on the day *Reno* was decided, "let today be the first day of a new American Revolution—a Digital American Revolution, a revolution built not on blood and conflict, but on language and reason and our faith in each other."[30]

## Political Engineering

At the same time that John Perry Barlow and Julian Dibbell were teaching the world about cyberspace self-rule, a crucial group of non-governmental actors was already exercising extraordinary powers of Net governance. Unlike Barlow and Dibbell, these men weren't newcomers to the Internet scene. They were as native to the Internet as it is possible to be, for these were the storied "founders" of the Internet itself—men like Larry Roberts, Robert Kahn, Vint Cerf, Jon Postel, and Dave Clark. Unlike Barlow and Dibbell, the founding engineers weren't terribly interested in communicating to the public. Many of them viewed terms like "cyberspace" or "virtual reality" as the wild imaginings of the technologically illiterate. Their working methods and network designs nonetheless contributed to the growing sense that the Net would be ruled in an unprecedented way.

The achievement of the Internet's founders is well known. They were academics or government employees, mostly Americans, who were funded by a deep-pocketed U.S. Defense Department. In the 1960s and 1970s they successfully created a universal language for computer networks, called the TCP/IP protocol (Transmission Control Protocol/Internet Protocol) or sometimes just the Internet protocol, that remains the foundation of the Internet we know today. This protocol, and other aspects of the Internet's architecture, rested on the founders' self-consciously revolutionary beliefs about networks. In technical jargon, they created a network with "open architecture," or "end-to-end" design.[31] In nontechnical terms, the founders embraced a design that distrusted centralized control. In effect, they built strains of American libertarianism, and even 1960s idealism, into the universal language of the Internet.

More specifically, the Internet's design was unprecedented because it was *open*, *minimalist*, and *neutral*. It was open, because it was willing to accept almost any kind of computer or network to join in one universal network-of-networks. IBM mainframes, AT&T networks, the U.S. Defense Department, and, eventually, personal computers could now all interconnect. It was minimalist, because it required very little of the computers that wanted to join. Becoming part of the Internet was like joining the Unitarian-Universalist church—the central dogma was not very demanding. Finally, it was neutral between applications. Some networks, like the telephone network, were specifically designed for a given purpose (in the case of the telephone network, talking). The Internet treated e-mail, downloads, and every other type of early application the same. This allowed new and better applications (like e-mail, the World Wide Web, and peer-to-peer technology) to evolve and replace the old.

The importance and dominance of the founders' creation is remarkable. As a universal language it spread like Esperanto was supposed to. It now so dominates data networking that it has no competitors or natural predators. It has achieved a universality that surpasses other universals of our era, including Microsoft Windows among operating systems and Lonely Planet among travel guides.

By the early 1980s, the founders, under the leadership of Vinton Cerf, had begun efforts to institutionalize what they saw as their communications revolution. To this end, they created a series of institutions with working methods designed to preserve the values of the founders. Most important of these was the Internet Engineering Task Force (IETF), founded in 1986 as the central standards body for the Internet.[32]

The IETF was, in practice, a series of ongoing meetings where Internet engineers would plot the future of the Internet's standards. But it was soon characterized as more: as a prototype form of a new type of government. Paulina Borsook's widely read 1995 *Wired* article, "How Anarchy Works," described the IETF as the "kind of direct, populist democracy that most of us have never experienced."[33] This band of engineers wasn't just a bunch of guys tired of shopping for electronics. They were "the masters of the metaverse" engaged in "a radical social phenomenon."[34] The genius engineers hadn't just built a good network. They had solved certain intractable problems of human governance along the way.

Territorial government is often characterized (or caricatured) as "top-down." It issues commands in the form of laws that apply within its borders; it enforces these commands through the use of coercion or force; and one reason why citizens obey is that the costs of not doing so (punishment) outweigh the benefits of disobeying. The engineers' method of governance was the opposite. For them, difficult decisions were not imposed by fiat but rather emerged organically in a "bottom-up" fashion through discussion, argument, and consensus. The engineers seemed to be the embodiment of deliberative democracy in action.[35] In the words of Dave Clark, an Internet founder: "We reject: kings, presidents, and voting. We believe in: rough consensus and running code."[36]

What does Clark's adage mean? When the Internet engineers faced difficult problems, their answers or solutions would not be based on majority support (as in a voting system) or fiat (as in kings or presidents). Rather, decisions emerged through a "rough" or "working consensus" among the relevant experts and were adopted voluntarily after long debate and efforts at practical implementation, based on what appeared in practice to work best. As Barlow later described the process, "the consensus is . . . institutionalized by the willingness, which is purely voluntary, of different sites to adopt that solution as part of their technology. New solutions win by virtue of adoption, and they don't get adopted if they're bad solutions."[37] It was an era in which the Internet was changing the rules of business, making companies like AOL and Netscape billion-dollar firms overnight. It seemed only natural that the Internet would also change the rules of politics. The information age would replace tired ideas like voting, legislation, and territorial representation with flexible, consensus-driven rules, created by informal communities organized by interest and expertise rather than the arbitrary condition of location.

In its golden age, the IETF used this informal governance framework to promulgate standards that deepened, formalized, and ultimately popularized the basic internetwork design from the 1970s. Popular Internet features like the modern e-mail system and the World Wide Web are the products of this era, along with countless other protocols whose operations are invisible to the average user. This kind of solution to what were difficult public problems, managed without government involvement, led people to believe that a new form of ordering human affairs might be emerging. When the post-territorial visionaries looked for a model of Internet governance, the engineers were their main inspiration.

## The Internationalists

The movements described thus far all assumed that the Internet would cause governmental power to shift downward from nation-states toward individuals and private groups. But some, while agreeing that the Internet was eroding the influence of the nation-state, thought it would have the opposite effect and move governance upward. The Internet's ubiquitous nature, and the conflicts of territorial laws it generated, led these internationalists to believe that territorial rule would need to be supplemented, and eventually replaced, by global governmental institutions.

In her popular book *The Death of Distance*, Frances Cairncross summed up the internationalist attitude toward the Net when she argued that governments would need to work together through international bodies or else "find national rules and standards frequently undermined wherever they differ from those elsewhere." [38] AOL's Steve Case echoed this sentiment, urging nations to "revis[e] outdated and 'country-centric' laws on telecommunications and taxes that could thwart the growth of the medium" and instead embrace "international standards—from security, to privacy, to taxation."[39]

The principal attraction of the internationalist strategy was its solution to the problem of overabundance of territorial regulation and tyranny of the unreasonable introduced in chapter 1. International law can apply all over the world, as it does, for example, when it prohibits torture (The Torture Convention), establishes minimal rules of airline safety (the Convention on International Civil Aviation), and bans certain barriers to trade (the World Trade Organization). If the nations of the world agree to a single global law for questions like libel, pornography, copyright, consumer protection, and the like, the lives of Internet users become much simpler: no conflicting laws, no worries about complying with 175 different legal systems, no race to the bottom. Legal compliance becomes like an all-inclusive resort in the Caribbean: pay one price and everything is taken care of.

Such a system of universal rules would benefit governments as well. As French Interior Minister Jean-Pierre Chevenement explained in 2000 in response to the rise of Internet data havens, "The idea is to produce a global text so there cannot be 'digital havens' or 'Internet havens' where anyone planning some shady business could find the facilities to do it."[40] Rather than suffer through the mutually destructive effects of unilateral attempts to govern the Net, nations should come up with a compromise global solution that would make all (or most) nations better off by halting the Net's most destructive effects. As Cairncross noted, governments could either "fight fruitlessly to protect their diminishing sovereignty, or find ways to manage their relations with other countries and the private sector so they could get at least some of what they want."[41] Internationalization entailed a relinquishment of national sovereignty, to be sure. But at least nations (especially powerful ones) retained some influence in international organizations, however diffuse.

Not only would internationalism solve the problem of conflicting laws, it also offered the promise of *better* laws. National governments are sometimes too close to (or too reflective of) their populations. They sometimes reject the rational or best solution to a global problem in favor of a local tradition or in obedience to a powerful local interest group. Many believed that international standards applied to the Internet could eliminate the parochialism of territorial legalism. International standards could reflect a kind of collection of best practices from around the world—the opposite of the tyranny of the unreasonable. An international approach could not only clear up confusion and conflict, but it could also wash clean the prejudice and ignorance hiding in the basement of national government.

It was just a new means of communication. But the arrival of the Internet in the 1990s tapped into something much deeper, causing many to hope that the new network might really change things, somehow liberate us from the world we live in and even do something to change the human condition. Behind every vision of Internet utopianism lay the hope that connecting every human on earth might make the world a better place. Humanity united might do better than our lousy systems of government, throw away the construct of the nation-state, and live in some different but better way.

According to each of the visions, one thing seemed clear: the system of territorial government was broken and needed to be replaced. Whether the replacement was international organizations, self-governing Internet communities, or rule by Internet engineers might not really matter. What mattered was that territorial government seemed to be melting away and becoming increasingly irrelevant.

three 3

# The God of the Internet

If you had met Jon Postel in 1998, you might have been surprised to learn that you were in the presence of one of the Internet's greatest living authorities. He had a rambling, ragged look, living in sandals and a large, unkempt beard. He lived like a modern-day Obi-Wan Kenobi, an academic hermit who favored solitary walks on the Southern California beach. When told once by a reporter that readers were interested in learning more about his personal life, he answered: "If we tell them, they won't be interested anymore."[1]

Yet this man was, and had been for as long as anyone could remember, the ultimate authority for assignment of the all-important Internet Protocol (IP) numbers that are the essential feature of Internet membership. Like the medallions assigned to New York City taxicabs, each globally unique number identifies a computer on the Net, determining who belongs and who doesn't. "If the Net does have a God," wrote the *Economist* in 1997, "he is probably Jon Postel."[2]

Jon Postel was a quiet man who kept strong opinions and sometimes acted in surprising ways. The day of January 28, 1998, provided the best example. On that day Postel wrote an e-mail to the human operators of eight of the twelve "name servers" around the globe. Name servers are the critical computers that are ultimately responsible for making sure that when you type a name like google.com you reach the right address (123.23.83.0). On that day Postel asked the eight operators, all personally loyal to Postel, to recognize his computer as the "root," or, in essence, the master computer for the whole Internet.

The operators complied, pointing their servers to Postel's computer instead of the authoritative root controlled by the United States government. The order made the operators nervous—Paul Vixie, one of the eight, quietly arranged to have someone look after his kids in case he was arrested.[3]

Postel was playing with fire. His act could have divided the Internet's critical naming system into two gigantic networks, one headed by himself, the other headed by the United States. He engineered things so that the Internet continued to run smoothly. But had he wanted to during this critical time, he *might* have created chaos. Together with his eight comrades, he could have made ".com" addresses unreachable for most users of the Internet. As technologist Keith Moore put it, "if we break the root, everything fails."[4]

Postel's e-mail was a reaction to changes that he and other founders didn't like. By 1998, the Internet was becoming commercial and contentious in ways its inventors had never imagined. Stakes rose, fortunes were made, and the vision and authority of the founders were under threat. One new player was the U.S. government, which, after being silent for years, had began to ask questions and assert its claims over the network. Another was a widely detested corporation named Network Solutions that had taken over day-to-day administration of Internet domain name registration. The community that invented the Net was losing control over its creation.

Postel's act was an effort to maintain the Internet's founding vision of an open, noncommercial network run by selfless experts for the benefit of all. His e-mail, backers said, was a warning shot to show the U.S. government who was really in charge. Network Solutions, in the words of one Postel supporter, held the "com" but Postel still controlled the "dot."[5] The founders of the Internet wanted to prove that they retained the power to "break" the Internet and thereby prevent anything from happening without their consent. This chapter tells the story of their motivations, their efforts, and their failure.

## Why Root Authority Matters

What Postel and the U.S. government were fighting over is something called "Internet naming and numbering authority," or "root authority."

For those deeply versed in the Internet's history, root authority matters automatically, in the way you might care who the president of the United States is without even knowing exactly why. But for those less familiar, it requires explanation.

To communicate on the Internet, your computer needs a unique number, or address, known as an Internet Address. The numbers look like this: 128.143.28.135. Someone has to decide who gets which numbers, and how many they get. In addition, someone has to give out the valuable "domain names" that are shorthands for the numbers, like evite.com, or cowboy.org. Those domain names, furthermore, are organized by their top-levels—dot-com, dot-net, and so on—and someone needs to decide what "top level domains" will exist and who will administer them. These decisions are the job of the "naming and numbering authority."

Making such decisions may seem merely technical, like the authority to assign phone numbers or license plates. But these decisions had enormous significance. Most attention concerning root authority has focused on ownership of "domain names," the globally unique name associated with an Internet address. There can only be one website at www.barcelona.com. Should it belong to the city in Spain, or to Whit Stillman's 1994 romantic comedy?[6] The answer does not respect national boundaries. The root authority decides, on behalf of every Internet user everywhere in the world. Valuable domain names are worth millions of dollars, and the domain name system itself underlies billions in electronic commerce.

Not only does the domain name system affect valuable Internet-related property rights, it also has the potential to serve as a powerful tool of Internet enforcement and to shape the nature of the Internet itself. As country clubs and medical associations know well, control over membership is a powerful tool for making people follow rules. Already today, a basic form of such enforcement is used to protect registered trademarks on the Internet. If you somehow managed to register harrypotter.com, Warner Brothers or J. K. Rowling could complain to the Internet naming authority, and you'd quickly lose the name. No court case, no trial; simply a direct divestiture of the domain name. It's a prime example of what David Johnson calls "electronic," as opposed to physical, force.[7]

The power over domain names and numbers could also be used as a broader enforcement tool against other types of unwanted conduct.

As we'll see in chapter 5, the U.S. government demands divestiture of domain names and IP addresses for offenses like selling drug paraphernalia or copyright infringement. One can imagine a future where divesture of IP addresses is a common form of enforcement. As punishment, individuals, institutions, or even whole countries could lose domain names, IP addresses, or even Internet membership.

This is why root authority matters. But how exactly does one "get" or "hold" this authority? No one understands the answer to this question completely. Stated most simply, root authority is the power to issue orders respecting domain names and numbers and have those orders obeyed. There are many ways such power might arise: from reputation, from actual administration of the computers in question, or from legal authority. In truth, the system long operated without a clear idea of exactly who held the ultimate power over the root, or why.

This ambiguity about who possesses root authority led to the earliest and most consequential battle for control of the Internet. As we saw in the last chapter, Postel and the Internet's founding generation viewed themselves as the acting authority over most Internet matters. They had designed the Net's architecture, they were the experts, and they had day-to-day control over most aspects of its operation. But they lacked any legal claim to govern the Internet—a problem they generally overlooked.

The U.S. government had a different type of claim. In the United States you usually own what you pay for. While the founding engineers may have invented the Internet and run it for years, nearly every aspect of the Internet's development was funded pursuant to U.S. government contracts. The U.S. government believed these contracts gave it ownership of the naming and numbering system.[8] Beyond this technical legal claim, there was a general sense that the highest questions of Internet policy remained for the U.S. government to decide, as the Internet's ultimate custodian. As Wayne State law professor Jonathan Weinberg, formerly at the Federal Communications Commission's Office of Plans and Policy, put it, "the mindset in the U.S. government was that this really was *our* Internet."[9] The problem was that the United States had long acted as an absentee custodian. From the 1970s through much of the 1990s, the U.S. government was passive, happy to let the engineers do their thing. "The U.S. government did not plan to be in charge of a critical Internet chokepoint," writes Miami law professor Michael Froomkin. "Its control of the root was, more than anything, accidental."[10]

## The Early Days

None of this seemed to matter much in the early 1970s, when the early Internet's naming system—all of it—consisted of one file, named "hosts.txt," maintained by the Stanford Research Institute pursuant to a Defense Department contract. It was a simplicity that suited a small research network, but it couldn't last. As the network grew complicated in the 1970s, it came to require a naming system and day-to-day naming maintenance. Some time in 1977, a young computer scientist agreed to take on the thankless job of keeping the early system working. It was one of those fortuities that change lives, for that young man was Jon Postel.

Despite being vested with what at the time was an inglorious and largely administrative job, Postel earnestly devoted himself to building and running the Internet's naming and numbering structure. He quietly proposed the top-level domains like dot-com, dot-edu, and dot-net that are now familiar to hundreds of millions. In his spare time, he co-wrote the "Simple Mail Transfer Protocol," a system we know better today as e-mail.[11]

It was these early years of quiet labor that built Postel's reputation for dedicated service and fair dealing. Said fellow founder and friend Vint Cerf, he "inspired loyalty and steadfast devotion among his friends and his colleagues . . . personify[ing] the words 'stewardship and selfless service.'"[12] Another Internet engineer, David Crocker, wrote, "We always knew that his views came from legitimate beliefs and we never had to worry that he was somehow considering political or personal advantage. We might not agree with him, but we always knew he was driven first by a concern that the right thing be done."[13] Postel earned the nickname "Jon the Protocol Czar," subtitled "Unfailing Arbiter of Good Taste in protocols."[14]

Under Postel and the Stanford Research Institute (SRI)'s joint stewardship, the modern domain name system was in full operation by the mid-1980s. The first registered dot-com domain name, issued

Jon Postel (Irene Fertik, USC News Service. Copyright © 1994 USC)

on March 15, 1985, was "symbolics.com," and registration was free.[15] By 1988 the U.S. government had made a formal contract with Postel's employer, USC's Information Sciences Institute (ISI), giving Postel the authority to continue doing what he had been doing for more than a decade: running the Internet's naming and numbering system. It was common at this time to refer to Postel as "the" naming and numbering authority.

As the 1980s came to an end, Postel enjoyed an authority over the domain name system and related Internet policy that was essentially uncontested. He was the man to go to for any naming or numbering problem, the "benevolent dictator" of the network. And as the Internet began to really grow, so did Postel's reputation. Said Cerf, "Jon was our resident hippie-patriarch."[16] The quiet loner, long overshadowed by more vocal or more senior founding engineers, began to enjoy a stature in the Internet community rivaled by few. He was a man revered—some called it "the cult of Jon."[17]

There was just one small and seemingly unimportant hole in Postel's otherwise comfortable authority. The responsibility for keeping the naming system up to date, and for managing the physical computers that hosted the naming system, rested with Stanford Research

Institute, pursuant to a defense contract. SRI had been a friendly, non-profit, and effectively passive partner. Unfortunately for Postel, SRI's role, and his, were about to change.

As the 1990s began, it was East Coast bureaucratic reforms that began to loosen Postel's grip. In the 1980s, the Defense Department adopted regulations that required most defense contracts to be open to commercial bidding. As SRI's contract to administer the root expired, the Defense Department "recompeted" the contract. In May of 1990, a giant defense contractor named "Government Systems Inc." won the bid, and quickly outsourced it to a small, unknown firm named Network Solutions Inc. (NSI). This meant that Postel (through his employer, USC) and Network Solutions would share authority over the naming system in various ways. Network Solutions became the sole registrar for the main nonmilitary domains (dot-com, dot-net, dot-org, and dot-edu).[18] But Postel retained "policy" authority: the power to decide, for example, the number and content of the top-level domains.

In some ways, this new arrangement fortified Postel's position. He still made big-picture decisions, and Network Solutions just executed the details. But in fact the transfer of partial authority to Network Solutions was a crucial turning point in Internet history. For the first time, administration of part of the Internet's naming system would be in the hands of a for-profit company. And also for the first time, a private firm with interests at odds with the founding vision would be exercising real authority over their creation. Perhaps even more significantly, Network Solutions became the custodian of the physical root server. As a result, the text files that make up the root were transferred to the Network Solutions offices in Herndon, Virginia, one hour west of Washington, D.C. The Ark had left the temple, never to return.

At first relations between Network Solutions and the engineers were relatively peaceful. But this changed in the mid-1990s when a new and unfamiliar element entered the picture—money, in large quantities. In 1995, Network Solutions won the right to charge for registering individual applicants for domain names: $100 for a two-year registration, and $50 per year thereafter. While that didn't seem like much, by the late 1990s, millions of domain names had been registered and Network Solutions' revenue was growing at an annual rate of greater than 110 percent. Revenue ballooned, as Network Solutions, with minimal operating expenses, collected over $200 million in 1999.[19] Network Solutions realized that it had hit a gold mine and began to see its monopoly over domain-name registration as worth fighting for.

Network Solutions' newfound wealth and its attempts to maintain that wealth led the engineers to view the firm as greedy, controlling, and monopolistic. Columnist Dan Gillmor expressed prevailing attitudes when he called Network Solutions "an arrogant, monopolistic enterprise that throws its weight around like the proverbial 800 pound gorilla. Except in NSI's case, this gorilla is just plain mean."[20]

## The First Attempt to Take Root Authority

As private firms like Network Solutions began to enter the picture, some of the founders decided it was time to make their operational authority over the Internet more concrete.[21] The immediate impetus was fighting the power of Network Solutions by providing alternatives. But there was much more at stake. In the early 1990s the founders undertook a course of action that would have formalized the control of Internet policy that they already assumed they had. But the plan led to direct conflict with U.S. government, which assumed it had the final authority over Internet policy.

An early leader of the founders' efforts was Vinton Cerf, perhaps the best-known of the Internet's founders, the celebrated "father" of the Internet. Cerf was already famous by the 1980s as the co-designer of the TCP/IP Internet network protocol. Cerf was also a close friend of Jon Postel. Both went to Van Nuys High, in the San Fernando Valley north of Los Angeles, and were Ph.D. students under the same supervisor at UCLA.[22] But where Postel was quiet and built his reputation slowly, Cerf was an early Internet star, with an obvious genius and ready charisma. Where Postel was famously casual—even a bit scruffy—Cerf favored a well-trimmed beard and a three-piece suit. And while Postel would come to challenge U.S. authority over the Internet, Cerf was a pragmatist who ultimately recognized the role that the U.S. government might play in ensuring the stability of the network. Yet despite their different styles, the friends shared the same vision. Both had a deep faith in the original vision of the Internet, and both believed in the wisdom of the policy guidance of the Internet community.

In June 1991, as the Pentagon was selling the root contract to the highest bidder, Cerf was in Copenhagen announcing plans to found the Internet Society.[23] The society, or "ISOC," was populated almost exclusively by Internet founders. It was "an attempt to self-privatize Internet governance" writes Milton Mueller.[24] The ISOC was designed to provide a governing structure, institutional home, and source of funding independent from the U.S. Defense Department and, more generally, the U.S. government.

Vint Cerf, "Father of the Internet" (Declan McCullagh)

These aspirations did not go unnoticed. In March 1995 Robert Aiken, an engineer working at the U.S. Department of Energy (and a member of the Federal Networking Council), wrote a message to the Internet Society that would demarcate the first lines of conflict between the engineers and the U.S. government. In an e-mail titled "inquiring minds want to know," he asked a simple and public question to the Internet Society: who, in its opinion, has the legal authority to control the Internet? As he put it:

> I would like a straightforward answer from the ISOC [Internet Society]. IS ISOC claiming that it has jurisdiction and overall responsibility for the [Internet] top level address and name space—as some (see below) believe it does? If yes—how did ISOC obtain this "responsibility",—if NO then who does own it?[25]

Cerf responded on behalf of the Internet Society. In a long and carefully worded e-mail, he stated his view that the Internet Society was the appropriate body for determining the highest questions of Internet policy. His message admitted the historical role of the U.S. government. "A reasonable case can be made that the IANA [Internet Assigned Numbers Authority] authority . . . could be associated directly and historically with agencies of the US Government."[26] But things, Cerf argued, had changed since the 1980s. "It was recognized by many in the 1990s that the Internet had outgrown its original scope and had become an international phenomenon." He concluded, vaguely, that governance was an open question that should be agreed upon. But his ultimate view seemed to be that it would be better to transfer authority away from the U.S. government and to the Internet Society. "My bias is to try to treat all of this as a global matter and to settle the responsibility on the Internet Society as a non-governmental agent serving the community."[27]

It was in 1997 that the Internet Society made its most focused and ambitious effort to make its authority over the Internet concrete. In anticipation of the scheduled expiration of Network Solutions' contract in 1998, the Internet Society launched a plan to give itself and affiliated entities full authority over questions of Internet policy. It was an effort that might be compared to that of the American colonists: the engineers were trying to convert a day-to-day, functional independence into something formal and legally recognized.

To carry out the plan, the Internet Society worked with the powers and institutions that it thought would make the plan work. One important group, to whom the Internet Society conceded much, were trademark owners who insisted that their property rights be respected in any deal. To try to reach consensus among relevant actors, the Internet Society agreed to include trademark owners on a blue-ribbon international panel, named the International Ad Hoc Committee (IAHC), that would set up a structure for the future of naming and numbering authority. Its membership was, as Ross Rader writes, "like a who's who of the inside track of the Internet," with spots also reserved for the appointees of the World Intellectual Property Organization and the International Trademark Association.[28] Network Solutions was not invited. As for the U.S. government, the sole representative was George Strawn, from the U.S. National Science Foundation, the Internet's benefactors.[29]

The IAHC created a plan that went by a characteristically unwieldy name, "Generic Top-Level Domain Memorandum of Understanding," or gTLD-MoU for short. The gTLD-MoU itself looked like an international legal document—not unlike a United Nations resolution. The spirit of gTLD-MoU (what its proponents called the "MoUvement") was to eliminate the Network Solutions monopoly and also create a general independence from the United States government. It would have put much authority in the control of an organization named CORE

(International Council of Registrars), a Swiss corporation, itself mainly under the control of the Internet Society.[30] The gTLD-MoU would have, as an initial matter, added seven new top level domains (including .shop and .nom), to be managed by CORE registrars.

The gTLD-MoU operated on the presumption that the Internet Society had the de facto authority to set high Internet policy. As member David Crocker wrote in refuting criticisms that the Internet Society lacked this authority, "such concerns miss the reality of [Jon Postel's] 10+ years of oversight and authority and miss the unavoidable reality that the Internet is now global."[31] The gTLD-MoU sidestepped difficult legal questions. As Crocker concluded, the "plan is self-enabling," and "hence challenges about prior authority are rendered meaningless."[32] Internet Society president Don Heath, a Cerf protégé, when asked by a reporter whether he might need the approval of the United States to implement gTLD-MoU, stated that the United States "has no choice."[33]

Great efforts were made to give the gTLD-MoU the trappings of official status and inevitability. The International Telecommunications Union, a branch of the United Nations, volunteered to serve as the official repository of the gTLD-MoU, lending a certain intergovernmental credibility. The gTLD-MoU was formally opened for signature to all interested members and companies in the Internet community. Secretary General Pekka Tarjanne gave a speech, calling the gTLD-MoU a new form of "voluntary multilateralism."[34]

There was even a formal signing ceremony for the gTLD-MoU in Geneva, on May 1, 1997. Along with members of the Internet society, major telecommunications firms like MCI made an appearance, along with major computer manufacturers like Digital. Sentiments of global comradeship were in the air. Isabelle Valet Harper from Digital said "this is not an end but a beginning. It is the beginning of a time when we can all work together."[35] Bruno Lanvin from the United Nations offered a "virtual bouquet" of lilies of the valley to the Internet community around the world.[36] Heath called the Geneva signing the beginning of "effective Internet self-governance."[37] Soon thereafter, the gTLD-MoU inspired a group of Internet Service Providers to release a tentative "Internet Constitution" that began:

> We the People of the Internet Community, in order to promote more complete interoperability of the individual Networks that constitute

the Internet, insure harmonious relations between the various Networks that constitute the Internet, and to secure the Blessings of Liberty to all the Networks that constitute the Internet, do ordain and establish this Constitution. . . ."[38]

Meanwhile, with the gTLD-MoU signed the Swiss organization CORE began to act as if it were soon to become the Internet's naming and number authority. In anticipation of its pending replacement of Network Solutions, CORE collected money from companies interested in becoming part of its new Internet naming system. It confidently announced that January 1998 would mark the implementation of the new authority, and the formal transfer of all the authority vested in Network Solutions to the Internet Society. CORE established a policy oversight committee, signed contracts, and collected more than $1 million.[39] The MoUvement was underway.

## The United States Reacts

Neither the United States nor any other government was invited to the Geneva signing ceremony. The absence of traditional governments was perfectly consistent with the dominant beliefs about the novel nature of Internet governance. The gTLD-MoU had implicitly declared a right independent of the United States to set Internet policy. The theory seemed to be that the United States wouldn't care and thus would freely transfer most of the naming and numbering authority away.

But the United States did care—a lot. The point man for U.S. policy was Ira Magaziner, Bill Clinton's friend and Internet policy czar. Magaziner told Clinton as early as 1994 that the "commercialization of the Internet" would be a boon to the U.S. economy that should be a top priority for the U.S. government.[40]

Magaziner later said that he had several distinct ideas about how best to foster the growth of the Internet and promote the Internet as an engine of commerce. The first was deregulatory—that the Net must remain free from "micro-regulations." Magaziner worried about the bit-tax idea floating around European capitols, and about calls to bring the Internet under the control of agencies like the Federal Communications Commission. Treating the Internet as a target for regulation, he was convinced, would have "killed e-commerce." Magaziner also thought that the Internet needed "predictability and security" to avoid various forms of piracy and related subversions. Big business had made clear to him that it would not invest billions in the Internet unless its basic architecture was secure. The Department of Defense and national intelligence agencies had similar concerns about Net security. Underlying all of these ideas was a belief that, in the end, the United States and no one else possessed ultimate authority over the Internet's deep structure, including naming and numbering authority. As Magaziner said, "The United States paid for the Internet, the Net was created under its auspices, and most importantly everything Jon [Postel] and Network Solutions did were pursuant to government contracts."[41]

As the fight over naming and numbering began to heat up, Magaziner formed his own team of experts. He put together an inter-agency working group chaired by Brian Kahin of the White House office of Science and Technology, and made up of people like Becky Burr from the Commerce Department, Elliot Maxwell from the Federal Communication Commission, and others from the Justice and State Departments. Their job was to figure out what was going on, and what the United States should be doing about it. Magaziner and the working group had great respect for Postel and Cerf, and great confidence in the expert engineers' ability to run the Internet on a day-to-day basis. But when it came to the Geneva process and the question of ultimate policy control, they parted company.

Ira Magaziner (Copyright © 2005 The William J. Clinton Foundation)

The working group chafed at the MoUvement's pretensions of Internet policy authority independent of the United States. They did not believe that the kind of stability that the U.S. government provided could be replicated by an uncertain and vague new governance arrangement based in Geneva. Most importantly, they feared that unless the U.S. government asserted its authority over the Net, it might fall prey to overregulation.[42] That may sound like a paradox—government action to prevent government action. But the involvement of the United Nations-affiliated International Telecommunications Union, an agency with a broad governmental membership, led the group to fear that the

Geneva process might lead to European or other countries using naming and numbering power to impose new and more invasive global controls on the Internet.

Through 1997, as the gTLD-MoU gained support and signatures, resistance to it increased. In addition to the interagency working group, more vociferous groups that disfavored the gTLD-MoU for one reason or another turned to Congress to vent. Andrew L. Sernovitz, a flamboyant business lobbyist, testified to Congress about a "Swiss conspiracy" that was plotting to hijack essential American infrastructure. The MoUvement, he maintained, "is in the process of setting up a full administrative infrastructure for the Internet in Switzerland, entirely outside of U.S. oversight,"[43] and "a puppet organization controlled by Dr. Jonathan Postel, Mr. Don Heath, and technocrat trustees of the Internet Society."[44] He further accused the "handful of academics who run IANA" of a "grave betrayal of the national trust," and charged other backers of the gTLD-MoU process of illegal dealings with the Libyan government.[45]

Even some in the Internet Society were beginning to have their doubts. Ira Magaziner met Vint Cerf in Washington, D.C. in the summer of 1997 to convince him that the Geneva process couldn't work. Cerf "got it," Magaziner later said.[46] "He understood the Internet was changing, and that the idea of a privately governed Internet would not work because it was not accountable to anyone except itself. He understood that such an organization wouldn't fly with the U.S. government, or foreign governments, or business." According to Magaziner, he and Cerf shared the "common goal" of keeping the Internet "as free as possible from government control, while at the same time giving the imprimatur of government control for purposes of security." They were both "looking for a government structure that would guarantee flexibility and freedom."[47]

The conflict between the Geneva process and the United States came to a head in December 1997, when Magaziner and his working group arrived at the Washington Hilton to attend an Internet Engineering Task Force (IETF) gathering. Two meetings took place. In an open session, representatives from the interagency group listened to the engineers discuss and explain the gTLD-MoU process. The mood became tense, as it became clear that some of the engineers were issuing an implied threat to the U.S. government. One of the IETF members began to discuss the technical community's (untested) ability to "break the root"—to wreck the domain name system and create Internet chaos. As presenter David Crocker later said, the goal was to educate the interagency group, who were "completely dismissive about technies. Openly, regularly, and insultingly."[48]

More importantly, in a second, private meeting, Ira Magaziner and Jon Postel met. Magaziner had enormous respect for Postel. "Jon was a wonderful guy, whom I loved," he would later say. Magaziner had even traveled to California earlier in 1997 to discuss Internet governance issues with Postel and "show him how much I respected him."[49] Nonetheless, in their Washington, D.C. meeting, Magaziner delivered a clear message: the United States—not the Internet Society, CORE, or Jon Postel—would decide the future of the Internet naming and numbering.[50] Magaziner had made it clear to Network Solutions that it was to ignore any commands, even from Jon Postel, to add the seven new domain names pursuant to the gTLD-MoU plan.[51]

According to the original Geneva plan, January 1, 1998 was the date on which the new era in Internet governance was to begin. But on that day, nothing happened. The United States had put its foot down, and the MoUvement was over.


## Postel's E-mail

It was in this context that, on January 28, 1998, Postel decided on a more radical course of action. Magaziner had demonstrated his power to block additions to the root file controlled by Network Solutions, and had put the gTLD-MoU on hold. Postel decided it was time to show that he could sidestep Network Solutions altogether and transfer root authority wherever he wanted, whether the United States agreed or not. By changing which computer the world would recognize as the root, Postel's plan would make it clear that the deepest aspects of naming and numbering authority resided with the founders of the Internet.

Postel did not make the decision alone. Some, like the Internet Society's Don Heath, had long maintained that Postel had the power to transfer root authority without the permission of the U.S. government.[52] As Heath put it, "The government has stayed out of the

Internet for 10 years. Why are they getting involved now?"[53] Postel was also egged on by anarchist-millionaire John Gilmore, who strongly urged him to challenge U.S. authority.[54] Whatever his reasoning, at some point Postel decided that it was time to demonstrate to the United States the power still held by the Internet community.

On the afternoon of Wednesday, January 28, Postel sent the e-mail replicated below to eight of the twelve operators of the Internet's regional root servers. In the normal course of affairs, the twelve regional root servers would synchronize their information with Root Server A, the master root server owned by the U.S. government and operated by Network Solutions. But Postel asked the regional servers to take the "small step" of recognizing his own server, located on the University of Southern California campus, as the authoritative root. As he wrote:

> Date: Wed, 28 Jan 1998 17:04:11-0800
> From: postel@ISI.EDU
> Subject: Root zone secondary service
> Cc: postel@ISI.EDU, iana@ISI.EDU
>
> Hello.
>
> As the Internet develops there are transitions in the management arrangements. The time has come to take a small step in one of those transitions. At some point on down the road it will be appropriate for the Root domain to be edited and published directly by the IANA.
>
> As a small step in this direction we would like to have the secondaries for the Root domain pull the Root zone (by zone transfer) directly from IANA's own name server.
>
> This is "DNSROOT.IANA.ORG" with address 198.32.1.98.
>
> [ . . . ]
>
> -jon.[55]

The wording was low-key but the meaning unmistakable. Postel was trying to prove what Heath had said: that the United States had "no choice" but to let the engineers control the root. It was a tall order, but all eight operators complied, despite the evident danger of a U.S. reaction. Later, Gerry Sneeringer, the operator of Root Server D, explained that Postel's personal authority made the difference. "If Jon asks us . . . we'll do it. He is the authority here."[56]

As the regional servers complied, root authority divided. Four regional servers—at NASA, the U.S. military, the Ballistics Research Lab, and Network Solutions—continued to recognize the U.S. government/Network Solutions as root authority. The remaining eight servers obeyed Postel's command and recognized his USC computer as the root of the network.[57] The Internet was now, in effect, two gigantic networks: One, largely military, headed by the U.S. government's computer in Virginia, and the second headed by Postel's computer in California. As Paul Vixie, operator of Server K, said, "watching the events of that week was like watching a sailboat stare down a battleship."[58]

Users of the Internet did not notice any difference, for Postel set up his computer to replicate the computer at Network Solutions. But the fact was that Postel was in a position to modify or even break the network. With the agreement of the eight regional servers, he might have tried to effectuate the gTLD-MoU, adding the seven new top-level domains. More radically, with a few keystrokes and the consent of the regional servers, Postel held the power to eliminate ".com" or ".net" for much of the world.[59] While few realized what was going on, it was a striking moment in Internet history.

There remains much dispute about Postel's motives. Some, like David Crocker, have argued that Postel's real target was the monopolist Network Solutions.[60] It was just "a shot across the bow," meant to preempt any effort by Network Solutions to "go rogue" and try to seize root authority itself.[61] Others, like Postel's brother Tom, maintain that the importance of the event has been overstated, and that it was nothing more than a technological "test."[62] But Craig Simon, who has devoted much of his Ph.D. dissertation to analysis of Postel's actions, concludes that "Jon was seeking to put physical control of the root where he honestly thought it belonged—under IANA."[63] Similarly, Syracuse professor Milton Mueller argues that "there can be little doubt that the redirection was a direct challenge to U.S. Authority."[64]

But the reaction of the United States would prove decisive. At one o'clock the following morning, U.S. national security officials roused Ira Magaziner from his slumbers at the World Economic Forum in Davos, Switzerland to tell him that they had "noticed something very strange happening with the Internet routing system."[65] Within the hour, Magaziner called Postel in Southern California. And to help put pressure on Postel, he got one of Postel's USC supervisors on the line.

Ira Magaziner recalls the following conversation:

*Magaziner*: "Jon, what is going on with the Internet Root?"

*Postel*: "We were simply conducting a test."

*USC official*: "[Gasp]. You were doing what?" [tone of disbelief and anger]

*Magaziner*: "Jon, you don't have the legal right to conduct a test. You cannot conduct a test without DARPA's (Defense Advanced Research Project Agency) approval. You will be in trouble if you continue this; both you and USC will be liable."

*USC official*: "Hell, we could have lawsuits up the kazoo because of the impact of this on commerce. It could bankrupt the university. Jon, you have to stop this immediately."

*Postel*: "Sorry, I was just doing a test. I didn't mean to do anything wrong."

*Magaziner:* "We don't want to cause you any trouble. Put things back as they were and we'll all agree to call this a test."[66]

The U.S. government's threat of legal force was effective. Within a week, Postel ended the "test" and restored full root authority to servers under government control. Magaziner kept his word as well, telling reporters that Postel had agreed to finish the "test" and move things back the way they were. But from this point on, Magaziner also made it clear that the United States would consider any unauthorized changes to the root file a criminal offense.[67] And since that time, the root file and presumptive root authority has remained, without exception, in the hands of the U.S. government. The day after Postel's actions, the United States released its "Green Paper," setting forth its initial vision of Net governance, asserting total authority over the Internet Root, and completely ignoring the claims of gTLD-MoU, CORE, and the Internet Society.[68] The Green Paper marked the beginning of a different age of the Internet, one in which powerful governments would begin to use threats of force to make their wills known.

Sadly, the stress of events may have taken their toll on Jon Postel. Nine months later, his heart failed. The once-god of the Net was dead, and an era was over.

*Part 2*

# Government
# Strikes Back

four

# *Why Geography Matters*

A visitor to the dell.com web page finds a message prominently displayed in the upper left-hand corner: "Choose a Country/Region." The cisco.com page likewise asks users to "Select a Location." Yahoo's web page has a "Yahoo International" link that connects to a global map with over twenty-five hyperlinks to specialized web pages tied to particular countries (like Denmark, Korea, and Argentina) and regions (like Asia).[1] Everywhere on the web, sites ask viewers to identify their geographical location.

Geographical links are puzzling for those who think of the Net as a borderless medium that renders place irrelevant. But the puzzle disappears when we see that, globalization and the supposed death of distance notwithstanding, national borders reflect real and important differences among peoples in different places. As this chapter shows, geographical borders first emerged on the Internet not as a result of fiats by national governments, but rather organically, from below, because Internet users around the globe demanded different Internet experiences that corresponded to geography. Later chapters will show how governments strengthened borders on the Net by employing powerful "top-down" techniques to control unwanted Internet communications from abroad. But in order to understand fully why the Internet is becoming bordered, we must first understand the many ways that private actors are shaping the Internet to accommodate differences among nations and regions, and why the Internet is a more effective and useful communication tool as a result.

## Why Borders Matter

The most immediate and important difference reflected by borders is language. People in Brazil, Korea, and France don't want English-language versions of Microsoft products. They want a version they can read and understand.

Microsoft learned this lesson when it tried to distribute an English version of Windows operating system in tiny Iceland. Redmond executives thought the market of 500,000 worldwide Icelandic speakers did not justify translation costs and figured the English version would suffice because most Icelanders spoke English as a second language.[2] But Icelanders felt that Microsoft's plan would imperil their language, which has retained basically the same grammar, spelling, and vocabulary for more than a thousand years. "It's a very big danger because schoolchildren need computers, and the language of computers soon becomes the language of the kitchen," said Kristjan Arnason, a professor of Icelandic at the University of Iceland.[3] After the Iceland government threatened to mandate local use of different operating systems (Apple came in Icelandic), Microsoft relented and wrote an Icelandic version.[4] The lesson was not lost on Microsoft's web business: Microsoft now has seventy-five different web pages keyed to the geographical regions where it does business, most of which are written in the dominant local language.[5]

In the 1990s, it was widely believed that English would overrun the Net just as the Net would overrun borders. *The Economist* confidently stated in 1996 that "English may now be impregnably established as the world standard language: an intrinsic part of the global communications revolution."[6] A *New York Times* article written the same year, titled "World, Wide, Web: Three English Words," asserted that "if you want to take full advantage of the Internet there is only one real way to do it: learn English."[7] Al Gore made a similar point when he recounted an episode during a visit to central Asia. "The president of Kyrgyzstan told me his eight-year-old son came to him and said, 'Father, I have to learn English.' 'But why?' President Akayev asked. 'Because, father, the computer speaks English.'"[8] Gore was triumphant, but many decried the seemingly inevitable dominance of English on the Net. French president Jacques Chirac described it as "a major risk for humanity."[9] In short, English seemed on its way to becoming the Net's universal language, much as TCP/IP had become the universal protocol that made Net communications possible.

Like many early predictions about the Internet, this one proved to be wrong. In the late 1990s, 80 percent of online information was in English.[10] By the end of 2002, less than 50 percent of the pages on the World Wide Web were in English;[11] and by 2005, about two-thirds of Net users were nonnative English speakers.[12] Everyone expects these flights from English dominance of the Net to continue.[13] A seemingly essential feature of the Net circa 1999 turned out to be a temporary blip based on the fact that English-speaking Americans, who dominated early Net use, created the Net (and especially the World Wide Web) in their image. As the rest of the world has connected to the Net, it has begun to reflect the fact that less than 8 percent of the people in the world speak native English.[14] Yahoo could have insisted that non-English speakers learn English in order to use its portal. But to draw users who don't speak English, and to compete with local portals written in local languages, Yahoo decided to build portals to meet local needs, including linguistic needs.

Language is only one way that Internet users vary by geography. Borders also mark off differences in culture, currency, climate, consumer norms, and much more. These local variations translate into different preferences and expectations among Net users in different places. The "choose a country" links try to satisfy these preferences and expectations. People in Japan are interested in Tokyo's weather and the value of the yen, not the weather in New York or the price of American movie tickets. Costa Ricans shop online for bathing suits, T-shirts, and sunglasses, not sweaters and overcoats. A Croatian who buys a Dell computer on the Web wants not only instructions he can understand but also the address and phone number of a local repair service, as well as a real-space return address, in case problems arise. Australians speak English, but they don't want a portal that gives them dinner menus, concert times, and traffic patterns in Miami.

The Internet has been celebrated for allowing open, universal communication. "Information wants to be free," John Perry Barlow famously declared.[15] But information does not, in fact, want to be free. It wants to be labeled, organized, and filtered so it can be discovered, cross-referenced, and consumed. The organization of information has always been a key component of successful communication.[16] Some-times the organization is based on content. You buy the *New York Times* for the quality of its reporting and analysis, and because you trust the editors to distinguish news from trivia. Sometimes the organization is based on language; you would be dismayed if the *New York Times* published editorials in Russian. And often it is based on geography. The Sunday *New York Times* published in New York has an elaborate "Metro" section, a real estate section, and an extensive sports page that focuses on New York teams. The Sunday *Times* published in Chicago has truncated New York coverage, no real estate section, a smaller sports section, and various inserts advertising local Chicago events.

Information filtering is especially crucial to the Net, where it is so easy to publish, and where the danger of information overload is thus so great. In the late 1980s, the Internet already connected massive amounts of information on computers at universities, major research firms, and government institutions. This information, however, was notoriously hard to find, even for computer mavens. "It was akin to walking down each aisle of a library, scanning each book just to figure out what is there, but doing this all in the dark!"[17] Once you happened upon something pertinent, you had to download and read the entire document; if you came across references to other relevant work on the Net, you had to start the process all over again, for there was no easy system of cross-referencing.[18] The Net became a revolutionary information technology only after Tim Berners-Lee developed the software and protocols of the World Wide Web, which made general browsing and hyperlinking possible, thereby making it much easier to organize, discover, exclude, and deliver content.[19]

The Internet gives firms potential access to every home and business connected to the Net, anywhere in the world. But this unprecedented opportunity presented an unprecedented challenge: How do you match the information about products, services, and other items to the varying preferences of Net users scattered across the globe? Ironically for a medium that was supposed to destroy borders, geography turns out to be one important way to make the match. Most people most of the time have interests that cluster by geography; at the very least, the probability that two people share the same outlook and concerns declines with distance.[20] Firms that do a global business realize this. The "choose a country" links are their crude way of mapping the borders of the real world on to cyberspace so as to better serve Net users in different places.

Geography is not, of course, the only way, or always the most effective way, to tailor information on the Net; many Listservs, web pages, and blogs shape information along many different dimensions besides geography. In addition, while neighbors tend to have a lot in common compared to people on the other side of the globe, they can still have radically different tastes, habits, hobbies, and the like. Internet "personalization" services respond to the many differences among peoples, like these, that don't correspond to geography. Amazon.com famously gathers data about customer purchases and related preferences, and creates individual "stores" with personally tailored recommendations. "Really Simple Syndication" (RSS) and related systems collect information from selected web pages and blogs, and "feed" it to a single page, enabling individuals to tailor precisely the content they receive on the Net to match their unique tastes and interests.

Even though the Internet permits unprecedented individualized content tailoring, geography will remain a good proxy for interests and preferences, and the geographical shape of Internet information will remain significant. Amazon stores differ greatly among family members, neighbors, and citizens in the United States. But in terms of language and content, the different Amazon stores among individuals in the United States are similar when compared with individual Amazon stores in Japan and France. While Internet firms dream about the possibilities of fine-grained one-to-one marketing, it remains very expensive, and potentially privacy-invasive, to collect, organize, and cross-reference loads of personal data about each individual. For many purposes, geographical targeting on the Internet provides a cost-effective way to match information with consumers, just as in real space.

## The Importance of Place

Futurist and investment guru George Gilder was one of the darlings of the 1990s Internet. In his turn-of-the century book, *Telecosm*, Gilder proclaimed the advent of "infinite bandwidth" and the coming age of the "fibersphere" in which distance would be irrelevant.[21] Bandwidth is the amount of data that can be sent through an Internet connection in a particular time. E-mails without attachments take up little bandwidth; web pages with graphics take up more; digital music and audiovisual files take up quite a lot. The more bandwidth, the faster the communication. Infinite bandwidth means instant communication, no matter where you are and no matter how bulky the message.

In the 1990s, Gilder was not the only, or even the most prominent, believer in bandwidth. "We'll have infinite bandwidth in a decade's time," predicted Bill Gates in 1994.[22] But Gilder famously put his money (and, through the influence of his newsletter, *The Gilder Technology Report*, many others' money) where his mouth was, pumping companies like WorldCom and Global Crossing that were laying millions of miles of fiber-optic lines across the country and around the globe. The premise of the great broadband rush of the late 1990s was that Internet traffic would double every one hundred days. "Like the attic of a house gets filled, no matter how much bandwidth is available, it will get used," wrote Jack Grubman, Salomon Smith-Barney's then–star telecommunications analyst, summing up the mood of the era.[23]

No one seemed to have noticed the tension between the twin predictions of infinite bandwidth and infinite demand for bandwidth. But in the end, it didn't matter, for neither prediction turned out to be true. By the early 2000s WorldCom, Global Crossing, and many other telecommunications firms that bet the store on bandwidth were bankrupt, drowning in a glut of unused fiber cables that continues to the present.[24] Bandwidth today is not even close to infinite. Depending on where you work or live, many Internet communications take noticeable time to complete, and some big files take quite a lot of time to send or receive.

Bandwidth limitations illustrate an important but poorly understood fact: the efficacy of Internet communications depends on the real-space location of both data and the underlying Internet hardware through which the data travel (routers and exchange points, and the fiber-optic cables, phone lines, cable lines, and microwave and satellites transmitters and receptors that interconnect them). Neither the data nor the hardware is distributed equally around the globe. This real-space fact about the Internet means that where you are in the world determines the content and quality of your Internet experience.

Consider the "last mile" of Internet connection between your home and the local network access office, today typically a cable, DSL, or dialup connection. For bandwidth to be infinite it has to be infinite along the *entire* connection, including the last mile. This means that consumers would have to be willing to pay for infinite bandwidth coming to their homes—not just for DSL, or cable, which are only so-so technologies, but rather for significantly more expensive fiber-optic connections. Not surprisingly, consumers balked. In the late 1990s and early 2000s, they were hesitant to pay even for DSL or cable access, priced at around $50 per month. Broadband—let alone "infinite bandwith"—arrived far slower than anyone had predicted. It was this lack of consumer demand for infinite bandwidth (coupled, in some cases, with fraudulent accounting to hide that fact) that killed WorldCom and similar companies, and made Gilder's prediction of "infinite bandwidth" a joke.

Even before the last mile, the efficacy of Internet communications depends on the real-space location of data and data consumers, and on the geographical distribution of the underlying Internet hardware through which the data travels. When a computer user in Boston types something in Yahoo's search engine, it can be expensive and time-consuming for this request to travel through the mass of Internet hardware to Yahoo's California servers, and for Yahoo's information, including its bulky graphics, to travel back through the same hardware to Massachusetts. This is why so many web firms, including Yahoo, pay companies like Akamai to negotiate Internet traffic jams and serve their content from regional and local "cache servers" (digital copies on local computers) located around the globe, closer to the information consumer. It is also why Cisco and many software companies ask customers to "select a location": downloading large software packages is faster from a nearby computer than from one across the globe.

The geography of Internet hardware also explains why so much Internet activity—content production, domain names, software design, server farms, and the like—clusters in urban centers. Big cities were supposed to be "leftover baggage from the industrial era," in

Gilder's memorable phrase.[25] Not only would the concentration of capital and labor in cities be unnecessary in an era where anyone could send and receive any information instantly from anywhere, but the delights of city life could be reproduced on the Net as well. "The telecosm can destroy cities because then you can get all the diversity, all the serendipity, all the exuberant variety that you can find in a city in your own living room." And, according to Gilder, a relentless miniaturization and decentralization would destroy the ugly side of cities. "All of the monopolies and hierarchies and pyramids and power grids of industrial society are going to dissolve before this constant pressure of distributing intelligence to the fringes of all networks."[26]

But Gilder was, once again, wrong. Companies that develop telecommunications infrastructure respond to consumer demand that is naturally concentrated in dense and wealthy population centers.[27] They lay the fiber-optic cables that make up the Internet's most powerful interconnections along the same routes that link cities by train and phone.[28] "Instead of trailblazing into the wilderness, opening a path to new settlements, digital networks have been built to reinforce existing connections between centers of power and influence in the world's great cities and metropolitan areas," explains urban theorist Anthony Townsend.[29] Powerful Internet connections, in turn, attract commerce. "Businesses want to be where they can get directly onto high-speed lines, and they don't want to have the potential for disruption or lots of bottlenecks," says Mitchell Moss of New York University. "Large metropolitan areas are where the big information users are, and they generate the demand for infrastructure. And once the infrastructure is in place, it generates more users in a snowball effect."[30] Far from destroying cities by making place irrelevant, the production and consumption of Internet content, and the infrastructure to support it, are concentrated in cities.[31]

The importance of place is manifesting itself in other surprising ways. Despite the supposed death of distance, Internet traffic—the sending and receiving of e-mails, and communications between users and web pages—appears to decline with distance and is increasingly concentrated within localities, countries, and regions.[32] This makes sense. In its early days, the Internet was dominated by scholars, scientists, and students who were more cosmopolitan than most, and more likely than most to surf and to correspond across borders and in multiple languages. But as the Internet grows into an everyday tool for the masses, the average user is less and less likely to have overseas correspondents or interest in overseas or foreign-language content, and more likely to use the Internet in local languages for local tasks.[33]

The distribution of bandwidth also reflects the evolving localization and regionalization of the Internet. In the 1990s, Internet traffic operated through a centralized hub-and-spoke system, with communications between countries in Europe or Asia typically being routed through giant exchange points in the United States. This U.S.-centric structure is being replaced by regional European and Asian hubs. "Today more bandwidth links key European cities to each other than to the U.S., making Western Europe the first hub to emerge from North America's shadow," says Telegeography, a firm that maps bandwidth geography, in a 2005 report.[34] "Intra-regional links between Asian networks are also growing much faster than any other region's." In brute physical terms, the Internet is becoming a connection of national and regional networks.

There is a final reason why real-space geography matters. The death of distance was supposed to allow for direct buyer-seller relations, eliminating the need for costly intermediary services like warehousers, retailers, and distribution networks, and making the location of the buyer and seller irrelevant. Every firm was no more than a click away from every consumer, and firms could reach consumers anywhere and sell to them directly. Amazon.com at its founding appeared to embody these aspects of what Bill Gates called "friction-free capitalism."[35] It took orders over the Net in Seattle from anyone anywhere, got books from local independent wholesalers, and shipped them directly to consumers around the world. It owned no brick and mortar retail stores, it carried little inventory, and it had no physical presence outside Seattle.[36]

But Amazon's early business model didn't work. Successful product distribution from a single city turned out to be terribly inefficient. Without a standing inventory, customers' orders for more than one book could not always be filled at the same time, requiring costly multiple deliveries. The problems cropped up in reverse when consumers wanted to return items. To address these problems, Amazon built giant warehouses with giant inventories scattered around the globe close to its customers, and invested heavily in real-space distribution networks.[37] Like hundreds of other Internet retailers, Amazon learned that e-commerce is not frictionless, and that attention to real-space middlemen was necessary to make it work.

## Putting Borders on the Net

"The Internet was designed without any contemplation of national boundaries. The actual traffic in the Net is totally unbound with respect to geography."[38] Vint Cerf, who uttered these words, should know; he helped design the computer protocols that made the Internet possible. And yet the "father of the Internet" is only partially right. Yes, the Internet he designed did not contemplate national boundaries. But no, for the reasons we have just seen, the Internet is not "unbound with respect to geography." Cerf's central mistake, a mistake typically made about the Internet, is to believe that there was something necessary or unchangeable about the Net's original architecture.[39] The "choose a country" links were primitive attempts to change Net architecture in ways that firms found useful. More sophisticated methods of geographical identification were soon invented.

Cyril Lionel Houri, whom we met during the *Yahoo* case in chapter 1, was a pioneer in this field. Houri seems to embody the view that the Internet is erasing borders. He speaks in the software idiom of Silicon Valley, but his words are wrapped in a French accent spiced with the inflections that his Jewish parents brought from their native Tunisia when they moved to France. Houri grew up in Paris and went to the elite Institute Polytechnique in Toulouse, one of the so-called grandes ecoles ("great schools") from which most of France's intellectual, political, and business leadership is drawn. Four years after graduating, however, Houri abandoned the French elite to live in New York. He went to work in computing, and he helped write the code that enabled market traders to move billions of dollars around the world daily. If this product of France's nationalistic culture could find his way to Manhattan's Silicon Alley, then surely national boundaries were crumbling.[40]

But Houri was destined to prop up, not destroy, national borders. On a trip home to Paris in August 1999, he discovered something that upended his career, not to mention conventional thinking about the Internet and territory. Staying in his parents' apartment, he flipped on his laptop after dinner to check his e-mail before bed. As the computer came on, Houri saw a portal he was accustomed to seeing in New York. Blinking cheerfully at the top of his screen was a banner advertisement for an American flower delivery service, accompanied by a 1-800-FLOWERS number usable only in the United States.

Cyril Houri (Courtesy of Cyril Houri)

In that moment, Houri realized that the logic of the Internet did not point inexorably toward the flattening of frontiers. He saw that, on the contrary, a borderless flower-delivery service made no sense at all. He also grasped that people would pay for software that took the boundaries of real space and re-created them on the Internet, so that flower deliverers and a thousand other e-tailers could know where their customers were. There would be big money, he thought, in a technology that prevented people outside America's borders from seeing the American ad, and that substituted a French ad for a French audience and a German ad for a German one. The same technology would allow news and entertainment sites to segment their content according to the whereabouts of their audiences. All it would take was a program to locate web surfers in real space. So Houri founded a firm named Infosplit that was devoted to doing just that.[41] And as we saw in chapter 1, he played a major role in the French court's revolutionary use of the technology in the *Yahoo* case.

The idea of locating Net users in real space was not new. Ever since the Net became commercialized in the mid-1990s, Internet firms have tried, with various degrees of success, to discover the geographical identity of their customers. The "choose a country" and "choose a server" links described above are one such attempt. Some websites ask users to type in an area code and promise to access the site from certain places. Some porn sites warn surfers in places where pornography is illegal not to enter the sites. Others require users to send geographical identification (such as a driver's license) by fax or snail mail before allowing access to a page. Yet others check the address associated with a credit card as proof of geographical identification.

But all of these techniques of real-space localization are time-consuming and for the most part unreliable. It is easy to lie about where one is, or ignore warnings not to access pages in places where doing so is illegal. Even if there is no incentive to lie—as with pages that ask you to choose a language or a server—the old-fashioned geo-location techniques were still slow and antithetical to the Net's culture. As Sanjay Parekh, the founder of Digital Envoy, another geo-ID firm, wondered during an "aha" experience similar to Houri's: "The entire point of the Web is to bring you information simply and quickly. Why do I have to scroll through dozens of countries before accessing the site? Surely there has to be a way for [the site] to recognize where I am."[42]

At the turn of the century, Houri's Infosplit, Parekh's Digital Envoy, and a half a dozen other firms such as Quova (which acquired Infosplit in 2004), Akamai, and NetGeo set out to make geographical identification on the Net easy, reliable, and invisible. Instead of requiring Net users to take extra steps to reveal or prove real-space location, they devised a way to make geo-location automatic. And they did so using the very features of Internet architecture that supposedly defied geography.

As we saw in chapter 1, IP addresses reveal little about a computer user's physical location. But the information packets that make up Internet communications travel via giant computers whose locations in real space *are* easy to identify. A "tracing" packet can report the list of computers through which a communication travels, much as a car driving along a network of highways collects a receipt at each toll. Just as one could determine the origin of the car's journey by looking at this collection of receipts, computers can trace the path of each information packet to determine the computer node closest to the computer from which it originated—usually, the servers of businesses and universities, or the Internet connection points for Internet Service Providers.[43] This information is then cross-checked against other IP databases that offer different clues about the geographical location of computers on the Internet.

No single database, by itself, suffices to identify the location of Internet users. But when the various databases are cross-referenced and analyzed by powerful computer algorithms, the geographical location of Internet users can be determined with over 99 percent accuracy at the country level. A web operator using this system can automatically determine the location of computer users seeking access to his page, and can display a page tailored to the user's locale. The identification process is invisible to the visitor—all she sees is content designed for her locality.

Net geo-identification services are still relatively new but are starting to have their effects on e-commerce. Online fraud, and in particular online identity theft, has been a big challenge for e-commerce, causing firms and consumers to lose billions of dollars each year.[44] Geo-identification is helping to solve this problem. When you make a credit card purchase in real space, the card company knows where in the world you are making the purchase. If the geographical pattern of your buying is unusual, they take steps to verify that the card is being properly used. Geographical identification on the Net works in a similar fashion. If stolen credit card numbers are used on the Net from an untypical or high-risk location, or in two places at once, red flags go off.

Geo-ID is also improving Internet advertising by making it possible, as Houri and Parekh envisioned, to display ads automatically in the correct language, geared to local conditions. When a firm advertises on Google, it can pay extra to target its campaign by nation, region, or city.[45] As a result, when you type in to Google the terms "massage" or "house renovation" from a computer in Boston, local ads for these services appear on the right-hand sponsored links. Geo-identification software is also speeding the delivery of electronic products, enabling Akamai and similar firms to deliver content automatically from the closest "cache" website, without having to ask the consumer where she is.[46]

Another example is the zoning of entertainment. An important hurdle to the distribution of entertainment on the Net has been that certain programs cannot lawfully be viewed in certain places. Major League baseball teams, for example, give exclusive broadcast rights to local television stations. This angers not only the local New York and Boston fans who would like to watch Yankees–Red Sox games on TV. It also angers those outside of New York and Boston who want to watch Yankees–Red Sox games on the Net, but who were prevented from doing so because Major League baseball could not, with the original technology of the Net, broadcast games to fans outside New York and Boston while honoring its commitment not to broadcast in New York and Boston. Beginning in 2003, however, Major League teams began streaming games using geo-identification software that blocked viewers in prohibited areas, earning over $130 million in Internet broadcast revenues in 2004.[47] Without the geo-ID technology, explains the CEO of MLB's online division, "we simply could not offer our product."[48] For similar reasons, and in similar ways, online movie businesses, web gambling firms, and software manufacturers, under the influence of the *Yahoo* decision, are using geo-identification technology to ensure that their digital products do not enter countries where they are illegal.[49]

Net geo-identification is not foolproof. While country identification is remarkably accurate, state and city identification is less reliable. Slippage at the subnational level is caused in part by the tens of millions of America Online users who use AOL's proprietary proxy server in Virginia, which makes it seem like all AOL users reside there. Another problem is that Internet anonymizers (intermediate web servers that disguise the user's IP address) and remote Internet connections can, despite countermeasures by geo-ID firms, still sometimes defeat the identification process.

Imperfections like these will always exist. But geo-ID does not have to be perfect to be effective. Fairly accurate identification suffices in most real-space contexts, and it will do so on the Internet as well. Moreover, IP-based systems of identification are being supplemented by scores of other geo-ID techniques. The increased use of Wi-Fi, for example, will make it easier to track people geographically through radio signals and satellites. And rising Net activity on portable devices like web-enabled phones will permit easier geographical tracking through the Global Positioning Systems (GPS) that are built into the phones.

The various geography-sensitive elements of the Internet discussed in this chapter—"choose a country" links, language differences, bandwidth distribution, geographical identification technology, and much more—show that geography remains crucially important, especially in the Internet era. They also show that the Internet's sensitivity to geographical difference happened naturally, via market mechanisms, as content providers and hardware and software makers responded to varying local demands. But there was another, much more powerful interest that was sensitive to geography and that, in various ways, also wanted to border the Internet: territorial governments. The next three chapters consider governments' responses to the borderless medium.

# five 5

## *How Governments Rule the Net*

In 1966 a retired British Major named Paddy Roy Bates took a liking to a small, abandoned concrete platform in the North Sea nicknamed "Rough's Tower." Rough's Tower was a World War II gun tower used by the British to fire at German bombers on their way to London. By 1966, nobody wanted the rusting contraption, so Bates renamed it the "Principality of Sealand" and declared independence from the United Kingdom, six miles away. He awarded himself the title of Prince Roy, and proceeded to issue Sealand passports and Sealand stamps with pictures of his wife, Joan, an ex-beauty queen.[1]

Sealand has had a colorful history, but before 1999, nothing suggested that a chunk of concrete and steel off the English coast might have anything to do with the history of the Internet. That year, Bates agreed to let a young man named Ryan Lackey move to Sealand and begin transforming it into a "data haven." Lackey's company, "HavenCo," equipped Sealand with banks of servers, and Internet links via microwave and satellite connections.[2] Borrowing an idea from cyberpunk fiction, HavenCo aimed to rent computer space on Sealand to anyone who wanted to escape the clutches of government. It promised potential clients—porn purveyors, tax evaders, Web gambling services, independence movements, and just about any other government-shy Internet user—that data on Sealand servers would be "physically secure against any legal action."[3] HavenCo, the company boasted, would be "the first place on earth where people are free to conduct business without someone looking over their shoulder."[4]

Sealand, off of the English Coast (Kim Gilmour)

HavenCo was the apotheosis of the late 1990s belief in the futility of territorial government in the Internet era. Lackey's company was premised on the commonplace assumption that governments cannot control what happens beyond their borders, and thus cannot control Internet communications from abroad. "If the king's writ reaches only as far as the king's sword, then much of the content of the Internet might be presumed to be free from the regulation of any particular sovereign,"[5] wrote Duke law professor James Boyle, generalizing the point.

In the end, though, HavenCo didn't realize Lackey's dreams. National governments have been able to assert control over the local effects of offshore Internet communications. They have done so not by going after computer sources abroad, but rather through coercion of entities within their borders. This chapter shows how this method of control works, and assesses some of its limitations. By witnessing the struggle to control extraterritorial harms, we can learn something not only about the history of the Internet, but also about the complex relationship among law, territory, and government power.

## Beyond Borders

Many stores in New York's Chinatown sell counterfeit Gucci bags and Rolex watches at a fraction of the usual cost. While some are junk, some of the more expensive counterfeits are good enough to compete with the originals. They come from manufacturers overseas, in China, Thailand, or the Ukraine, that are far beyond the territorial control of the United States, and might as well be in Sealand. Since only a tiny fraction of these fakes can effectively be stopped at the border, HavenCo's logic would suggest that the United States and other nations are powerless to stop the trade in counterfeits.

But the counterfeits' story shows the opposite. It shows how governments control the illegal local effects of extraterritorial conduct, even when they lack the power to punish overseas producers, the resources to stop the illegal goods at the border, or the will to punish domestic consumers.

The most important targets of the laws against counterfeits—trademark laws—are local retailers.[6] If the fake Rolexes come from Thailand, it doesn't matter much that the United States can't go after the Thai manufacturers, because Wal-Mart won't sell you one. Wal-Mart doesn't sell counterfeits because doing so would be an obvious breach of a law from which it cannot hide. Wal-Mart's physical assets, its corporate headquarters, and its founding family all are in the United States, making it hard for the firm to evade U.S. government action. This is why trademark law cares little about end users. It isn't even illegal to own a counterfeit watch; it is only illegal for Wal-Mart to sell you one.[7]

It is true, of course, that even by controlling Wal-Mart, Macy's, and Sears, the United States doesn't *eliminate* counterfeit goods. Gucci and Rolex lose potential income each year to counterfeit purchases. But it doesn't follow that the trademark laws are useless. The law need not be *completely* effective to be *adequately* effective.[8] All the law aims to do is to raise the costs of the activity in order to limit that activity to acceptable levels. We do not conclude from the persistence of occasional bank robberies that laws against theft are ineffective, or even suboptimal. Often, the law accepts small evasions because achieving perfect legal control, though possible, is just too expensive.

Similarly, the fact that there are sellers—like the stores in Chinatown—who are willing to assume the legal risk of selling counterfeits does not mean that the trademark laws are ineffective. To be effective, trademark law need only throw enough sand into the workings of the counterfeit market so that Gucci and Rolex continue to make smart profits. Certainly, government could do more to dry up the counterfeit market. It could hire more enforcement officers, invest more in border control, criminalize the purchase of fake goods, or increase the punishments dramatically. But the system can be adequate to its task even though the government could do more, and even though compliance is not perfect. Government regulation works by cost and bother, not by hermetic seal.

The fake Rolex example teaches a crucial lesson about how law actually works. We tend to think of law as like the Ten Commandments—a series of direct, individualized directives (thou shall not kill, steal, or bear false witness). And while some laws do work this way, many do not. It is easy to overlook how often governments control behavior not individually, but collectively, through *intermediaries*.[9] Pharmacists and doctors are made into "gatekeepers" charged with preventing certain forms of drug abuse. Bartenders are responsible for preventing their customers from driving drunk, and gun manufacturers have in recent years been held liable for the injuries of shooting victims.[10]

Similarly, to control offshore Internet communications from places like Sealand, governments threaten local Internet intermediaries: the people, equipment, and services within national borders that enable local Internet users to consume the offending Internet communication. Government action against such local intermediaries makes it harder for local users to obtain content from, or transact with, the law-evading content providers abroad. In this way, government affects Internet flows within their borders even though they originate abroad and cannot easily be stopped at the border.

## Extraterritorial Control Through Local Intermediaries

How precisely does control of local intermediaries relate to the government's ability to influence offshore content providers? Most illegal acts can be understood as transactions involving three relevant parties: the "source" (the manufacturer), an intermediary (the Chinatown shops), and a "target" (the purchasers):

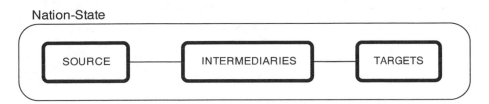

Havens move the illegal source outside the limits of the government's physical control. A simple haven strategy can be pictured as follows:

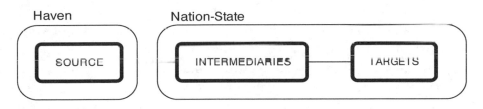

The counterfeit Gucci bags from Thailand follow this example. The source of the illegal conduct—the manufacturer of the counterfeit goods—has moved overseas. Yet, as we see in that example, both the intermediaries and the targets remain within the physical control of the government. This leads to an important insight: effective control over *any* of the three elements of the transaction permits the government to control conduct within its borders. In the counterfeit goods example, control over the intermediary sellers or (if the government had the resources) the actual purchasers could effectively control the illegal transaction.

One might think that the source can diminish the problem of government control by eliminating the intermediaries. Such *disintermediation* is what many think the Internet is supposed to be all about.[11] On the Net, after all, you don't need a stock broker to lose money, and you don't need to visit a bookstore to buy books. That evasion technique, disintermediation, is pictured here:

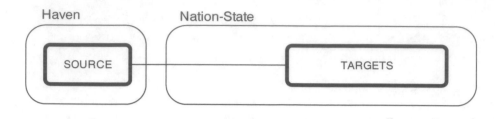

Haven   Nation-State

SOURCE —————————— TARGETS

In principle, this is a powerful strategy. It leaves the government with the sole option of trying to hunt down the "target" end users, who might be numerous and expensive to find (more on this later). So, if the Internet, as advertised, is eliminating intermediaries, doesn't this mean that traditional governmental power is doomed?

The problem with this theory, which pervaded Internet thinking in the late 1990s, was its central premise. The rise of networking did not eliminate intermediaries, but rather changed who they are. It created a whole host of new intermediaries, the most important of which (for our purposes) are ISPs (Internet Service Providers), search engines, browsers, the physical network, and financial intermediaries. In short, the Internet has made the network itself the intermediary for much conduct that we might have thought had no intermediary at all prior to the Internet.

But if governments control the Net through intermediaries, why can't content providers evade this control by just circumventing intermediaries? The answer is that it is hard to get rid of intermediaries because the elimination of intermediaries is in many cases the same thing as the elimination of the underlying conduct. Specialized intermediaries exist, after all, because they allow people to do things that would be difficult, or even impossible, for them to do themselves. It doesn't make sense to speak of making telephone calls without some entity to connect calls. Car manufacturers exist because, though it might be possible for people to make cars on their own, the cost would be enormous. To truly act without any intermediaries means acting by oneself. There are few things that one can do without the direct or indirect assistance of someone else. And so in the Net context, scores of intermediaries are needed to make the Net experience work. Most of the time, they are invisible, but they are there. And they can be controlled.

What about moving the intermediaries themselves offshore, beyond the range of government control? Here is what such a move would look like schematically:

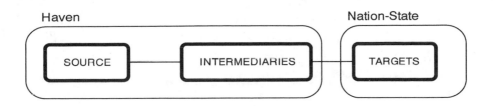

This model is no more realistic than the one that eliminates intermediaries altogether. In the Internet context, there are *always* local
intermediaries. The most basic, of course, is the actual computer
through which individuals access the Net, and which nations can
regulate. Behind that are many more that we have already discussed:
the physical communications lines, the network nodes, search engines, ISPs, and the like. If you try to access an unregulated offshore
ISP through a long-distance telephone call, the phone system becomes an important intermediary. If you unplug your line and connect by Wi-Fi, the computer remains an intermediary, as does a
physical network standing behind a Wi-Fi connection. And so on.
Local intermediaries are a defining, and therefore ineliminable, aspect of the Internet.

We have discussed the enforcement options that remain when the
source of illegal materials moves overseas. But what if, in response to
enforcement, end-users or "targets" also leave the country? This is
the possibility of "total exit" pictured here.

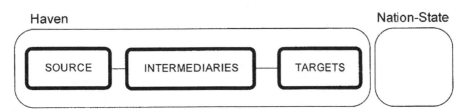

The creation of an exile community is indeed a kind of final escape
from undesirable laws. Moses and the Israelis fled Egypt in search of
(among other things) a better legal system. And today, more prosai-
cally, lovers of high-stakes gambling can move to Las Vegas, and
serious marijuana users can make their home in Amsterdam and enjoy a different kind of life. But at some point this becomes less of a
challenge to government power than an acceptance of it. If you move

from the United States to Germany to escape highway speed limits, that is less what we think of as evasion, and more like what we think of as emigration.

## Finding the Internet's Intermediaries

In the 1990s, Lawrence Lessig revolutionized cyberlaw thinking with his sustained analysis of the premise that "code is law."[12] What Lessig meant was that the architecture of the Internet—its hardware and software—was a different and potentially very powerful way of controlling Internet behavior. One of Lessig's aims was to throw cold water on the hyperlibertarianism of the early Internet days by showing that sometimes government does a better job than private firms (especially monopolies) of designing Internet code in ways that serve user interests. Another aim was to show that the government could control the Internet by controlling its hardware and software.[13] What we learn in the remainder of this chapter sheds a different light on Lessig's thesis. When government practices control through code, it is practicing a commonplace form of intermediary control. Sometimes the government-controlled intermediary is Wal-Mart preventing consumer access to counterfeit products, sometimes it is the bartender enforcing drinking age laws, and sometimes it is an ISP blocking access to illegal information. In what follows we work through what have

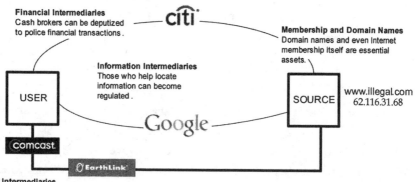

The Nation-State

**Financial Intermediaries**
Cash brokers can be deputized to police financial transactions.

**Membership and Domain Names**
Domain names and even Internet membership itself are essential assets.

**Information Intermediaries**
Those who help locate information can become regulated.

USER

SOURCE    www.illegal.com
62.116.31.68

comcast

EarthLink

**Transport Intermediaries**
The owners of the physical network are an obvious first target.

emerged as the primary intermediaries of government control over the Internet.

### *Transport*

As far back as 1995, the Germans raided the Bavarian offices of Compuserve, and later indicted and tried the German manager of Compuserve Deutschland. The offense: failing to prevent child pornography, much of which came from outside Germany, from reaching German citizens.[14] The prosecution made Compuserve think twice before allowing illicit content through its German portal. In 2001, the British government threatened British ISPs with criminal prosecution for distributing illegal adoption sites, including sites located abroad. The result: British ISPs blocked the sites to keep people in Great Britain from accessing them.[15] Today, German, French, and British laws require local ISPs to screen out illegal content once they are notified of its existence.[16] A European Union Commerce Directive imposes the same basic rule—a rule that, in practice, causes ISPs to err on the side of caution in removing content.[17]

Internet Service Providers are the obvious first target for a strategy of intermediary control. It can be great fun to talk about the Internet as a formless cyberspace. But, as we saw in chapter 4, underneath it all is an ugly physical transport infrastructure: copper wires, fiber-optic cables, and the specialized routers and switches that direct information from place to place. The physical network is by necessity a local asset, owned by phone companies, cable companies, and other service providers who are already some of the most regulated companies on earth. This makes ISPs the most important and most obvious gatekeepers to the Internet.[18] Governments can achieve a large degree of control by focusing on the most important ISPs that service the vast majority of Internet users. "Pressure applied strategically to the concentric ISPs serving smaller ISPs—one or two "dolls" up in a Matryoshka sequence of destination ISPs—can cover large swaths of subscribers," explains Jonathan Zittrain.[19]

As the examples above suggest, the command-and-control Europeans are, in the Western world, pioneers in using ISPs to control unwanted Internet content. Regulation-sensitive Americans have been relatively hands-off, and in fact the United States expressly immunizes ISP from liability in many contexts for the illegal acts of third-party users.[20] At the other end of the spectrum, the true champions of information-transport control can be found in the East. As the next chapter shows in detail, China has from the beginning maintained extremely close control of every element in the Internet transport pipeline. Saudi Arabia has a less aggressive, but still extensive, nationwide filtering system. According to a 2004 report by the OpenNet Initiative, the Saudi government puts proxy servers between the government-owned Internet backbone and servers outside of the Kingdom. If a Saudi ISP user requests illicit content on a foreign server, the request travels through the intermediate proxy server, where it can be filtered and blocked.[21] All the user sees is a "block page" stating that "[a]ccess to the requested URL is not allowed!"[22] Saudi Arabia is most aggressive about blocking pornography, websites that promote drug use, Web gambling sites, information about tools to circumvent the government's filtering, and sites that promote religious dialogue between Muslims and Christians.[23]

### Information Intermediaries

Norwegian Andreas Heldal-Lund describes himself as "a skeptical atheistic freethinking pacifistic positive engaged and tolerant heathen who bases his life on modern secular humanism."[24] He lives in Norway and is a member of both the "Norwegian Society of Heathens" and "Human-Etisk Forbund," a national secular humanist organization. He is also perhaps the Church of Scientology's greatest living irritant. Heldal-Lund has since 1996 devoted much time to a website, "Operation Clambake," that exposes the deepest secrets of the Church and attempts to debunk its teachings.

For the Church of Scientology, Heldal-Lund's activities presented a serious problem of information control. A major benefit of rising through the ranks of the Church's strict internal hierarchy is access to carefully guarded teachings and writings. But in 2002 Operation Clambake's website began to host many of the important teachings of the Church.[25] Suddenly, writings that were meant to take years of preparation to read (and cost tens of thousands of dollars in training) were available to everyone on the World Wide Web.

Unable to shut down Clambake's Norwegian service provider, the Church turned to a different technique. It sent letters to Google, the Web's most popular search engine, demanding that Google take down Clambake's sites under an American law, the Digital Millennium Copyright Act.[26] According to the Church, Clambake's materials were an infringement of copyright that Google was legally obliged to block.[27] Google complied, and for a while a search for "the secret library of Scientology" failed to deliver anything related to Operation Clambake. Eventually, for reasons that remain mysterious, Google restored many of the Operation Clambake sites. The Clambake story nonetheless sheds light on an under-recognized fact: search engines like Google routinely block links because of possible governmental action.

Google receives a constant stream of letters in the United States—about thirty per month—insisting that it remove specified pages from its search results, usually because of alleged copyright or trademark infringement.[28] Google complies with most of these requests. Many of these pages are located on servers outside the United States, beyond the direct control of U.S. law.[29] But the government, or those invoking its laws, can block the offshore content provider by going after the local search engine instead.

As with information transport, Europeans are more aggressive about using search engines as Web content-blockers. In 2002, Jonathan Zittrain and Ben Edelman found that Google in France and Germany (google.fr and google.de, respectively) blocked more than one hundred sites that were available on google.com. "While google.fr and google.de use google.com's database concordance of 2,469,940,685 web pages (Google's count as of October 20, 2002), the French and German sites seem to screen search results corresponding to sites with content that might be sensitive or illegal in the respective countries," explained Zittrain and Edelman.[30] Most of the sites blocked in France and Germany unsurprisingly concerned Nazism, hate speech, white supremacy, and related sites that are banned in those countries but lawful in the United States.

The general technique of controlling information intermediaries has extraordinary potential. Consider how often you rely not just on search engines to find information but also on blogs, online newspapers, and other intermediaries that point you in the direction of useful information. It is one thing for government to crack down openly on forbidden information. But it can be harder to notice that information has become more difficult to find. It is hard, in other words, to know what you don't know.

### Financial Intermediaries

In the early 2000s, online cigarette vending looked like a promising business, especially on Indian reservations that typically place no taxes on cigarettes sales. A 2001 survey found that of eighty-eight online cigarette vendors, forty-nine were on reservations and most of the rest were in low-tax states.[31] The basic advantage of buying online in bulk is convenience and tax avoidance. In New York State, for example, state taxes amount to about $15 per carton. It is thus unsurprising that, by 2004, online cigarettes were a $1 billion industry, or 3.1 percent of industry volume.[32]

All that changed in 2005. The Federal Bureau of Alcohol, Tobacco, and Firearms, joined by several states, decided to crack down on online sales. They didn't bother actually charging the vendors with anything. Instead, they went after crucial financial intermediaries—the major credit card companies. The bureau simply ordered Visa, MasterCard, and AmEx to stop taking online cigarette orders or face the consequences. Government officials argued that the online sites weren't doing enough to comply with age verification laws, and weren't making sure that states receive their sales tax.

Was the government right? Online cigarette companies are hardly the only ones who do not charge state sales tax on online sales, and as for underage buying, the tobacco vendors insisted that they do maintain controls. Experts agreed online purchases by minors were not a serious problem, or no more serious than any other way that minors get access to cigarettes. But the vendors will never have a chance to test their theory in court. The credit card companies accepted the government's position, and that was that.

"Not since the dot-com bust have so many sites gone south so quickly," reported the *New York Times* in the spring of 2005. Scores of online vendors went under in a two-week period. They "lost the means to do business profitably, and are either limping along or have shut down their operations altogether."[33] Without access to credit card payment, the cigarette websites might have tried other financial intermediaries, like PayPal. But PayPal capitulated too, just as it did in a similar situation when New York officials threatened it with fines for financing illegal offshore Web gambling.[34] Checks or direct deposits from local banks would in the end fare no better, since local officials could go after these new intermediaries with the same tools it used against the others. There might be other ways for the determined purchaser to buy online cigarettes, but at some point buying cigarettes online becomes enough of a legally dangerous pain in the rear to kill the business model.

As the cigarette example shows, governmental targeting of financial intermediaries can cripple an online industry, particularly one that is premised on convenience of payment. Could the online pharmaceutical industry prosper if the seller didn't take credit cards? Could Amazon or eBay stay in business without convenient lines of credit? Probably not. And that is how, without ever laying a finger on online sellers, the government can impose its power, often without even needing to go to court.

### The Domain Name System and Internet Membership

In the fall of 2000, Al Gore and George W. Bush were fighting for the American presidency, aided by hundreds of millions in campaign contributions. That gave James Baumgartner, a student at the Rensselaer Polytechnic Institute, a clever idea. As a commentary on the role of money in the election, he opened the website voteauction.com as a place for otherwise uninterested voters to sell their votes to the highest bidder.[35] Its slogan was "Bringing Capitalism and Democracy Closer Together." With so much money being spent trying to influence elections, why not just pay the money directly to the voter? Baumgartner billed Voteauction as "the only election platform channeling 'soft money' directly to the democratic consumer."[36]

The site actually worked. As the *Chicago Tribune* reported in early October of 2000, 521 unidentified people in Illinois had agreed to sell their presidential votes. The top anonymous bid for the 521 votes was $8,500, or $16.31 per head.[37] While Baumgartner intended the site as satire, the Chicago Board of Election Commissioners decided there was nothing funny about offering to buy and sell votes, and it moved to shut down Voteauction as quickly as possible. And it chose a novel means. Instead of targeting Baumgartner, or trying to hunt down the vote-sellers themselves, it went after an essential asset—the name "voteauction.com."[38]

In short order, an Illinois judge imposed an injunction not on Voteauction but on its U.S. domain name registry, Domain Bank, which had a standard domain name registration agreement prohibiting domain name use for "illegal purposes."[39] Domain Bank banished voteauction.com's domain name as if it were the itinerant Mr. Bungle, "shutting down voteauction.com all over the world."[40] One week later, voteauction.com opened up under a new domain name, "vote-auction.com," registered in Switzerland with the International Council of Registrars (CORE).[41] But CORE too had a prohibition against illegal uses in its standard domain name registration agreement, and after extensive telephone and e-mail discussions, vote-auction.com was shut down.[42] Voteauction later began trying to publicize its numerical IP address, http://62.116.31.68, but that address is obviously much harder to find, and by then the voting was over.[43]

In 2003, John Ashcroft's Justice Department began a controversial crackdown on Web vendors of drug paraphernalia—purveyors of bongs, vaporizers, and other favorites. Its method: the seizure of the website domain names themselves. The Justice Department explained that seizing property used in the commission of a crime is a routine matter. And rather than shutting down the sites, the Justice Department, in effect, hijacked them. Visitors looking for a new pipe would instead read:

> BY APPLICATION OF THE UNITED STATES DRUG ENFORCEMENT ADMINISTRATION, THE WEBSITE YOU ARE ATTEMPTING TO VISIT HAS BEEN RESTRAINED BY THE UNITED STATES DISTRICT COURT.[44]

Since its experiment with drug sites, the Justice Department has also begun seizing the domain names of sites that facilitate copyright infringement, replacing them with warnings against piracy. "I believe this is one area—intellectual property rights—where there is a deterrent effect from aggressive and effective criminal prosecution," said Ross Nadel of the San Francisco U.S. Attorney's Office. Nadel predicted that the government would redirect users to a privacy warning page following future domain name seizures.[45]

Tight control over domain names is another looming and particularly effective way for nations to control Internet behavior. As discussed in Chapter 3, we take it for granted that the Internet's "membership policy" is neutral and open. But that's contingent, already under attack from several quarters, and a fact that could gradually change. Countries know that as a general matter, membership rules have always been a powerful means of control, whether it's at a country club or the World Trade Organization. There may come a time, and that time might be soon, when accurately disclosing who you are is a condition of Internet membership. There may soon come a time when abusing your privileges as a member of the Internet could lead to expulsion from the club.

As these and other examples show, government has many types of intermediaries it can use for indirect control. None of these examples should obscure the most basic means of control: the direct physical coercion of individuals.

## Targeting Individuals

Tore Tvedt ran a Norwegian organization called Vigrid, devoted to the worship of Odin, other ancient Norse gods, and the ideology of the Nazi party. Fearing Norwegian hate-speech laws, Tvedt had a clever idea. He placed his anti-Semitic propaganda on a server in the United States, beyond the reach of Norwegian authorities. Unfortunately for Tvedt, he didn't do anything to put *himself* out of the reach of Norwegian authorities. One day in 2002, the Norwegian police simply arrived at the home of Tvedt and placed him under arrest. [46]

Tvedt illustrates the simplest and most direct strategy that governments use in response to illegal Internet content from abroad—physical arrest of individuals inside their borders. Sometimes, as with Tvedt, they do so to dry up the *supply* side of unwanted Internet communications. What happened to Tvedt also happened to Duane Pede and Jeff D'Ambrosia, two Americans who lived in the United States and were convicted of running an Internet gambling site from an island off the coast of Venezuela.[47] Other times, governments crack down on individuals in order to dry up the *demand* side. When the FBI closed down Landslide Productions, a Texas-based website that gave paid subscribers access to hundreds of Russian and Indonesian child porn sites, they discovered a database full of subscribers worldwide.[48] Authorities in the United States, Canada, and Great Britain used this information to arrest thousands of Landslide customers within their borders.[49]

Some may be skeptical of the effectiveness of arresting a few law violators when so many are violating the law. But this skepticism overlooks the deterrence effects of individual enforcement. In the late 1960s, economist and Nobel laureate Gary Becker argued that lawbreakers were rational, and that their decisions to break laws reflected a calculation of costs (including the chances of getting caught and the possibility of fines or jail time) and benefits (the financial and other rewards of crime).[50] The government, Becker argued, doesn't need to catch every lawbreaker to control lawbreaking. It just needs to increase the likelihood and severity of punishments to the point where for most people the costs of committing crime are less than the benefits. The economics of deterrence led Becker to argue that government shouldn't waste too much money looking for criminals but instead should just raise the sanctions for breaking the law. You might think more than twice about parking illegally if a parking ticket meant a month in prison.

Matters are not, of course, as simple as Becker suggested. Fear of punishment is not the only reason people obey the law. Reflecting this intuition, academic work since Becker's article has pointed out the limits on the amount of deterrence that can be achieved just by increasing punishments. Some people, for example, are poor enough that they don't fear fines, or are so pessimistic about their future prospects that going to jail may not seem so bad. And of course there's an upper limit on what most governments can threaten. For various social and moral reasons, parking violations do not usually result in one-month prison sentences. If governments punished relatively minor wrongs (like Internet gambling) as severely as serious crimes (like bank robbery), the law would lose its ability to send a message about what citizens should not do, and what they *really* should not do.[51]

So there are limits to deterrence through individual enforcement. But Becker's basic point—that even criminals respond to incentives— is sound. Enforcement against individuals is rarely an isolated strategy but usually part of a unified strategy that involves various means of intermediate control as well. The interesting and difficult question is how much individual enforcement adds, especially in situations like those of mass disobedience that often prevail on the Internet, such as music filesharing. The point for now is simply that enforcement against individuals has at least some effect and is part of an integrated governmental strategy to crack down on law evasion.

## Challenges

Our discussion of the techniques of government control over the Internet is not meant to suggest that the techniques always work perfectly. They do not. Nor do we mean to suggest that government control over Internet activities will always be as successful as when these activities take place outside the Internet. They will not, as consumers of pornography, web gambling, and free digital music know. At one level, these points are unsurprising. Every great technological innovation has the potential to lower the cost of violating law. The telephone, at least before wiretapping, made it easier for criminals to plan their activities. The record player and the radio increased the incidence of infringement of copyright-protected music. Transportation advances (the automobile, the airplane) made it easier for criminals to plan and commit crimes from abroad, or to commit crimes in one place and flee to another.

The same is true of the Internet, as porn and web gambling show. But as we have emphasized throughout this book, law has never been perfect. It succeeds by lowering the incidence of prohibited activities to an acceptable degree. The Internet will not, as Barlow and other romantics suggested, make it so easy to violate so many laws that the nation-state itself will cease to function. But in certain areas, techniques of law avoidance will prove more effective than in others. The interesting and difficult questions are how such new techniques of control will fare against new techniques of avoidance—and what the ultimate results of such arms races will be. We consider three main issues: small nations, intermediary minimization, and mixing.

The techniques of intermediary control are generally less effective in small nations, where opportunities for Internet intermediary control are diminished. The United States and France can control offshore Internet communications through intermediaries more readily than Fiji and Ghana because the larger countries have a larger array of intermediaries to go after. We learned in chapter 1 that France was able to influence the local effects of Yahoo's U.S. servers because Yahoo had many assets, including a subsidiary, in France. But Yahoo doesn't have a presence or assets in Fiji or Ghana. Nor do information intermediaries like Google or Blogger. That doesn't leave a country like Fiji without options. It can choose to block the Internet altogether, and it can still order its necessarily local intermediaries—for example, ISPs—to filter forbidden materials. But some of the techniques available to large-market countries are just unavailable to those with smaller markets.

Even in powerful countries, intermediaries, while impossible to eliminate, can in some contexts be relatively hard to control. The story of Web gambling in the United States provides a good example. In response to the rise of web gambling services in Caribbean countries like Antigua, U.S. enforcement officials focused their attention on local financial intermediaries—the credit card companies and Internet payment systems (like PayPal) that made it possible for Americans to ante up online. In 2002, New York's redoubtable attorney general, Eliot Spitzer, used threats of prosecution to convince every major American credit card provider and online payment system to stop honoring web gambling transactions. "With this agreement, we will cut off an enormous line of credit that was a jackpot off illegal offshore casinos," Spitzer proclaimed.[52] This technique seemed to work pretty well, driving half of Antiguan web gambling firms out of business, and (in the words of the Antiguan prime minister) leaving a "significant, negative impact upon the [Antiguan] economy."[53]

But Spitzer's efforts did not end matters. As we'll see in chapter 10, Antigua brought an action against the United States in the World Trade Organization. The web gambling firms fought back as well. Instead of relying on credit cards, they began to ask customers to wire money from local banks to offshore banks to use for chips.[54] Because there are thousands of local banks in the United States, this strategy dramatically multiplied the number of intermediaries in the United States that enforcement officials must crack down on. And this, in turn, means that financial control of offshore web gambling is more complicated and expensive for local officials, for now they must go after thousands of intermediaries rather than just a dozen or so.

This arms race increased the costs to government of controlling gambling. But at the same time, of course, it increased the costs to gamblers themselves, who must now arrange to transfer money from banks rather than type in a credit card number, and who face heightened chances of legal jeopardy. It is difficult to generalize about when and under what conditions these swings of regulation and evasion will reach equilibrium. The government's resources dwarf those of private entities, and can, with sufficient focus and will, be expected to prevail in most contests. But the government does not always have the focus and will to prevail, often because at some cost the activity in question is simply not worth cracking down on further.

This latter point relates to the third technique of avoidance: mixing. Why is it so easy to get Internet porn in the United States? You might think it's because Internet porn is inherently difficult to control, but there's more to it than that. As we saw in chapter 2, the American Congress reacted quickly to the initial flood of Internet porn, passing the Communications Decency Act in 1996—a law that would have done much to drive pornography behind ID-protected walls. But the problem for government's efforts to control pornography is that it's hard to distinguish it from stuff the U.S. government doesn't want blocked, like artistic expression, sexual education, and news. As a result, the government's interest in stopping porn collided with its constitutional commitment to free speech. The Supreme Court, as we saw in chapter 2, concluded that the law's effort to crackdown on Internet porn swept up too much protected speech along the way. When a new technology that makes it much cheaper and easier to make and distribute pornography combines with the fact that pornography is hard to distinguish from deeply valued protected speech, the result is an increase in the incidence of available pornography.

This is the technique of "mixing" legal and illegal conduct. For law avoiders, it means structuring conduct so that a given business—for example, pornography—can only be stopped at the expense of giving up things that government and society value highly—like artistic expression and an open environment for speech. Mixing gives the government no choice but to lose what it likes when it bans what it doesn't like. It means taking advantage of deeply held national values, like commitments to open commerce, free speech, or respect for citizen privacy. That can be enough for a country like the United States to leave an activity, like pornography, basically unregulated. It doesn't mean the United States cannot control pornography, for the United States could in theory adopt techniques used in countries like Saudi Arabia that worry less about the incidental effects on protected speech. What it means is that the United States would be forced to compromise in ways it is unwilling to do.

Nation size, intermediary minimization, and mixing can all affect the success of national Internet control. We address additional challenges to Internet control in chapter 10. But while these challenges should not be overlooked, they should not be overstated either. Along other dimensions, the Internet, like all previous communications technologies, increases government power. For example, it enhances the government's ability to monitor the everyday activities of its citizens, to know about, and thus potentially to control, what is going on in every recess of the nation, and to convey government information and propaganda. These Internet-related powers are often held in check in countries like the United States that value privacy and free speech. But as we will see in chapter 6, in the hands of a government like China that does not share these values, the Internet enables frighteningly unprecedented control by the government over individuals.

## Epilogue

On August 3, 2003, HavenCo founder Ryan Lackey went to Las Vegas to give an astonishing speech at DefCon, the annual convention for computer hackers. His talk was titled "HavenCo: What Really Happened."[55] HavenCo, he revealed to the world, had never been the success it was portrayed to be. The story of the giant server farm, hidden deep in the recesses of Sealand, was a lie: HavenCo's equipment consisted of "five relay racks standing mostly empty."[56] The "dozens" of customers HavenCo claimed were, at the best of times, roughly ten, almost all online casinos.[57] And now, Lackey reported to the crowd, HavenCo was dead.

HavenCo died for two related reasons. The first was the absence of cooperative intermediaries, especially financial intermediaries. "Sovereignty alone," said Lackey, "has little value without commer-

Ryan Lackey, founder of HavenCo, spent long periods living on Sealand (Kim Gilmour)

cial support from banks, etc."[58] Banks wouldn't cooperate with
HavenCo, one suspects, for the same reasons that U.S. financial institutions are not cooperating with online cigarette sales. Local pressure
on these crucial intermediaries influences how they interact with providers of information content.

Sealand itself also turned out to be susceptible to the pressures of
powerful governments. More than anything else, Prince Michael, the
ruler of Sealand, wanted recognition as an actual country. HavenCo's
unseemly activities, he began to believe, were an impediment to that
dream. The Prince began to insist that HavenCo adhere to "norms of
international practice and custom" and demanded that nothing "offensive" be available from his sovereign nation.[59] But of course, the
hosting of "offensive" content was HavenCo's raison d'être. Without
it, HavenCo was nothing. The company sank into a slow decline, shed-
ding customers and losing money, until finally came what Lackey called
the "nationalization" of HavenCo in November 2002, when Sealand
kicked HavenCo off the island. Sealand today nominally owns what
remains of HavenCo—a jumbled pile of network equipment, rotting
and obsolete.

# China

"Long live prostitutes" was the title of Wang's posting. Fifteen years old, living in China, and full of teenage bluster, Wang had collected fifty-four reasons to think Chinese politicians worse than prostitutes. The list included:

- There is no indicator that prostitutes will disappear, but there are many indicators that the government will collapse.

- Prostitutes allow others to oppose them, unlike the government which arrests opposition and "re-educates" them through labor.

- Prostitutes have no power, unlike those who use their power to suppress others.

- Prostitutes do not need you to love them, unlike that group which forces you to love it.

- Prostitutes win customers with credibility, unlike those who maintain power with lies.

- Prostitutes sell flesh, unlike those who sell soul.[1]

Liu Di was a psychology student at Beijing Normal University who called herself the "Stainless Steel Mouse" and ran an "artist's club" through her personal website. In 2002, in one of her many stunts, the twenty-two-year-old urged her followers to distribute Marxist literature:

Let's conduct an experiment of behavioral art: disseminating communism on the street! We can print copies of "The Communist Manifesto." However, we should take "Communist" out of the title. Then, like sociologists, we ask people on the street to sign their names onto the Manifesto.

Liu Di wrote an essay titled "How a national security apparatus can hurt national security." Echoing typical criticism of governments everywhere, she called China's security apparatus "limitless," or possessed of "a tendency to expand, without limits, its size and functions."[2]

Wang's message and the writings of Liu Di appeared on obscure Internet sites. Nonetheless, they came to the attention of the Chinese authorities and provoked swift action. Soon after Wang posted his message, it was deleted. He was arrested in Henan and subjected to an unspecified punishment. Wang's story was printed in the *People's Daily* as a warning, with the headline "15-Year-Old Youth Punished For Making Reactionary Argument That the Government is Prostitute"[3]

The State Security Protection Bureau arrested Liu Di on her university campus on November 7, 2002. Her site was shut down, and she was jailed and forced to share a cell with a convicted murderer. When human rights groups and other Chinese Internet users protested, the government responded by arresting five Net users who had signed a petition calling for Di's release. The State Security Bureau told Liu Di's parents that their daughter was charged with "being detrimental to

state security."[4] Liu Di was held for a full year, then released subject to permanent surveillance and banned from speaking to foreign journalists or traveling outside of Beijing.[5]

These examples of political control are one side of the Chinese Internet. But if you visit China, you'll be struck by a different and seemingly paradoxical reality—information technology

Liu Di, Internet writer who was arrested for her essays (AFP/AFP/Getty Images)

and mass media are flourishing as never before. By 2005, China's aggressive broadband rollouts had created nearly as many Chinese broadband users as in the United States.[6] One hundred million people in China had Internet accounts, there were 4 million Chinese blogs, countless chatrooms, and scores of commercial sites like eBay China and Ctrip.com, a travel reservation site.[7]

Facts like these led many, including the *New York Times*'s Nicholas Kristof, to believe that China's Communist Party must be losing power. As Kristof wrote in a 2005 column, *Death by a Thousand Blogs*, "the Chinese leadership . . . is digging the Communist Party's grave, by giving the Chinese people broadband."[8] Like many others, Kristof believed that the Internet, once it reaches a country, is an unstoppable liberating force. Kristof's colleague Thomas Friedman put it this way: "the Internet and globalization are acting like nutcrackers to open societies."[9]

This chapter explains why this conventional wisdom is wrong. Some people, when they see pornography and web gambling and hate speech flourishing on the Internet, wonder whether the techniques of intermediary control and individual deterrence can do the job. But as the China example shows, a government's failure to crack down on certain types of Internet communication ultimately reflects a failure of interest or will, not a failure of power. The developing Chinese Internet shows what a government that really wants to control Internet communications can accomplish.

The Chinese government does not try to control everything on the Internet. William Farris of the Congressional-Executive Commission on China states that the Chinese government is "drawing an increasingly clear line. You can talk about what you want, but no direct threats to Government."[10] It is trying to create an Internet that is free enough to support and maintain the world's fastest growing economy, and yet closed enough to tamp down political threats to its monopoly on power. The government is doing this by grafting Chinese nationalist ideology onto the network itself, in the process literally changing the nature of the Internet in China. Because of linguistic and cultural differences with the West, and because of the government's extraordinary system of monitoring and filtering, the Chinese Internet is becoming less and less like its Western counterparts—it is pulling away from the rest of the world.

China is not only an extreme example of control; it is also an extreme example of how and why the Internet is becoming bordered by geography. Only time will tell whether the China strategy will work, or whether the sheer volume of information will erode the government's influence and render the Internet in China open and free. But so far, China is showing the opposite: that the Internet enjoyed in the West is a choice—not fate, not destiny, and not natural law.

## President Clinton and the China Democracy Party

When President Bill Clinton visited China in 1998, he pledged to spend time talking about freedom of information and human rights. While in Shanghai, Clinton stopped at an Internet café to mingle with young Internet users. He said afterward, "I had an incredible experience in one of these Internet cafés in Shanghai." Access, he declared, was now open to all. "Even if they didn't have computers at home, they could come to the café, buy a cup of coffee, rent a little time and access the Internet."[11] Clinton later joked about China's prospects for controlling the Net. "There's no question China has been trying to crack down on the Internet—good luck. (laughter). That's sort of like trying to nail Jell-O to the wall. (laughter)."[12]

While Clinton was visiting China, Wang Youcai, a political activist, decided to test Clinton's theory. On the morning of June 28, 1998, Wang went with two friends to the Civil Affairs Bureau in Hangzhou, China. The bureau is located near the famous and picturesque West Lake, former summer residence of the emperor, about eighty miles south of Shanghai. As part of a careful plan devised via e-mail, Wang decided to register, openly, an opposition political party, with a name similar to President Clinton's party: the "China Democracy Party."[13]

Wang was aware of the risks but felt the time was ripe. Clinton was in China; the regime had begun to signal some degree of political relaxation—yet another "Beijing Spring" in the history of Chinese politics; and the China Democracy Party had the liberating power of Internet technology on its side. Even if the registration failed, Wang had set up overseas websites, and used a U.S.-based e-mail newsletter ("VIP Reference") to communicate his ideas to thousands of mainland Chinese. The China Democracy Party would, they thought, follow a long history of overseas Chinese opposition movements and conduct its resistance in cyberspace. Wang was putting the Internet's capacity for political liberation to the test.

Wang's application was, unsurprisingly, rejected. The next day, June 29, police officers came to his home in Hangzhou. While his wife and children watched, they took Wang away. As his wife, Hu Jiangxia, later said, "Plain-clothes police came to our house around one o'clock and talked to my husband about his activities and about the China Democracy Party. They took him away just before four o'clock."[14] The detention came just as Clinton arrived in Shanghai, 80 miles from Wang's home.

Wang and others were formally charged, several weeks later, with "fomenting opposition against the government."[15] His wife wrote an impassioned letter to President Ziang Zeming. Does he "deserve to be treated like this just because of the pursuit of democracy and freedom[?]" she asked.[16] Her letter, available only outside of China, went unanswered.

On December 18, Wang was tried in a Hangzhou court without a lawyer. Facing a possible penalty of life imprisonment, he pled not guilty and conducted his own, unsuccessful, defense. His trial lasted only a few hours.[17] He was sentenced on December 21, 1998, to eleven years imprisonment and three years deprivation of political rights for subversion.[18] Around the same time, most of the other founding members of the China Democracy Party were tried and imprisoned. Wang and his colleagues had become Clinton's Jell-O, nailed to the wall.

Three days before Wang's sentencing, President Jiang Zemin gave a landmark speech commemorating the twentieth anniversary of economic reforms that began in 1978. President Clinton, during his visit earlier that year, described "a genuine movement toward openness and freedom."[19] But here Jiang spoke on a different topic: the necessity of absolute information control. "From beginning to end, we must be vigilant against infiltration, subversive activities, and separatist activities of international and domestic hostile forces," said Jiang to thunderous applause.[20] Standing before a giant golden hammer and sickle mounted between large red curtains, he announced his vision. "Only by sticking to and perfecting China's socialist political system can we achieve the country's unification, national unity, social stability, and economic developments." He concluded that "The Western mode of political systems must never be copied."[21]

Wang Youcai's imprisonment is an example of a Chinese government strategy best expressed by the Chinese proverb "killing chicken to scare monkey." In other words, China practices Gary Becker's selective deterrence with a vengeance. Arrest and detention of those who criticize the government is the simplest method of killing the chicken to scare the monkey. But China uses the Internet to employ an array of more subtle methods to deter political activists. And it is doing much more on the Internet than practicing deterrence: It is changing the nature of the Internet itself.

## Information Borders

What do the following websites have in common?

- Sex.com

- The U.S. Bankruptcy Court for the District of Massachusetts

- GALA: Gay and Lesbian Acceptance

- Depression Reality: Information and Support

- The University of Michigan Health System

Each of these sites, external to China, was blocked or is blocked by the Chinese government as a threat to the Chinese State.[22] We know this because in 2002, Jonathan Zittrain and Ben Edelman manually dialed a Chinese Internet provider long distance, and in the guise of a Chinese end user, went looking for blocked websites. The results were the first-ever openly available list of sites that the Chinese government is blocking, or was blocking at the time.[23]

How does the Chinese government block sites outside its borders? China has surrounded itself with the world's most sophisticated information barrier, a semipermeable membrane that lets in what the government wants and blocks what it doesn't. In technical terms, it is a "firewall," rather similar to the security firewalls placed around corporations. Only this one is placed around the entire country.

China's information barrier was built primarily by Cisco, the Silicon Valley network vendor. In the early 1990s, Cisco and other companies developed products to let American corporations filter employee access to the Internet. Companies wanted the Internet, but they didn't want their employees on ESPN or playboy.com all day. Cisco demonstrated to Chinese officials long ago that the same products could be used to effectively block unwanted materials from entering China. It showed that it could be done flexibly, in a subtle fashion, and without loss of performance. Hence, the modern "Great Wall of China" is, in effect, built with American bricks.[24]

China's information barrier works because Internet data enters or leaves China at a limited number of points. At each of these "gateways," Chinese officials have ordered Chinese Internet carriers like China Telecom to deploy Cisco's equipment as a checkpoint. The key product is the "router," a sophisticated network computer that "routes" Internet traffic to the correct destination. Since a router knows how to *get* information to the right location, it can easily be reprogrammed to *lose* information instead. That's all that a basic filter is: an instruction to drop information from or for certain addresses.

In practice, the government provides a list (the "access control list") of all of the banned sites, identified by their IP address (e.g., 127.37.28.1) and their URLs (e.g., wutangclan.com). These sites, presumably, are obtained by the labor-intensive search conducted by the Internet Police or other agencies. Companies like China Telecom feed

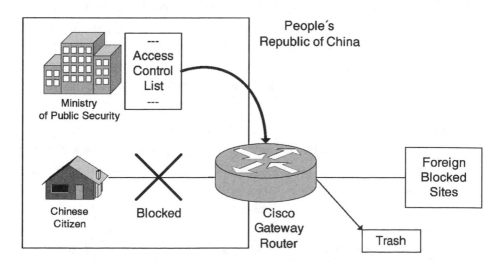

their gateway routers the list of blocked addresses provided by the government. Subsequently, any message, or packet, carrying a forbidden address is simply dropped and never reaches its target. John Gilmore's idea from chapter 1 that the Internet "interprets censorship as damage and routes around it" is thus reversed: the router itself has become the censor.

But doesn't this filtering, which happens at high speed (what an engineer would call "wire-speed," or the speed of light), come at a performance cost? Not really. It can be more efficient to drop packets of information than to route them to their proper destination. Imagine how much easier and faster the mailman's job would be if he were allowed to dump half his mailbag into the garbage. The same goes for routers: the Cisco and other routers can block Internet traffic without a significant negative impact on performance. As a result, China gets an Internet just as fast as any other country's but limited to what China wants its citizens to see.

Chinese censorship is not only efficient but also subtle. No screen appears saying "Blocked by the Chinese State." Instead, the blocking takes on the appearance of technical error. A user who tries to reach, say, freechina.net, will get a "site not found" screen, a network timeout screen, or any one of a number of HTTP error codes.[25] And it can be difficult for an end user (and researchers) to know whether the problem is in fact censorship or technical difficulties. The mandated list of blocked sites changes as political events develop. For example, sometimes the *New York Times* website is available on computers in China, and sometimes it isn't.[26] This uncertainty, coupled with the general unreliability of the Internet, helps mask efforts at censorship.

So what does the Chinese government block? In 2005, Zittrain and a new team of Harvard researchers repeated Zittrain's original study and concluded that "China operates the most extensive, technologically sophisticated, and broad-reaching system of Internet filtering in the world."[27] They found that Chinese filtering had grown to focus even more carefully on the principal perceived threats to the Communist Party: Tibetan independence groups and human rights sites like Human Rights Watch or Amnesty International; religious or spiritual sites, such as Christian, Muslim, Jewish, Hindu, and even new-age churches; and, of course, any and all information related to the banned Falun Gong religious movement. And finally, the Party justifies the border blocking as a kind of defense against Western "dumping" of information on China. As the Party says, "Western countries, headed by the United States . . . dump on China massive amounts of information of all kinds, including their political models, value systems, and lifestyles, in order to oppose and edge out socialist values."[28]

China's border barriers are important. But ultimately they are not its most important form of Internet control. Some may imagine that Chinese citizens are dying to read an uncensored version of the *New York Post*, but that isn't so. Domestic interest in foreign sites within China is low to begin with, because the sites don't focus on China and usually aren't written in Chinese. As a result, the real centerpiece of China's system of information control is its internal controls.

## Internal Controls

In the spring of 2005, China watchers and Microsoft haters found common ground when Microsoft admitted that its "MSN Spaces" service, allowing users to set up blogs in China, would block all titles like "freedom" and "democracy." A blog site titled "democracy" generated an error message as follows: "This message includes forbidden language. Please delete the prohibited expression."[29]

Microsoft is not the only American company helping the Chinese government to censor within its borders. Say you're using a Yahoo China online discussion forum and you type "It's time for an independent Taiwan and multiparty elections in China." In all probability, no one will react. The reason? Yahoo China, with the help of a time delay and a human or software filter, will block your message before it hits the chatroom.[30] As we saw in chapter 1, Yahoo, the former champion of free-speech rights in the United States, plays an entirely different role in China. It employs a host of censorship systems that continually monitor and filter what people see.

Just as Cisco's routers patrol the boundaries of China, American commercial service providers like Microsoft and Yahoo run an even more sophisticated program of internal information control within China. Through these and other methods of internal control, China has created a system—originally called the "golden shield" by the Ministry of Public Security—that complements China's external barrier.

Beginning in 2000, the Chinese Information Industry Ministry issued regulations defining the different kinds of content banned from discussion forums. In addition, as we saw in chapter 1, major commercial operators like Yahoo agreed in 2002 to a binding "self-discipline pact." The pact obliges signatories "not to produce or disseminate harmful texts or news likely to jeopardize national security and social stability, violate laws and regulations, or spread false news, superstitions and obscenities."[31]

In 2003, a group named Reporters Without Borders decided to test the effectiveness of the internal Chinese filters.[32] It wanted to see what would actually happen if political postings were made. Was it all just a lot of talk—or would posts actually be taken down? The results give us rare insight into the operation of an active censorship regime. They show a censorship system that is far from perfect, yet nonetheless prevents effective debate of topics the government does not want discussed.

The reporters, working from overseas, logged on to websites and began typing forbidden words. The first thing they learned was that all messages containing a set of forbidden words were automatically screened by software and never reached anyone. In their testing, any message or posting on a discussion forum stating words like "human rights," "Taiwan independence," "pornography," "oral sex," "BBC," or "Falun Gong" was filtered by machine and lost forever.

What about more subtle messages? The reporters found a subjective sliding scale at work, betraying a human intelligence. More sensitive or controversial messages would be blocked or quickly deleted. Less sensitive messages would last a little longer, but then also eventually be deleted. Direct criticism of government officials—such as demands for new political leadership—were in the former category, either never reaching the forum or facing near-immediate deletion. Conversely, less controversial subjects, like discussion of the Chinese role in the war in Iraq, lasted longer. But the important thing was that the messages did not last: most of those that even made it to the discussion group were eventually taken down within the hour.

In time, the user-accounts used to post messages were blocked and kicked off the discussion list. Had the reporters actually been in China, there is some possibility they would have been arrested and prosecuted for subversive acts. Why would the ISPs erase messages and delete users? The reason is simple: threats directed at ISPs themselves. As the Congressional-Executive Commission (CEC) set up by Congress in early 2000 to monitor China's conduct has observed, systems "known for allowing cutting-edge postings on politically sensitive topics routinely disappear from the Internet altogether."[33]

The scale of human involvement in China's internal censorship system may be changing. The CEC reported that the Chinese government funded research in software designed to identify the political viewpoint of information. It described a "Falun Gong Content Examination System" that designates pro–Falun Gong information as "black," anti–Falun Gong information as "red," and articles dealing with Buddhism and health care as "neutral." "The system can be installed on personal computers, servers, and at national gateways, so that as soon as a user tries to visit a web page that is pro-Falun Gong, the system can filter the page and immediately notify authorities."[34] While the effectiveness of the Falun Gong content examination software is hard to verify, it is clear that China will continue to invest in ever-more automated internal control and filtering systems.

Increasingly sophisticated filtering systems are not, of course, the only methods of internal control. The Chinese government also deters unwanted political communication (and in the process enhances its monitoring capabilities). For example, it requires bloggers to register with the central government, and it closely polices Internet cafés.[35] In the early 2000s, authorities conducted major crackdowns that closed thousands of "illegal" cafés across the country.[36] Today, regulations in cities like Shanghai, where Clinton went, require users to register with their national ID card before logging on. Regulated cafés also feature cameras pointed at computer screens and, occasionally, roving police officers who simply watch what users are doing. Far from being a liberating force, the Internet café in China has become a major site of government surveillance.

## Promoting Nationalism

Ma Zhichun lives in central China and meets the exacting qualifications necessary for his job. He is less than forty years old, a university graduate with a background in journalism, and has extensive experience using the Internet. Ma's job is "Internet Commentator" for the Siquan City External Propaganda Office. He is paid to secretly influence public opinion, as found on chatrooms and elsewhere, in directions that favor the government. As Ma explains his job, "the key is to seize the initiative."[37]

It is wrong to say that the Internet has failed to promote a new political consciousness in China; it just hasn't been the kind the West had hoped for. Sometimes, to be sure, dissidents have used the Internet to the government's disadvantage, and sometimes political sentiment on the Net has exposed the political corruption of individual officials. But what has emerged, usually with the tacit support of the government, is Internet support for a different ideology: Chinese nationalism, often laced with virulent anti-American or anti-Japanese sentiment. The government is using the Internet, in other words, to direct anger away from the Communist government and toward China's foreign "enemies."

In May of 1999, an American B-2 bomber, using an outdated map, dropped four 2,000-pound bombs on the Chinese embassy in Belgrade, destroying the building and killing three Chinese citizens.[38] Government-operated media immediately suggested, on the Internet and elsewhere, that the bombing was no mistake. As anti-American riots erupted, the *People's Daily*, China's largest newspaper, helpfully created a chat-forum called the "Anti-Bombing Forum" (later changed to the "Strong country forum.") According to Shanthi Kalathil of the Carnegie Endowment, the forums played a "small but significant role in legitimizing among an elite, wired section of the population the Chinese government's position that the bombing was deliberate."[39] They also provided the first outlet for anti-American rage on the Internet, setting a pattern that has been followed and encouraged.

In 2001, an American EP-3 surveillance plane was confronted by two F-8 Chinese military jets off the southeastern Chinese coast. The American plane collided with one of the F-8s, killing the Chinese pilot and forcing the American plane to conduct an emergency landing.[40] The Americans were held by the Chinese government for a time, and the Internet chatrooms erupted as never before. "If little Bush goes on squawking, we should rope together his 24 white pigs and parade them through the streets," read one reported posting.[41] The official online and paper media fed the fire. "On this planet only the stuck-up United States is this rude and unreasonable."[42]

Japan has not been left out. In 2003, Internet chatrooms buzzed with anger after reports of police breaking up a giant orgy held in a Chinese hotel by Japanese businessmen. In the spring of 2005, the Japanese government approved the use of a controversial textbook which among other things refers to Japanese occupation troops as "liberators." Anger on Chinese chatrooms spilled into the street and raged for weeks. Protestors stormed Japanese department stores and chanted anti-Japanese slogans, fueled by chatroom rage.[43] According to reports, the protests were well within the control of the government and sometimes even orchestrated by it. One protest organizer explained, "We provided the police with the names of the people participating and the slogans we would use."[44]

For anyone acquainted with twentieth-century Chinese history, there is something very familiar about government-sanctioned anger against "enemies." During the Cultural Revolution it was "old ways" and whoever had been chosen as the reactionary of the week. China is today a very different place than it was in the 1960s or the 1990s. The

Anti-Japanese protests stirred by Internet chatrooms (Frederic J. Brown/AFP/Getty Images)

99

government, however, is not above defining enemies and not above using public rage as a political tool. Even after the September 11, 2001, attacks on the United States, there were mixed reactions from Chinese Internet users. Though China itself has been the victim of terrorist attacks, Americans who live in China were shocked by the responses. Some Chinese did express their horror at what had happened, but just as common was a sense that America was getting what it "deserved." A censorious government says much by what it doesn't choose to block. Left untouched was one well-reported post: "Airplanes? Why not an atomic bomb?"[45]

## Changing the Network

In the middle of all this control we must keep sight of a crucial fact. Unlike Burma or Cuba, China is not stopping technological progress in exchange for totalitarian control. Quite the opposite: China wants to have the fastest and most sophisticated information network in the world. It is spending tens of billions to achieve this goal.[46] It is following the South Korean model—mass investment in Internet infrastructure. China wants to become one of the most advanced networking countries on earth while continuing to maintain control of information.

Consider the story of video-on-demand. In the 1990s and early 2000s there was much talk in the United States of the promises of "video-on-demand," the delivery of movies and video to consumers' homes. Despite industry blather, there were few examples of actual deployments, and no examples of such systems making money. Enron did report more than $100 million in revenue from its video-on-demand business and projected the value of the unit at $20 billion. But the service had, in fact, never launched.[47] Video-on-demand was notable in the United States largely as a means of defrauding investors.

Yet visit the campus at Beijing University, better known as BeiDa, and you're in for a surprise. The dorm rooms at BeiDa are crowded, holding six students in a room an American would find crowded for one. Yet the computers in the crowded dormitories of BeiDa are equipped with advanced video-on-demand capabilities. Indeed, a broad range of films are available, including popular commercial releases from Hong Kong and Hollywood. The students, of course, take it for granted. But it is in small ways like these that urban China, while still behind, is becoming more wired, and more Internet driven, than its Western counterparts.

Conventional wisdom has suggested this will never work—a country cannot open itself up to the Internet *and* maintain fierce political control over its citizens. As Tom Friedman wrote of China in 2000: "What makes the Internet so dangerous for police states is that they can't afford not to have it, because they will fall behind economically if they do. But if they have it, it means they simply can't control information the way they once did."[48] A country could either reject the network and remain a technological backwater, or let the Internet in and lose all control.

But none of that is true if the center of gravity shifts, if China has the power to create its own sphere of influence over network norms. In raw numbers, China is becoming its own network center of gravity. According to a recent survey, the number of Chinese Internet users had risen to 103 million by July 2005, making China second only to the United States in number of Internet users.[49] The size of the Chinese domestic Internet now exceeds the world Internet of 1997. That size means more power to control the most basic building blocks of network design: network standards.

In the United States, Wi-Fi, or wireless Internet technology, is widely hailed as the harbinger of easy, open, and anonymous Internet access. Oftentimes, in any large city, you just turn your computer on and find that you're connected. Cafés and campuses across the United States and Europe are just two of the locations that have gone wireless. Wi-Fi is fast, usually anonymous, and often free.

While China likes the promise of wireless technology, it doesn't like the anonymity and anarchy of the American standard. In the early 2000s, China therefore took up the fight for its own, closed, Wi-Fi standard. In December 2003, citing "national security" concerns, it mandated that a technology known as the WAPI, the "WLAN Authentication and Privacy Infrastructure" be incorporated into every Wi-Fi device used within its borders by June 1, 2004.[50] What WAPI does is simple: it makes a wireless network closed rather than open, by forcing every user of a wireless network to register with a centralized authentication point.[51]

China's WAPI initiative, however, ran into trouble with world trade rules. "This is the most ludicrous trade barrier I have ever come across," said Frank Vargo at the time, a representative of the U.S. National Association of Manufacturers.[52] Certainly part of China's motive was to give business to local companies, since it refused to give foreign companies access to its encryption standard. But there is something deeper going on here. As the founding engineers knew, control over the Internet's standards is how network norms are created. As China seizes control over certain standards, it can put its mark on what kind of products reach its markets and ultimately have a say in what the network is like. The WAPI effort, noted Dave Eberhart, was "a long-term move to make the Chinese WAPI the world standard, dissing long-standing [standards bodies]."[53]

Under pressure from the United States and threat of World Trade Organization intervention, China ultimately suspended its absolute requirement of selling WAPI with every Wi-Fi. But China hasn't given up on the standard, which it is still pushing. The real significance of this episode is for the future of standard-setting. Rebecca MacKinnon, a China expert, puts it this way: "What happens when the next wireless standard is invented in China and performs to government specifications? That's the aspect of this episode that should not be ignored. China is doing what it can to influence the network protocols of the future."[54] Its actions portend a future when China does battle with other nations, most likely the United States, over major Internet standards.[55]

The billions spent building the Chinese network are also having their effects. Physically, the Internet within China looks more and more like a giant office network, centralized by design.[56] In the spring of 2005, China announced its latest buildout—the "Next Carrying Network," or CN2, a massive new intra-Chinese network that will be incredibly fast, but also built by a single, government-owned company and easily filtered at every step. While such things are hard to measure, Internet maps suggest that growth in China's domestic bandwith is rapidly outpacing the speed of its international connections.[57] Network-wise, China will soon be like a country with a great internal transport system but relatively few roads leading in or out. That means information coming from abroad will be that much slower to arrive, that much more likely to get stuck in a network traffic jam.

## Countermeasures

Some technologically savvy readers may be thinking that these controls will be ineffective because Chinese users can get around them. It is an article of faith among techno-optimists that China's controls are fallible and therefore destined to fail.

It is of course true that technologically savvy users can avoid many and perhaps most of the Internet controls imposed by the Chinese government. But as we have argued throughout this book, governmental controls need not be perfect to be effective. The real question is whether and how circumvention of control by a few savvy users will make any difference to China's political evolution. Any movement toward democracy and Western-style government must compete with the nationalist ideology that the Communist Party is weaving into the Internet itself. The effect of the government's control of the media, including the Internet, is not to kill all discussion of democracy, but to put any democratic movement at a major comparative disadvantage.

Consider the all-important chatrooms, where discussions of democracy are banned. Not a problem, some say—even on the most closely monitored chatrooms, people will talk about "cabbages" when they mean "democracy." As one blogger wrote, "No democratic movement in the history of mankind has ever stalled just because the word 'democracy' could not be uttered."[58] True, inventing secret languages can make it hard for the government to understand and censor ideas. But it also makes it hard for ordinary Chinese to have any idea what you're talking about. As Harvard law professor Bill Stuntz puts it, a secret code "is only effective if people know it, and if other people know it in any significant number, the government will likely also know it, and so can block it. It's a perfect catch-22. The secret code either won't work, or its users will be caught."[59]

At a broader level, if you're talking about carrots and cabbages instead of multiparty elections, the Communist Party is already ahead. The cabbage discussion must be seen in context: it is competing with open and fervent discussions of China's greatness, along with complaints about the latest Japanese or American "outrage." In the history of nations, arguments for tolerance and democratic values have not always beaten out nationalist fervor among the masses. And in China, so far, Internet-driven nationalism appears to be beating democracy

CHINA

103

hands down—especially when the democratic movement is saddled with extensive controls.

The ultimate effect of the Internet and China's efforts to control it on China's political evolution is difficult for anyone to assess. But if this chapter suggests anything, it is that the West must abandon the facile yet still dominant assumption that these controls are meaningless or ineffective or bound to fail. We in the West are used to an Internet that is free. But the story of the People's Republic shows the contingency of the Internet's identity, a contingency that reflects its birth in the United States. China is an enormous force that is changing the Internet's identity. As law professor Peter Yu puts it, "the question is no longer how the Internet will affect China. It is how China will affect the Internet."[60]

seven

7

# The Filesharing Movement

Some people change history by accident, and Niklas Zennstrom counts as one of them. This soft-spoken and still largely unknown Swede, described by the *Washington Post* as a "younger, hipper version of Bill Gates," started two small companies in the early 2000s that have already done much to change how people exchange information in the twenty-first century.[1] His first company created a filesharing software application called "Kazaa" that was destined to become the most downloaded program in history. Millions of people used Kazaa to exchange billions of songs in open defiance of national copyright laws.

This chapter chronicles the filesharing movement, in which Zennstrom and Kazaa played a big role. At its height this movement led many to believe that filesharing might upend the central role of national copyright law in the distribution of information. With the benefit of hindsight, we can now see that this was not to be. And so in part, this chapter is a sequel to chapters 5 and 6, showing again the importance of law and national government, even for filesharing—a technology designed to be impossible to control.

This chapter also introduces a crucial new theme: the effect of technological change on the market and the legal system. Filesharing introduced a cheaper method of distributing music that sparked massive changes in the economics of music distribution and the behavior of consumers. These changes were a jolt to the copyright law system that seemed to many to render it irrelevant. What appeared a threat to copyright law, however, turned out simply to be the law's hesitation and adjustment in the face of a massive battle between the recording industry, technological upstarts, and music consumers over the spoils of a better music distribution system made possible by the Internet.

## Early Wars

As the 1990s ended, the music recording industry's mood was optimistic. A new and sturdy technology, the compact disc, anchored the best decade of sales ever. A handful of major labels, a textbook oligopoly, exercised near total control over the distribution of music.[2] And while the industry faced considerable expenses in the development and marketing of new artists, existing music cost little to manufacture and could be sold for up to $20 per album. The recording industry was rich, powerful, well-connected in Congress, and uninterested in changing a successful business model.

There was just one cloud on the horizon—the danger posed by the personal computer, the Internet, and something called "digital piracy." The Internet was a threat to the recording industry's business model because it held the potential to make the distribution of music nearly free. The conflict over music distribution can be understood as a battle over that "Internet surplus"—the difference between music distribution prices in the pre- and post-Internet worlds. It was a battle that would pit the considerable economic and political resources of the recording industry against the efforts of music consumers, programmers, and entrepreneurs like Zennstrom to seize that surplus for themselves.

The recording industry had long been aware of the threat that cheap music copying and distribution posed to its business model. Its first answer was a legislative campaign to preempt the threat. In the late 1980s, the recording industry secured legislation that put copying restrictions on "Digital Audio Tapes" (tapes capable of making copies as perfect as CDs), rendering the technology unattractive to consumers.[3] Through the 1990s the industry worked hard to further tighten the copyright laws in reaction to the threat posed by the Internet. It promoted a package of antipiracy laws that made digital copying harder, and it wrote laws to protect "digital locks" on CDs and DVDs, to increase criminal penalties for bootlegging, and to lengthen the copyright term.[4] With the help of a willing Congress, a friendly administration, and a team of talented lobbyists, the industry got most of the laws it wanted, and it seemed well prepared to deal with whatever threats might emerge.

Yet when the long awaited "digital onslaught" finally arrived, it came from an unexpected direction. The recording industry had easily put down an early generation of companies offering online music.[5] What the industry didn't count on was a decentralized, evolving attack on its business model. And that's exactly what the music filesharing movement was.

At the turn of the century, the first major attempt to seize the Internet surplus came from a college dorm. Shawn Fanning, an eighteen-year-old student nicknamed "the Napster," wrote a program that represented an entirely new kind of challenge to the recording industry's business model—the first easy-to-use filesharing program to make mass distribution of music free. Fanning released a simple program named Napster that collected and provided a centralized list of the music that most students had on their hard drives, and a convenient way to search that list. Using Napster, people could easily search through what amounted to a giant shared music collection, taking whatever they wanted. It was music for free, instead of $15–20 per CD; and that's what made Napster such a threat to the recording industry.

It wasn't long before the Recording Industry Association of America (the RIAA)—the music industry's "copyright cops"—detected Napster's launch. In December of 1999, the industry filed suit against Napster, calling the then-tiny firm a "haven" for music piracy operating on "an unprecedented scale."[6] Even though Napster was unknown, the industry forecast damages at $100 million.

The first and unexpected result of this lawsuit was to make Napster a media sensation. As a smiling Shawn Fanning appeared on the cover of *Time* magazine,[7] both the recording industry and the world became aware that something unusual was going on. The Internet's decentralization of communication had reached the distribution of copyrighted music and become obvious to the public. Suddenly, tens of millions of users were on Napster, trading billions of songs.[8]

Within a year after its launch, however, things had turned from sunny to gloomy for Napster. United States copyright law says you cannot copy songs without the owner's permission, and the U.S. recording industry owns most of the world's valuable copyrighted songs. Technically, of course, it was Napster's users who were trading files with the Napster program. But the fact that Napster brokered each and every search made credible the industry's charge that Napster should be responsible for what its users did. To make matters worse for Napster, its central server was geographically located in the United States. A U.S. court order to kill Napster's directory would be easy to enforce and lead to total system collapse.

Federal courts in California had little trouble concluding that Napster was a "contributory infringer" of copyright. As court after court found Napster illegal and ordered it shut down, the recording industry's legal strategy seemed to have paid off, and its lawyers began to gloat. Napster thought it "would drag the music industry kicking and screaming into the 20th century," said industry lawyer Russ Frackman. "But nothing could be further from the truth. Managing new technologies," he explained, "takes effort, education, and—once in a while—a lawsuit."[9] Even John Perry Barlow acknowledged Napster's impending death. "We may be forced to watch a few pointless public executions," said Barlow. "Shawn Fanning's cross awaits."[10]

## Kazaa Emerges

In the summer of 2001, Napster shut down for good after having exhausted its appeals. Millions of students returned to their dorm rooms that fall looking for new ways to satisfy their filesharing fix. The race to succeed Napster was on.

At the time, a program named Gnutella was the best-known alternative to Napster, and users migrated to it en masse. Within months, however, the Gnutella networks began to collapse. The U.S. government had shut down Napster because it kept music located centrally and did too much to help users download files illegally. Gnutella, by contrast, was a radically decentralized alternative to Napster with no central directory of files. It instead placed all power in the hands of users, who would send specialized search packets on the network to look for music on other computers. But without any intermediary servers to direct search and delivery traffic, the volume of Gnutella-user searches expanded exponentially with the number of users connected to the network. As a result, Gnutella worked for small numbers of people but collapsed for larger numbers.[11]

New filesharing contenders arose throughout 2001 and 2002, as firms like Aimster, AudioGalaxy, Limewire, and Bearshare vied to be the next Napster. Each had some solution to Napster's problems. But it was Kazaa, produced by Zennstrom, that beat all comers. Napster's sharing was limited to music, but Kazaa could share any kind of media—songs, movies, pictures, photos, even Word documents. More importantly, Zennstrom's Kazaa system took a middle road between Napster's centralized filesharing system and Gnutella's radically decentralized system. It established an ingenious system of "super-peer" computers. Super-peers were specially chosen Kazaa users whose computers performed the functions of Napster's central directory, but on a much smaller, decentralized scale. The super-peer system meant that, in contrast to Napster, the Kazaa program's sharing of music did not take place under the direction of Kazaa itself.

The Kazaa super-peer design also proved to be more rugged than other post-Napster filesharing services.[12] In practice Kazaa handled thousands, then hundreds of thousands, and finally millions of active

Niklas Zennstrom, co-founder of Kazaa
(Declan McCullagh)

users. By the summer of 2002, the winner was clear. Kazaa had grown larger than Napster at its peak.[13] By early 2004, the Kazaa program had been downloaded more than any other software in history—an astonishing 319 million times.[14]

Watching Kazaa rise out of the ashes of Napster, the recording industry decided to try to sue it out of existence. On October 2, 2001, seven months after Kazaa's release, the RIAA filed a lawsuit against Kazaa and several Kazaa cousins, including "Grokster," a company that had licensed Zennstrom's Kazaa software. "Defendants have created a 21st-century piratical bazaar" thundered the RIAA, "where the unlawful exchange of protected materials takes place across the vast expanses of the Internet."[15] The industry used the same basic legal theory that had worked against Napster. Kazaa, it insisted, was responsible for the illegal acts of its users, and the government should shut it down immediately.

Kazaa was organized entirely outside the United States to avoid the enforcement powers of U.S. authorities, and neither Kazaa nor Zennstrom showed up for the *Grokster* lawsuit.[16] But the remaining defendants that used Zennstrom's software appeared in the case to defend its legality. They recruited a talented team of lawyers, most from San Francisco firms, along with lawyers from the Electronic Frontier Foundation (EFF), the organization founded by John Perry Barlow.

The EFF and the other lawyers made two important arguments. The first built on the famous *Sony Betamax* case from the 1984, where the U.S. Supreme Court determined that the Sony VCR was a legal product even though it could be used for illegal purposes, such as copying shows from TV to build a home library. The Supreme Court explained that it is indeed legal to manufacture standardized technologies (like a VCR, or a photocopier, or even a pencil) that are used for both copyright infringing and legitimate purposes, as long as the technology was capable of "substantial noninfringing uses."[17] One of EFF's lead attorneys, a young Stanford lawyer named Fred Von Lohmann, had "a strong suspicion that the *Grokster* case would be *the* pivotal fight for the future of *Sony Betamax*."[18] He and the defendant filesharing companies contended that Kazaa fit within the *Sony Betamax* rule because it was a user-driven, general purpose technology that had significant legal uses, just like the VCR. And like Sony, but unlike Napster, Kazaa had no control over what its users did.

In addition to this legal argument, Von Lohmann and others tried to frame the case as one about the future of technological innovation. The industry, they implied, was trying to stop dead a new and important technology for the simple reason that it endangered their way of doing business. Courts applying copyright law, the EFF argued, needed to be careful not to kill technological innovation in the name of stopping copyright infringement. Copyright law had always been flexible enough in the past to permit new technologies to come to market, and the same should be true in the age of the Internet.

These arguments put the industry's lawyers on the defensive. District Judge Wilson wanted to know "whether [the defendants] do anything, aside from distributing software, to actively facilitate—or whether they could do anything to stop—their users infringing activity."[19] The Kazaa software was designed to answer this question in the negative, for Kazaa, unlike Napster, did not play a hand in facilitating music-swapping. The EFF could thus maintain that Kazaa was no different than the VCR, photocopier, and any number of technologies that are used for both licit and illicit purposes.

The EFF's arguments were hardly bulletproof. The defendant companies knew that the Kazaa software was predominately being used for illegal purposes. Indeed, they had advertised themselves as replacements for Napster and were making money off of the same business that Napster went down for. But the arguments were nonetheless good enough for Judge Wilson. On April 25, 2003, he ruled against the RIAA in an opinion relying squarely on *Sony Betamax* and stressing the importance of copyright's accommodation of new technologies.[20] Quoting the *Sony Betamax* case, he wrote: "Sound policy, as well as history, supports our consistent deference to Congress when major technological innovations alter the market for copyrighted materials."[21]

The RIAA thought Wilson's decision was kooky, and rushed to appeal. But to the surprise of many, in August of 2004 the federal appellate court in California went even farther than Judge Wilson. Echoing the language of innovation economists like Joseph Schumpeter, Judge Sidney Thomas discussed the potential death of the current recording industry in a whirl of creative destruction. "The introduction of new technology is always disruptive to old markets," said the court, "particularly to those copyright owners whose works are sold through well-established distribution mechanisms."[22] His answer was simple—trust the market. "History has shown" said Judge Thomas, "that time and market forces often provide equilibrium in balancing interests, whether the new technology be a player piano, a copier, a tape recorder, a video recorder, a personal computer, a karaoke machine, or an MP3 player."[23]

Kazaa and Grokster had won hands down, seeming to confirm John Perry Barlow's prophecy in 2000 that "the future will win; there will be no property in cyberspace."[24] For a brief time, it seemed to many that the government had given up on copyright enforcement in the file-sharing context, and that we had witnessed, in the phrase of Tulane law professor Glynn Lunney, "the death of copyright."[25]

## Copyright's Communications Policy

Senator Orrin Hatch had a strong reaction to the district court's decision in *Grokster*. Eight weeks after it was announced, Hatch declared that there's "no excuse for anyone violating copyright laws." He proposed amending U.S. law to permit the widespread destruction of computers used to download music illegally on peer-to-peer filesharing networks. "If that's the only way, then I'm all for destroying their machines" said Hatch. "If you have a few hundred thousand of those [destroyed machines], I think people would realize" the seriousness of their actions.[26]

But Hatch's and other congressional proposals to reverse the *Grokster* decision and enlarge copyright protection didn't get off the ground. And of course, there were many more things the government could have done if enforcing copyright laws were all that mattered. It could have banned or tightly controlled copying devices, from the VCR to TiVo and the CD-burner. Or it could have cracked down on copyright "thieves" with the same intensity that it chases terrorists, murderers, or bank robbers. These and other harsh steps would reduce copyright infringement enormously. But the government did none of these things. Why didn't it do more to stop filesharing cold?

The answer is that, despite the famed influence of the RIAA, protecting the music industry is not the government's only interest. The RIAA is a powerful lobby. But Congress also has many constituents who like to share music, and interest groups that represent them. Hatch's proposals would have been very harmful to many high-tech industries and to consumers, and these groups pressured Congress to oppose the senator from Utah. Such intense competition among groups and interests seeps up through the political process and causes government to hesitate, to take half-measures, and to look for compromise. The result is something far short of full copyright enforcement.

Congress's nonresponse to massive violation of copyright law is best viewed as a wait-and-see policy toward technological change. This is hardly anything new: in the history of copyright law, initial acquiescence in mass "piracy" is how the law typically responds to the arrival of new technologies. It's a point that can be hard to see in the rhetoric surrounding copyright today, but it is a pattern as old as copyright law itself.

In the 1900s, the music industry of the day complained bitterly about outlaws who were ignoring copyright and threatening (they said) the future of creativity. Who were these pirates? The early recording industry, of course. Their newfangled gramophones, player pianos, and talking machines threatened to negate the value of copyrighted sheet music. Composer John Phillip Sousa complained to Congress that "these talking machines are going to ruin the artistic development of music in this country." He recalled that, "When I was a boy . . . in front of every house in the summer evenings you would find young people together singing the songs of the day or old songs." But "today you hear these infernal machines going night and day. . . . The vocal chord will be eliminated by a process of evolution, as was the tail of man when he came from the ape."[27]

The point is clear in retrospect. Records and piano rolls in 1903, like online music in 2003, offered a better way to distribute music than the incumbent (sheet music) industry. There was powerful support for sidestepping copyright, undercutting the then-dominant industry, and serving the consumer directly. But it was all just a phase. In short order, the recording industry became part of the copyright system (through the "mechanical license"—the compulsory licensing system for sound recordings). The recording industry was transformed from a pirate industry to its present incarnation, as copyright's greatest champion.[28]

This same story recurred with radio in the 1920s and '30s, and again in the 1960s and '70s, with the advent of cable television. Cable came into business as a kind of pirate, capturing "free" broadcast signals on large community antennas and selling the signals to its customers. It was a new system of media distribution that took advantage, like Napster, of copyright arbitrage. Broadcasters cried foul. As the copyright office summarized their complaints in 1965, "[Cable operators] neither need nor deserve a free ride at the expense of copyright owners," and the "activities of the CATV operators constitute a clear moral wrong"[29] In 1975, film industry lobbyist Jack Valenti described the cable industry as a "huge parasite" that was "feeding and fattening itself off of local television stations and copyright owners of copyrighted material."[30]

While it was easy to think that the early victories in the *Grokster* litigation were a fundamental challenge to the centrality of copyright in the distribution of music, in a sense it was business as usual. Neither the early *Grokster* rulings, nor Congress's failure to do more to protect the music industry, reflected an absence of power. They instead reflected an intragovernmental discussion over how to balance conflicting interests in technological innovation and the protection of authors' rights.

## Counterattack

Despite its early losses in the *Grokster* litigation, the recording industry was not ready to give up on copyright in music. It convinced the Supreme Court to hear its appeal in the *Grokster* case in December 2004. And a year earlier, while the *Grokster* litigation was still proceeding in the lower courts, the industry took an even more radical step. Doing what it had threatened for years, it turned its legal arsenal against its own potential customers—the millions of American music listeners who swap files online.

The consumers were an easy target. The vast majority lacked the legal resources to defend a lawsuit, and almost certainly had violated U.S. copyright law. But why would an industry want to attack its customers? The recording industry, it seemed, preferred to be feared than loved. Said Cary Sherman, the RIAA's president, "The public has been educated and re-educated and re-educated again," [31] and "when your product is being regularly stolen, there comes a time when you have to take appropriate action."[32] As advertising consultant Lee Kovel put it, "They want to make a statement and strike fear. They don't care about PR."[33]

On September 8, 2003, the industry filed its first of thousands of lawsuits against individual American filesharers. "Illegal downloading of music is theft, pure and simple," said Frances W. Preston, president of BMI. "We must end the destructive cycle now."[34] Hugh Priestwood, a songwriter, had a personal message for filesharers. "I, not you, have the right to control what happens to [my songs], a right your technology does not trump."[35]

The lawsuits landed hard, seeking damages in the hundreds of thousands, more than most people's life savings. Copyright's harsh remedies were designed to deter corporate infringers—to make companies think twice about using pirated software. But most of the RIAA's defendants weren't companies—they were college students and teenagers and other time-rich, money-poor defendants.

In one well-reported case, Brianna LaHara, a twelve-year-old girl, was sued for several hundred thousand dollars for downloading songs like "If You're Happy and You Know It Clap Your Hands."[36] Brianna and her family, poor and living in public housing, were operating under the mistaken belief that paying for Kazaa made filesharing legal. "I thought it was OK to download music because my mom paid a service fee for it," said Brianna. "Out of all people, why did they pick me?"[37] RIAA chief executive Mitch Bainwol gave the industry line: "As this case illustrates, parents need to be aware of what their children are doing on their computers."[38]

By June 2005, the industry had sued nearly twelve thousand Americans. Some dismissed the significance of these lawsuits. Wayne Rosso, president of Grokster, scoffed and predicted that the lawsuits would have no effect. "Come on. Users know they can't sue 60 million of them. Who are they kidding?"[39] Fred Von Lohmann, the EFF lawyer, put it as follows. "I think this really suggests that the recording industry dinosaurs have completely lost touch with reality—over 57 million Americans are using file-sharing software today. That's more than voted for President Bush."[40]

The campaign, however, had its effects. "It doesn't take too many tickets to get everybody to obey the speed limit," said singer Hugh Priestwood.[41] Many people will ignore the lawsuits just as many people ignore speed limits. But as Gary Becker would have predicted, the lawsuits make networks like Kazaa that much less attractive, both to hardcore dedicated filesharers who move to more protected networks and also to ordinary Americans. The real point of the suits was not to eliminate filesharing but to marginalize it and thus prevent companies like Kazaa from becoming mainstream, legitimate businesses, and real competitors to the labels.

## Kazaa's Woes

As Kazaa's users faced a barrage of lawsuits, Kazaa, despite early victories in American and other courts, began to suffer from different problems. Although Kazaa was the most downloaded software in history, the company did not make Zennstrom or anyone associated with it wealthy. It suffered, in the words of Chris Oakes, from "the glaring absence of a revenue model."[42]

Why wasn't Kazaa lucrative? It's an interesting question, for Kazaa had an enormous consumer base, and companies can usually translate users into revenue in one of several standard ways. Some charge a small fee for every transaction, as in the eBay model. Some sell advertising, as in the Google model or the online newspaper model. Some sell or license their software, the model pioneered by Microsoft and its first major product, MS-DOS. Kazaa tried all of these, and more. But none worked, for reasons that can be traced to its organizational attempts to avoid government regulation. And therein lies a lesson.

First, Kazaa had trouble attracting legitimate advertisers. It's not fully clear why, but the answer is probably that the lawsuits against it made it a risky and unstable platform for advertisers. In any event, the dearth of traditional advertisers led a desperate Kazaa to turn to the bottom of the advertising barrel and use adware, parasite-like programs that install on users' computers to grab user information or to display ads at the right time. These kinds of moves disgusted consumer groups—by late 2004, Computer Associates had labeled Kazaa the number one spyware threat to American computer users.[43] Kazaa's advertising strategies were also undermined by outlaw competitors who rewrote the Kazaa software to remove its ads. "Kazaa Lite," for example, offered users the benefits of Kazaa without the "spyware aftertaste."[44]

With no luck attracting regular advertisers, Kazaa turned to bizarre and arguably unethical means try to convert its user base into cash. In 2002, Kazaa proposed a strange business model that would have turned its millions of Kazaa customers into a gigantic parallel processing computer. The idea, apparently, was that the computer could run in the background on millions of machines, and Kazaa could then sell the computer's time to interested clients.[45] Unfortunately, Kazaa didn't actually tell its users about the plan. Unbeknownst to its customers, it began secretly including "sleeper" software in its downloads, awaiting orders to awake and take over. It was all a bit spooky. "Return of the PC Snatchers," CNN called it, and in the subsequent uproar Kazaa abandoned much of the plan.[46] People were beginning to hate the company that was supposed to liberate them from the recording industry.

Kazaa also tried the traditional strategy of actually selling a product. Early on, it convinced companies like Grokster to pay for a license. But as Grokster found itself in a Los Angeles courtroom, the Kazaa license began to lose its attraction. Next, Kazaa tried Kazaa+, an enhanced version of Kazaa without the adware and with a few other features, for $29.95. Some people, like Brianna LaHara, actually paid for it. But in a classic "live-by-the-sword" problem, Kazaa had to face the fact that people could use Kazaa to distribute and receive Kazaa+ for free. In addition, Kazaa+ faced competition from "Kazaa Gold," a $39.95 product that promised protection from lawsuits. But Kazaa Gold was just one of many scams—it had nothing to do with the real Kazaa, and while it worked, it provided no protection from an industry lawsuits.[47]

Faced with a proliferation of copycats like Kazaa Gold, in 2003 Kazaa found itself in the incongruous position of complaining about copyright infringement. Kazaa actually sent a letter to Google demanding that it take down all sites hosting fake Kazaa clients.[48] Google complied, but Kazaa ultimately has had as much trouble as the recording industry in dealing with problems of copyright and trademark infringement. Ironically, its business model began to depend simultaneously on avoiding and enforcing copyright.

Finally, Kazaa had endless problems policing bad users who put fake files, porn ads, and other abusive content on the network. Those users, even more than the recording industry, destroyed Kazaa's reputation, not only as a company but as a product. By 2005, Kazaa users were weeding through a junkyard of corrupt files, deliberate fakes, and efforts to advertise porn sites that made the P2P experience a major chore. Kazaa was designed to make it hard to shut down—but that also made it hard to shut down its abusive users, many of whom were in the United States. Kazaa might have asked U.S. authorities to step in and help maintain order on the network. But Kazaa had organized itself to avoid U.S. governmental authority and could hardly ask U.S. officials for help.

In short, the Kazaa system ended up being much more of a tradeoff than people realized at first. Its decentralized design and organizational structure was better than Napster's for skirting U.S. copyright law. But the costs of its structure were an inability to rely on government to control fraud, disorder, and the copying of its product, as well as an inability to establish the credibility to attract revenues. Kazaa was designed to avoid government control but needed government's help to succeed. As Kazaa demonstrates, and as we discuss in more detail in the next chapter, many aspects of the Internet that business and individual users take for granted are the product of a stable legal environment that only governments provide.

By 2004, Kazaa was under siege. Its Australian offices and the homes of its Australian executives were raided by Australian police looking for evidence of illegal filesharing.[49] Meanwhile, usage levels were slipping worldwide as Kazaa's reputation for spyware and RIAA lawsuits took their toll. Yet as Kazaa began to wither, someone was watching Kazaa carefully. He was trying it out, learning from its successes and mistakes, and witnessing how hard it is to run a company that runs against the law. That someone was Steve Jobs, the storied founder of Apple Computer company, who was determined to make his own effort to seize that elusive Internet surplus.

## Apple's Bright Idea

Steve Wozinak and Steve Jobs founded Apple in 1976 on the bet that a personal computer might be a successful mass-market product. Thirty years later, Apple was destined to repeat the process for the music world. Steve Jobs bet that a legitimate online music site could succeed, and he called his bet "the iTunes download store."

Kazaa and Napster had launched under fire, beginning life at war with the recording labels. But Apple, older and savvier, knew better. Steve Jobs is a hybrid of Southern and Northern California, one of the few who moves with ease between the feuding worlds of media and technology. By virtue of Apple, Jobs is native to Silicon Valley; but he also founded Pixar, the Hollywood studio that produced *Toy Story* and *Finding Nemo*.

Instead of going to war with the recording industry, Jobs struck a deal in 2002. "We were able to negotiate landmark deals with all of the major labels," said Jobs.[50] Jobs's success may have resulted from his famous powers of persuasion, but it may also have reflected fatigue on the part of an industry tired of battling online music, and realizing, however slowly, that it might have to change.

iTunes launched on April 28, 2003, with massive publicity. Technically, it wasn't a filesharing system at all. It was a single, centralized downloading system that let customers buy songs using a computer

Steve Jobs introducing iTunes (Ian Waldie/Getty Images)

and an Internet connection. iTunes's deal with the recording industry reflected several compromises. On the price side, iTunes kept the same price on a per album basis that the labels were charging for CDs—about fifteen dollars. (To offer the service at all, Apple had to pay licensing fees to the record companies for permission to sell their products and had to guarantee minimum pricing levels.) But iTunes did change music pricing by creating a ninety-nine-cent song price, low enough, as Jobs put it, to be an "impulse buy."[51]

In another compromise, iTunes, unlike Kazaa, put limits on what people could do with the music they downloaded. Personal sharing and transfers were fine, but mass filesharing was off limits. As Jobs said, "You can burn as many CDs as you want for personal use, you can put it on your iPod, you can use it in your other applications, you can have it on multiple computers."[52] But on the flip side, Apple's control over the songs remained considerable. The songs were designed to prevent mass filesharing, à la Napster and Kazaa.

Many believed that iTunes would fail—that it would never be able to compete with "free." After all, Kazaa and its cousins offered the same product for nothing, with no pesky encryption. And iTunes did have its growing pains, launching with only 200,000 songs—a fraction of the song universe. But Steve Jobs had watched Kazaa's struggles carefully. He thought that many people were sick of the whole filesharing ordeal, and that at some price, they would rather pay for music online than spend hours evading detection. Kazaa, by the mid-2000s, was like a flea market—cheap, but littered with weird stuff and broken junk. In contrast, iTunes was more like a regular store—quality for a price. As Jobs put it, using Kazaa "you're spending an hour to download four songs that you could buy for under $4 from Apple, which means you're working for under minimum wage."[53] Using iTunes also eliminated the risk of being sued by the RIAA or arrested by the FBI. That gave iTunes, according to Steve Jobs, better karma. "On the good side, [services like Kazaa] are instant gratification, showing the Net was built for music distribution," Jobs said. "On the downside, it is stealing, and it's best not to mess with karma."[54] For those ninety-nine cents, iTunes offered reliable downloads and no lawsuit risk. For people who care about such things, it was a pretty good deal.

By June of 2005, iTunes had grown as popular as the major P2P services.[55] Surveys showed it was being used by about 1.7 million U.S. households per month, outpacing Kazaa and other services.[56] "One of the music industry's questions has been, when will paid download stores compete head-to-head with free P2P download services?" said Russ Crupnick, president of the NPD Group's music and movies division. "That question has now been answered. iTunes is more popular than nearly any P2P service."[57]

## Normalization

In the summer of 2005, the Supreme Court, after thinking things over, unanimously reversed the lower courts in *Grokster* and declared illegal the business model of the filesharing firms that used Kazaa software.[58] The EFF's Von Lohmann and the lower courts thought the case turned on the applicability of the *Sony BetaMax* rule to a new copying technology. But the Court did not rely on that rule. It instead decided the case on the entirely different ground that the Kazaa licensees were, in effect, crooked businesses, premised on an obvious intent of encouraging people to break the law. "Grokster and StreamCast are not . . . merely passive recipients of information about infringing use," wrote Justice Souter for the Court. "The record is replete with evidence that from the moment Grokster and StreamCast began to distribute their free software, each one clearly voiced the objective that recipients use it to download copyrighted works, and each took active steps to encourage infringement."[59] The Kazaa licensees were liable for the acts of its users, the Court concluded, because it "induced" them to break the law.

In so ruling, the Supreme Court agreed with lower courts that the case required a balance between innovation and copyright protection. "The more artistic protection is favored, the more technological innovation may be discouraged; the administration of copyright law is an exercise in managing the trade-off."[60] The Court's tradeoff was deeply influenced by its view that Kazaa and its cousins didn't represent legitimate businesses, whatever the merits of the technology. The Court was notably far less in awe of the Internet than it had been back in 1997, when it decided *Reno*, discussed in chapter 2. By 2005 the

Outside the U.S. Supreme Court after the *Grokster* oral arguments (Declan McCullagh)

Internet wasn't new and wasn't unfamiliar; it was, instead, simply one of a number of communication technologies that posed interesting legal problems.

The Supreme Court's decision and Apple's assumption of center stage appears to mark the beginning of the end of the online music wars, and a new equilibrium in the music industry.

The decision was a major boon for Apple. The Court effectively cursed Kazaa and by implication blessed the ascendant iTunes business model. By the fall of 2005, Apple was reporting quadrupled profits, and what Jobs called "the best year in Apple's history," thanks in part to the blessing of the Supreme Court.[61]

Meanwhile, within months of the Supreme Court decision, the RIAA was wielding the coercive powers assigned to it by *Grokster* to shut down the remaining U.S.-based filesharing firms. Firms fell before new, tough cease-and-desist letters waving the *Grokster* decision's inducement test. Testifying before Congress, Sam Yagan, developer of the P2P software eDonkey, explained why he was "throwing in the towel." "This threat of imminent litigation from the major music labels, coming in light of the Supreme Court's ambiguous ruling, led us to conclude that . . . we did not have the resources to endure the protracted litigation that the RIAA letter presaged."[62] Other P2P companies, like Grokster itself, turned to desperate efforts to try and adopt the iTunes model.[63]

But while the Court's decision is butchering online music filesharing firms, it does not mean anything close to the end of filesharing altogether. One response to the *Grokster* decision and RIAA suits will be further burrowing of filesharing into the depths of the Internet, masking the identity of both the filesharing service and its users. A new and important filesharing technology, Bittorrent, even faster than Kazaa, began its rise in 2004, and it and other new technologies will meet the needs of determined underground filesharers. In addition, services like "Earth Station 5," rumored to be based in the Jenin Refugee Camp in the Palestinian Territories, offer layers upon layers of intermediate servers designed to keep the identity of P2P users secret. "The next revolution of P2P file sharing is upon you," wrote Earth Station's founders. "Resistance is futile and we are now in control."[64]

The critical word here, of course, is "underground." Many of the characteristics of post-Kazaa filesharing—secrecy and anonymity— do much to accomplish the law's goals. As filetrading groups become smaller or more secretive to avoid government detection, they become harder to discover, not only for governments (which is the whole point of "darknets") but for ordinary users as well. This, in turn, means that fewer and fewer filesharers will be interested in smaller collections of free music that are harder to find. This is what Janelle Brown in 2000 presciently called the "Gnutella paradox,"[65] and it is akin to the catch-22 of secret codes that we met in the chapter about China. A service for mass filesharing has the greatest effect on national copyright law if it is easy to find and easy to use. But if it is easy to find and use, it is pretty easy for governments to control, if they want.

Ironically, then, the most rebellious filesharing programmers can become handmaidens of the government's will. What secretive darknets do is zone the music world, dividing music consumers on the basis of free time and computer ability. A minority, the Slashdotters, with all the time and expertise in the world, have disappeared into darknets, and won't pay for music. Others, meanwhile, stay with legitimate pay sites that are easy to use, easy to find, and reliable. And the dwindling computer illiterate, and those who love packaging and physical goods, may continue to make the trip to Tower Records.

Neither the Supreme Court's *Grokster* decision nor iTunes's success means that the recording industry has, in some sense, won. The industry is still in serious trouble. The money it expects to make—its salaries, benefits, and profit—all depend on charging high prices (at least $15) for a product that can be obtained on the Net for less, and sometimes for free. For the first time in decades, the recording industry faces something other industries call "price competition." As time passes, online music labels will undercut CD prices, and the recording industry will be forced to respond in two ways: cutting its own prices for its traditional product, and either partnering with or trying to destroy companies like Apple and Napster. The ugliness is not over, but the history of technological succession is rarely a dinner party.

The filesharing battles and the emerging normalization of online music fit a pattern described by Harvard Business School professor Debora Spar in her 2001 book, *Ruling the Waves*.[66] Spar explained how technological innovations—ranging from the compass to the telegraph to the radio to the Internet—"spark recurrent patterns of governmental evasion and control." When a revolutionary technology first enters the public realm, it emboldens outlaws and seems immune from government control.[67] During this period, "it's not that governments lack the interest or the wherewithal to govern new areas of technology; rather, its just that old laws are unlikely to cover emerging technologies and new ones take time to create—time, that, initially seems to favor the pirates and pioneers."[68] But eventually, the commercialization of the new technology needed to make it available to the masses fuels demands for property rights and government-enforced rules. After an initial period of uncertainty, the government responds to business and consumer demand to assert the control over the new technology needed to make it widely available. Government is crucial here, because only it "can defend firms' property rights," "regulate their interaction with a demanding consumer market," and "help to keep the pirates at bay."[69]

Spar captured what has happened with music distribution on the Internet in the 2000s. The Internet made possible great reductions in the price of music distribution, and filesharing entrepreneurs tried to seize that surplus for themselves and, along the way, pass much of it on to consumers. But doing so required violating copyright law and living an outlaw existence—a difficult position to maintain over the long term. The result was a kind of compromise in which national copyright law remained central but the distribution of the value in recorded music had shifted. The traditional recording industry loses profits, and newer companies like iTunes embrace the new technology, capture some of the Internet surplus, and pass on to consumers much of the savings in price that the Internet makes possible. In the end, though, the fact that even lower prices are charged for music on the Internet and CDs is testament to the importance of the political power of existing industries, even in face of a technological challenge, and to the abiding significance of national copyright law.

## Epilogue

When the Supreme Court announced Kazaa's legal fate in the United States in June 2005, Niklas Zennstrom had long since turned his attention to a new company. Bored with music, Zennstrom had begun to wonder about something else: given the Internet, why do phone calls cost money? In early 2004, he answered that question by founding a company, Skype, that provided the world's first effective and free Internet telephone service. By the time of the Supreme Court's decision in *Grokster* eighteen months later, Skype had become a worldwide telephone firm with over 40 million users, "making it not just the fastest-growing telecommunications company in the world but one of the fastest-growing businesses of any kind."[70] But this time around, things would be different. On September 12, 2005, eBay purchased Skype for $2.6 billion, making Zennstrom, at last, a wealthy man.[71]

*Part 3*

# Vices, Virtues, the Future

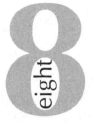

# eight 8

## Virtues and Vices of Government Control

Pierre Omidyar's self-composed one-line autobiography reads: "Technologist, founder of eBay, trying to make the world a better place."[1] As his life's progression suggests, of the many 1990s Internet billionaires, Omidyar's disposition and outlook may most truly reflect the ethos of the West Coast. During his early "technologist" period he had a pony tail, wore aviator sunglasses, and worshipped the Apple Macintosh. It was during this period, in 1995, that he started eBay in his spare time, as a kind of hobby. "It was just an idea that I had, and I started it as an experiment, as a side hobby basically, while I had my day job."[2] In media legend the inspiration was his fiancée, Pam, who wanted to meet like-minded collectors of PEZ dispensers. But Omidyar's account of his company's origins emphasizes a different point. "The whole idea there was just to help people do business with one another on the Internet. And people thought it was impossible because how could people on the Internet—remember this is 1995— how could they trust each other? How could they get to know each other? And I thought that was silly. . . . [P]eople are basically good [and] honest."[3]

It didn't take long for eBay to realize that not everyone was good and honest: As this chapter shows, eBay quickly learned that to prevent fraud, enforce its contracts, and ensure stability in its auction services, it would depend critically on government coercion and the rule of law provided by a stable country like the United States. These are a few of the many complex benefits that only territorial sovereigns can bring, and without which most aspects of the Internet that we love and cherish would not exist. In this chapter and throughout part 3, we study these largely hidden virtues of government control of the Internet. As the story of China has already made clear, and as we discuss further in what follows, government control of the Internet is not always a happy prospect, for governments often rule unwisely and often clash with one another in destructive ways. Our aim in this part is to give a balanced account of these virtues and vices, and to show how the future of the Internet will be shaped by domestic politics and international relations, as interest groups and countries fight for control and influence over the once-borderless medium.

## Early Days

AuctionWeb, as eBay was originally named, came online on Labor Day, 1995, and as just one of three pages Omidyar was hosting on his homepage. That homepage happened to be called eBay.com (short for Echo Bay technologies). AuctionWeb shared space with a small biotech startup and an unusual site dedicated to the Ebola virus. After a slow start—including no visitors on its launch day—eBay slowly began to attract buyers and sellers, mainly through word of mouth. As Omidyar said, "It just kind of grew. Within six months it was earning revenue that was paying my costs. Within nine months the revenue was more than I was making on my day job."[4] It turned out that Omidyar had tapped into something deep in the human psyche. People like to buy and sell junk.

At first, eBay was a tiny place, known to just a few users. Buying and selling was friendly and community-oriented, like so much on the early Internet. As Adam Cohen, author of *The Perfect Store*, writes, "Omidyar wanted his corner of cyberspace to be a place where people made real

Pierre Omidyar (Acey Harper/Time Life Pictures/Getty Images)

connections with each other, where a social contract prevailed. He wanted it to operate according to the moral values he subscribed to in his own life: that people are good, and given the chance to do right, they generally will."[5]

Despite the friendly atmosphere, some conflict was inevitable, even in those early days. Omidyar's solution was to turn to community enforcement. On February 26, 1996, he invented the "Feedback Forum." The Feedback Forum was the Internet's first organized reputation system. It allowed users to post information about people they had done business with on eBay. Here was Omidyar's message to the AuctionWeb community:

> Posted: February 26, 1996
> To: eBay Community
>
> I launched eBay's AuctionWeb on Labor Day, 1995. Since then, the site has become more popular than I ever expected, and I began to realize that this was indeed a grand experiment in Internet commerce. By creating an open market that encourages honest dealings, I hope to make it easier to conduct business with strangers over the net.
>
> Most people are honest. And they mean well. Some people go out of their way to make things right. I've heard great stories about the honesty of people here. But some people are dishonest. Or deceptive. This is true here, in the newsgroups, in the classifieds, and right next door. It's a fact of life. But here, those people can't hide. We'll drive them away. Protect others from them. This grand hope depends on your active participation. Become a registered user. Use our Feedback Forum. Give praise where it is due; make complaints where appropriate. . . .
>
> Now, we have an open forum. Use it. Make your complaints in the open. Better yet, give your praise in the open. Let everyone know what a joy it was to deal with someone. Above all, conduct yourself in a professional manner. Deal with others the way you would have them deal with you. Remember that you are usually dealing with individuals, just like yourself. Subject to making mistakes. Well-meaning, but wrong on occasion. That's just human. We can live with that. We can deal with that. We can still make deals with that. Thanks for participating. Good luck, and good business!
>
> Regards,
> Pierre Omidyar[6]

At the time, according to Omidyar, "I didn't necessarily think that was really going to work, but to my surprise, it did. Most of what I saw was positive ratings, not negative ratings. That's when it hit me: You know what, people really get a good feeling themselves when they can give praise to people who deserve [it]."[7] The feedback system, of course, survives to this day, and its method of creating reputations and community self-policing is the backbone of the eBay system.

Omidyar soon supplemented the feedback system with eBay's first dispute resolution system. An early loyal user, Jim Griffith, had become a fixture on the AuctionWeb Bulletin Board as "a friendly source of advice for new users."[8] "Uncle Griff," as he was known, was hired for $100 per month to be AuctionWeb's first customer support person, a responsibility that soon grew to include the resolution of disputes among buyers and sellers. Uncle Griff took his duties seriously, doing what he could to maintain peace, including persuasion, counseling, and good humor.[9] By all accounts Uncle Griff was successful at diffusing tension and resolving disputes.

In its early days, eBay appeared to be just the type of aterritorial, self-governing virtual community that John Perry Barlow and Julian Dibbell had written about in their early exploration of cyberspace. Uncle Griff, the community's virtual magistrate, didn't even live in California where eBay was located. He presided from his home in West Rutland, Vermont, but he could just as well have done his job from Japan or Africa. It soon became clear, however, that the online Feedback Forum and Uncle Griff would not suffice to keep order on eBay.

## Fraud

This virtual community, eBay, grew fast. It grew faster, in fact, than any other company in the history of the world. "Everyone was saying, 'No, no, there's no way it can continue to grow this fast.' But it has."[10] By the end of 1999, eBay had over five million users.[11] After a successful IPO, eBay was not only popular but rich—Omidyar's personal fortune stood at over $10 billion. But while large and successful, eBay still had the same old informal governance system centered on the Feedback Forum and Uncle Griff. Unfortunately for eBay, it quickly developed a new problem Omidyar didn't plan on: online auction fraud.

The Furby fraud of 1998 was the wakeup call for eBay. The Furby ("your emo-tronic friend") is a sort of robotic stuffed animal that resembles a cross between a cat and an owl. Unusual for a stuffed animal, the Furby speaks its own language (Furbish) and also has limited English skills. In 1998 it was an enormously popular toy and a hot eBay auction item. That was especially true of the rare "limited edition" and colored Furbies, which sometimes sold for as much as $1,000. The problem was that there were no limited-edition Furbies, and no colored versions that weren't just home-dye jobs. The limited edition Furby was a scam. As Internet-ScamBusters.org explained, "unethical promoters, scam artists, and hucksters have rushed into this hot market and 'invented claims' of rare Furbies in order to take advantage of unwary consumers."[12]

Faced with the Furby fraud and other reports of online auction fraud, eBay announced its first official antifraud program in January 1999. But it did little else, and both fraud and pranks, or at least the public's perception of them, continued to increase. In 1999, for example, a seller posing as "Richard Posner"—the famous federal judge and legal scholar who early in his career had written about markets for babies—listed for sale "one unborn baby."[13] The listing received great media attention before being shut down. In March 2000, Kembrew McCleod, a college professor, sold his soul on eBay to a New York real estate executive for $1,325. As McCleod said, "it doesn't matter whether they think it's art or ironic, as long as they send me the money."[14]

While these pranks were more fun than anything else, the fraud problems were not. In the spring of 1999, a serious Rolex scam garnered wide media coverage.[15] And a problem present since the early days—sports memorabilia fraud—continued to get worse. Who's to know whether a signed Reggie Jackson bat was actually signed by Reggie Jackson? In the late 1990s, the problem wasn't just that the fraudsters were selling fake autographs; they were also issuing fake certificates of authenticity and generating fake feedback ratings. By 2000, eBay faced a class-auction lawsuit, *Gentry v. eBay*, filed by allegedly defrauded buyers.[16]

eBay had long prided itself on being a friendly community first and foremost, a place where disputes were settled in a different way. But the legal and reputational risks to eBay of fraud were becoming clear. A federal report in 2000 found more than $4 million in losses from auction fraud alone.[17] While the actual incidence of fraud was still relatively low, the perception of danger, coupled with a string of hacker attacks, left eBay with little choice. As Omidyar said, "we've had to evolve our strategies and our policies from what I built in the beginning, which was a self-policing community of people, to one where we take a more active role in trying to help identify the bad actors."[18]

In 1999, eBay took an important step. It hired two hard-bitten crime-fighters who (like the couple in *The Thin Man*) were also a married couple. Angela Malacari came to eBay from law enforcement: she had served in the Drug Enforcement Agency's Violent Gang Task Force and as a special agent for the Immigration and Naturalization Service, where she was famous for breaking a large immigrant-smuggling ring.[19] Her husband, Rob Chestnut, was a federal prosecutor in the Eastern District of Virginia, where he had prosecuted the Russian spy and CIA employee Aldrich Ames.[20] With Chestnut and Malacari, eBay began an active policy of hiring former law enforcement officials that continues today.

Malacari became the head of eBay's fraud investigation team, or "ebay's Cop." [21] Her job: to prowl eBay for signs of fraud and prepare the case for law enforcement to prosecute. As she stated, "We try to provide law enforcement with precedent-setting cases."[22] Among her tools were secret in-house monitoring and data-mining software designed to detect suspicious behavior. Chestnut, meanwhile, worked on fraud and also became one of eBay's point men in Washington to get Congress to do more about cybercrime and its effects. In 2000, Chestnut testified before Congress: "It's our view that computer intrusions and attacks on commercial websites are serious crimes that require a forceful response." He asked Congress to "send a message to cyber criminals throughout the world that the U.S. government can and will protect e-commerce from criminal activity."[23] The contrast between the Malacari/Chestnut team and Uncle Griff could not be clearer. Griff's job was to be helpful, funny, nice, and settle what disputes he could. Malacari and Chestnut were hired to catch and imprison criminals.

By 2004, eBay's transformation was complete. Its website now boasted that "eBay's security team includes former law enforcement officials from around the world," and explained that eBay was "here to work with law enforcement in criminal investigations."[24] From its early reliance on the golden rule—Omidyar's advice to "Deal with others the way you would have them deal with you"—eBay had developed by 2005 to employ a full-time security staff of eight hundred people.[25] Critics grumble that "eBay is not only 'The World's Online Marketplace' but the world's online informant."[26]

Today, eBay's feedback system remains central to its business model and works for most of the billions of transactions on eBay. But eBay's level of integration with and dependence on law enforcement is remarkable. Pierre Omidyar defends the transformation from his founding vision. "The community really is no longer the way it was in the early days. My philosophy then was, let the community govern itself. That philosophy didn't really scale up. I would have wanted it to. But I realized in early 1998 that at a certain point, you have to say, well, there is a part of the community out there that isn't appropriate."[27]

## Coercion

What eBay learned over the course of its existence is a very old lesson about the first and most fundamental role of government. Political theorists have long argued that the clearest justification for a coercive State is the protection of citizens from harming one another through force, fraud, or theft. As Thomas Hobbes argued in the seventeenth century, human beings require "the terror of some power" to force them to behave. Without the order and stability provided by government, Hobbes claimed, men live in "continual fear, and danger of violent death."[28]

Hobbes exaggerated the role of government in securing order. As the eBay story shows, community norms, civil society, and an innate human tendency to cooperate and reciprocate play crucial roles in smoothing human relations. For the vast majority of transactions, the norms of eBay and the Feedback Forum are sufficient to maintain an order without law. The vast majority of eBay users are, as Pierre Omidyar had hoped, honest and good people.

But laws are not important for policing eBay's honest users. They matter for the people who are bad. Some percentage of eBay's customers is made up of people whose primary interest is stealing money or goods. It is for these people that law and government power is needed. As eBay came to realize, without the threat of law enforcement behind eBay's community system, it could be quickly overrun by criminal fraud.

It is true that, in the absence of government power, eBay might create alternative systems of enforcement. It might, for example, take possession itself of the goods and guarantee their quality. But then eBay would be a store, not eBay, and its cost structure would give it no economic advantage over traditional retail stores. The phenomenal success of eBay is made possible because eBay doesn't have to identity, verify, and play police officer. Instead, eBay more or less lets the market run itself. But for that to work, there must be harsh punishment of that tiny minority who want to break the rules. The eBay auction system, as libertarian as its origins may have been, depends on an oft-hidden virtue of government power to deter those who would destroy the system.

## Rule of Law

eBay's problems with fraud demonstrate its most obvious need for the coercive power of government. But its reliance on the government is actually much deeper. Every successful eBay transaction, as eBay constantly reminds its users, is a legally binding contract. Nonetheless, disputes and breaches of contract are not uncommon. And the legal enforceability of those contracts is ultimately essential to the eBay model.

In 1996, as we saw, eBay employed a simple means of dispute resolution—Uncle Griff. Uncle Griff did the best he could, and the small eBay community didn't resort to litigation. But he could not possibly handle all of the cases that came up as eBay grew. And so in 2000, eBay partnered with Square Trade, a firm established by former McKinsey Consultants who specialized in online mediation services. Mediation is simply a term for what Uncle Griff was doing all along— helping buyers and sellers resolve disputes through a consensual, non-judicial process in which a neutral party tries to work out the dispute in a nonconfrontational and informal way. Square Trade offered a more professional and institutionalized process than Uncle Griff for disgruntled buyers or sellers to identify the dispute, discuss it directly, and work with a professional mediator in "developing a fair, mutually agreeable solution."[29]

Square Trade's mediation service is a sensible private substitute for government-enforced resolution of contractual disputes. As in any other setting, most disputes on eBay do not warrant the actual use of courts and contract law. Many disputes result from misunderstandings that are easily cleared up; most people who buy a defective alarm clock do not sue the manufacturer, but rather take the clock back or throw it out. The same is true with eBay. The vast majority of conflicts are either resolved by the parties by themselves or with the help of a mediator. The connection to eBay's reputation rankings through the Feedback Forum makes Square Trade mediation particularly effective.

Mediation and related extralegal dispute resolution mechanisms are not, however, a complete substitute for real contract law. For a class of cases, and for the very ground rules that eBay lives by, government enforcement of eBay contracts is essential. Without enforceable contracts, many day-to-day matters might work fine—but eBay would be limited in its effectiveness, efficiency, and growth.

At the bottom of eBay's web page is a link for "user agreement." Most people ignore the user agreement, but in fact, every time you use eBay, you agree to "the terms and conditions applicable" to your use of eBay service contained in the agreement. "If you do not agree to be bound by the terms and conditions of this Agreement, do not use or access our services," warns eBay.[30] The terms in the user agreement form a contract that binds you to scores of obligations if you use eBay. And the government's promise, or threat, to enforce the obligations in this contract is crucial to eBay's viability.

Consider one of many examples—eBay's release from liability. It provides:

**eBay is a venue**.

**3.4 Release. . . .** [I]n the event that you have a dispute with one or more users, you release eBay (and our officers, directors, agents, subsidiaries, joint ventures and employees) from claims, demands and damages (actual and consequential) of every kind and nature, known and unknown, suspected and unsuspected, disclosed and undisclosed, arising out of or in any way connected with such disputes.[31]

This provision effectively says that eBay users cannot sue eBay for transactions that take place on eBay. The importance of this agreement and its enforcement to eBay should be clear. Were eBay subject to liability for everything that happened using eBay, its costs would increase dramatically. The contractual release is what prevents this from happening. But the release is only valuable if a court upholds it after someone tries to sue eBay over a transaction gone bad. By upholding eBay's release and preventing eBay from being destroyed by lawsuits, government helps make eBay a viable and cost-effective service.

Contract law is also crucial for eBay's handling of large transactions. eBay's Feedback Forum, combined with its Buyer Protection program (which reimburses the buyer up to $200 when the seller fails to deliver as promised), is certainly effective for small transactions— only obsessed people with a lot of time actually sue to recover small amounts of money. But one of the great surprises of eBay has been its ability—without altering its simple model—to serve as an auction site for large-ticket items like automobiles, computer equipment, and even, in one case, a World War II submarine. None of this was planned. In the case of cars, an eBay employee simply noticed one day that people were buying and selling real Ferraris in the toy car section of eBay.[32] It is one thing to buy a $10 Star Wars doll in an impersonal market from someone you don't know. But it is doubtful that many people on eBay would be willing to buy or sell a $120,000 automobile without some government-backed guarantee that the contract would actually be enforced.

Why wouldn't Square Trade mediation be enough? Here's one user's response, posted on an eBay message board: "Unfortunately there is a lot of hype going on about Square Trade and what it does for a person to be a member. Well, it's baloney. Square Trade is only a mediation service and can't do anything to affect your eBay or PayPal accounts."[33] In other words, if the other party doesn't cooperate, Square Trade won't get you your money back. What did the user recommend instead? If there's trouble, "file a Mail Fraud complaint with the USPS [United States Postal Service]. . . . I would guess that any seller finding a pair of USPS inspectors on their doorstep . . . would be rather quick to refund your money or 'find' the 'lost' package."[34] There is, in short, a user demand for coercive enforcement of promises that cannot be met by voluntary procedures.

This contrast between Square Trade mediation and the USPS inspector teaches something about what makes government action hard to replicate. Why does the user assume that a USPS inspector will have an effect that the mediators won't? There is a simple reason that government action is different—its power of legitimate physical coercion. The government has the power to arrest you, jail you, or sometimes even kill you, if you do not obey—and it may generally do so without fear of being punished itself. Physical coercion, meanwhile, can be relatively cheap for the government—but the costs to the individual of being imprisoned are enormous.

Physical coercion is not the only kind of coercion, or always the most relevant. The threat of reputational loss on eBay can be a threat, particularly for a repeat eBay user. The difference with physical coercion, however, is its severity and universality. Not everyone cares about an eBay reputation, but everyone values physical sanctity and freedom of movement. An eBay scofflaw may laugh at reputational sanction and mediators; the ability to laugh at arrest and imprisonment is less common.

To complete the point, we might ask: what would eBay look like in the absence of government-enforced contract law? One might think, based on the Feedback Forum, the Buyer Protection program, and Square Trade, that eBay could continue to run much of its ordinary business. In the absence of law, though, eBay would need something to make up the difference that the legal threat now provides. It is true that eBay itself might possibly provide greater security for buyers and sellers. And eBay might guarantee that *it* would make sure that the contracts would be honored. But as with fraud, the result wouldn't be eBay as we know it, but rather some very different business—and a much more expensive and less popular business. What has made eBay successful and profitable since day one is its hands-off, self-executing, low-cost nature. That, in turn, depends on a robust system of community norms, and also, underneath that community, the rule of law and government coercion.

## Between Anarchy and Despotism

The success of Internet companies like eBay, the success of the Internet itself, and indeed the success of many human endeavors depend on something invisible but essential: public goods like criminal law, property rights, and contract enforcement provided by government. Public goods are benefits (national defense, street signs, and clean air are other examples) that can usually be provided only by governments. The main reason that only government can provide these goods is that they benefit everyone. Private actors who considered supplying them couldn't force "free riders" to pay for them and thus wouldn't provide them in the first place. The government, by contrast, can force people to pay taxes to ensure that the goods are supplied adequately.[35] On a day-to-day basis, we aren't always aware of the government-provided protection against harm, and the enforcement of contractual and other rights that safeguard peaceful relations. But we do notice when they are missing: when contracts go unenforced, when property is stolen, and when fraud is rampant.

Many of the Internet visionaries we met in chapter 2 believed that Internet communities like eBay could govern themselves without any intervention or support from traditional government. But they overlooked how vital government-provided public goods are to private flourishing, whether it be commercial flourishing through buying and selling on eBay, or recreational flourishing like playing in a safe park with clean air. Private groups like eBay and its customers need government to keep their community from being overrun by villains. They also need government for much more: to regulate and support the capital markets that helped eBay raise billions of dollars to expand its operations and boost its marketing; to enforce trademark laws that protect eBay's brand from being diluted; and to build roads, ensure clean water, and provide police and fire protection in San Jose, California, where its headquarters are located.

This is the happy side of government. There is, of course, another side. Government is not a benevolent trustee of the public's interest, always doing what is best. In reality, government is often ugly and pathological. The counterpart to the private anarchy that faced eBay is the abuse of government power. We have already seen in chapter 6 the excess of which government rule of the Internet is capable. A highly repressive government can make much that is good about the Internet untenable. Matters are much better in a democracy, which has freedom of speech and press, independent courts, and regular, open elections. But of course, even governments in democracies have serious problems. With respect to each of the public goods described above on which eBay critically depends, there is a danger that government will go too far and overregulate private life. It might, for example, overpunish certain behaviors, as many believe it has done with drug sentencing. Or it might overregulate capital markets, as the Sarbanes-Oxley legislation following the Enron and WorldCom scandals arguably did when it imposed burdensome and expensive accounting requirements that many believe will stop small and medium-sized firms from accessing public capital markets. Or it might overprotect intellectual property rights and stifle innovation, as many believe was the case with the Sonny Bono Term Extension Act, which extended the term of all existing copyrights by twenty years.

There are systematic reasons why elected governments sometimes fail to do what is best for their citizens. One prominent reason is that groups within societies differ wildly in their ability to be heard by government and to get government to do what they want.[36] Industry groups, unions, farmers, and other well-organized factions have a disproportionate influence on what laws government passes. Sometimes the result can be roughly reflective of the preferences of the governed—especially when two or more well-organized groups face off. But sometimes the well-organized exploit the poorly organized. There are many well-known examples—farmers and crop subsidies, tenants and rent control, the AARP and Social Security, and millionaires and tax loopholes.

The Sonny Bono Act mentioned above is a prominent example. Many believe that this statute aided the highly organized and ailing recording industry at the public's expense. "The real impetus for term extension [came] from a very small group: children and grandchildren of famous composers whose works are beginning to fall into the public domain, thereby threatening trust funds," explained former congressional staffer William Patry. "These estates had considerable

141

political and financial impact with ASCAP, the music performing rights collecting society." But "at some point, a long term of protection loses all connection to acknowledging the author for his or her creativity, to providing incentives for the author to create, or to looking after the author's immediate family."[37]

Interest group capture of the legislature is not, of course, the only flaw in democratic government. The executive and judicial branches can also be corrupt or incompetent, and can fail to follow the law or reflect the wishes of the people. For every useful intervention that government makes in private life, there is a danger that it will go too far, and it often does go too far. It is difficult in the abstract to say where the line between government and private control should be drawn. Academics, policy makers, and pundits debate these questions daily and fiercely in discrete contexts, and the answers vary among such contexts.

Without denying the difficulties of where to draw this line, our main claims are modest. Public goods and related virtues of government control of the Internet are necessary across multiple dimensions for the Internet to work, and as a practical matter only traditional territorial governments can provide such goods. Anarchy—the absence of coercive government that the Internet visionaries cherished—will not work. Moreover, despite the well-known warts of democratic government, it remains the least-bad system known to history. With an open and free press, regular elections, and an independent judiciary, democratic governments are the best system that human beings have ever devised for aggregating the varied interests and desires of a sovereign people into a workable governing order, and for minimizing or correcting the many pathologies that invariably encumber governmental systems.

All governments exist somewhere on an axis between the anarchy that governments are supposed to redress and the despotism that governments sometimes employ. Some countries strike this balance better than others for reasons of history, tradition, or just plain luck. What may be surprising is the extent to which the Internet, or the applications that make it interesting, depends on this balance. For as we next show, the success of the Internet and its companies depends on the stability of the country beneath it.

## Expansion Abroad

In 1999, eBay opened its first overseas auction site, in the United Kingdom, and by the end of 2002 had established auction sites across Europe and Asia. As might be expected, different laws in different nations created new legal and business challenges. In the UK, for example, defamation laws are strict. When users received negative feedback, they often threatened to sue both eBay and the person who left the feedback, and so eBay had to create a process for handling defamation complaints. In Germany, meanwhile, eBay refused to allow the listing of Nazi goods from the beginning in order to comply with German law, a policy it later adopted for the U.S. website. [38]

The legal challenges in Europe were nothing compared to the challenges eBay faced in India. In 2004, eBay paid $50 million for a company named Baazee.com, India's then-largest online auction site, and in 2005 created the latest eBay outpost, eBay.in.[39] The new business met some expected challenges. Credit card usage in India is uncommon and listings on eBay India typically need to list multiple forms of bank transfers as payment options.[40] The number of Internet users in India is still relatively low—about 20 million.[41] Consequently, on an August 2005 visit to eBay.in, the number of listings was also low—only thirty-two listings under "Bollywood" (the name for India's film industry), as compared with 1,461 listings under eBay.com.

eBay.in's legal problems were also unexpected. Sometime in November 2004, members of the press discovered a listing for an oral sex video clip featuring a seventeen-year-old boy and sixteen-year-old girl, both students at a prestigious Delhi high school, for sale on Baazee (which at the time was owned by eBay). "Following investigations," said the police, "we have found that the sale was continuing on the online site and they did not act diligently. In this connection, we have arrested the CEO of the site, Avnish Bajaj." [42] Bajaj, an American citizen and the CEO of Baazee, was detained and charged with a violation §67 of India's Information Technology Act, which mandates imprisonment for anyone who "publishes or transmits or causes to be published" "lascivious" material.[43] As part of a spreading "Delhi Public School MMS sex scandal," the students were expelled, and the seller of the video clip, a student at India's prestigious Indian Institute of Technology, was arrested.

Bajaj was released on bail after, among other things, diplomatic intervention by the U.S. State Department.[44] But the lawsuit highlights how dependent eBay is on governments providing the elusive balance between anarchy and despotism. Without questioning the legitimacy of the Indian enforcement action, eBay could not operate long in a country where its officials are routinely imprisoned for social scandals. Overly aggressive local laws can doom eBay and other Internet businesses as much as a failure to prosecute fraud.

Nonetheless, eBay's pattern of overseas expansion appears to reflect a greater desire to avoid anarchy than to avoid despotism. One might expect that eBay would simply expand to the countries with the largest GNPs and richest citizens, as the locations of the greatest potential revenue. While market size is obviously important, eBay's and other Internet companies' record of expansion reflects another concern. It shows an interest in the rule of law and the likelihood of either fraud or repression affecting its business.

Of the world's fifty largest economies, eBay had, in the spring of 2005, set up shop in twenty-six. There were eBays in four of the world's five largest economies: the United States, China, India, and Germany (eBay Japan folded in 2002). But of the top twenty economies, eBay is only in fifteen. It has not set up shop in Russia, Indonesia, Thailand, Iran, and Turkey, despite the size of these markets. Russia is particularly important: it remains the tenth largest economy in the world, yet neither eBay nor other Internet multinationals are willing to invest in it.

Instead, eBay has set up business in much smaller markets that have better legal systems. For example, eBay operates an auction site in Poland, despite the fact that the Polish economy is about one-third the size of its Russian neighbor. eBay also chooses to operate in Malaysia but not in the larger Pakistani, Iranian, or South African markets. The same patterns are also evident in the investments of other Internet multinationals. Yahoo operates in twenty-seven countries, approximately the same number as eBay. It too gives Russia, the world's tenth largest economy, a pass. And it chooses to operate in smaller economies with predictable legal systems, like Denmark, over some larger economies like Columbia or Ukraine.[45]

What might explain these decisions? We can focus on Russia as the greatest anomaly. As mentioned, its economy is the tenth largest in the world—$1.4 trillion in purchasing parity in 2004—and while

Russia has many poor people, it also has a class of very wealthy people. Nonetheless, multinational Internet companies like eBay do not provide services there. At first glance this is a puzzle, since Russia is a far cry from the oppressive place it was when it was at the center of the Soviet Union. But Russia has the opposite problem. It suffers from private harms gone unchecked: insecurity of private property, corporate fraud, a failed criminal law system, organized crime and oligarch-dominated business, and ineffective respect for and enforcement of contract rights.[46] "Without a well-functioning public power of a certain kind there will be no prevention of mutual harm, no personal security, and no 'standing rule to live by,'" wrote NYU professor Stephen Holmes in a famous 1997 essay about Russia that remains largely accurate today.[47]

Post-Soviet Russia holds powerful lessons for companies like eBay and the government's role in Internet regulation. As viruses, online fraud, spam, and other abuses add up, the greatest dangers for the future of the Internet come not when governments overreact, but when they don't react at all. The old and primary role of preventing harm and protecting rights must be translated to the present for the network to continue to grow and prosper.

## Epilogue

In the summer of 2000, Pierre Omidyar left his day-to-day work at eBay. In Adam Cohen's account, Omidyar simply emptied his cubicle one day and left, without announcement or ceremony.[48] Omidyar had moved to another stage of life. As his autobiography suggested, it was time to do more to "make the world a better place." The company he had created had always been designed to run itself. Now it didn't even need Omidyar—its self-execution was complete.

The greatest praise we can offer for traditional territorial government is reflected in the eBay story. The chief virtues of government in this story are invisible: they are the background rule of law that makes a company like eBay viable, and even possible, as a self-executing business. This is not an accident. There is no place for eBay in an anarchy like 1990s Russia or the failed states of Africa, that lack the basic public goods that make thriving Internet businesses possible.

nine

# Consequences of Borders

Australia's Joseph Gutnick is a billionaire, a diamond and gold miner, a political player, a philanthropist, and a rabbi. On October 20, 2000, Gutnick awoke in Victoria to find himself accused of tax evasion and money laundering by the American business magazine *Barron's*. The article, "UnHoly Gains," suggested that Gutnick had engaged in shady dealings with Nachum Goldberg, a Melbourne money launderer jailed in 2000 for washing AU$42 million in used notes through a bogus Israeli charity.[1] Gutnick read the story, not in the print version of *Barron's* but on the online version of its sister publication, "wsj.com," a website on a server physically located in New Jersey. Gutnick was not the only Australian to read the story. Approximately seventeen hundred Australians subscribed to wsj.com, including many Australian business and finance leaders. An enraged Gutnick vehemently denied the illicit association with Goldberg. To protect his reputation, he sued Dow Jones & Company—the parent company of both *Barron's* and the *Wall Street Journal*—in an Australian court, taking advantage of tough Australian libel laws unleavened by the U.S. First Amendment.

The legal arguments in the *Gutnick* case mirrored those in the *Yahoo* litigation in France a few years earlier. Dow Jones argued that Australian courts were legally powerless (or "without jurisdiction") to rule on the legality of information on a computer in the United States, even if it appeared in Australia.[2] The Australian High Court, like the court in France, disagreed. For material published on the Internet, it stated, the place where the person downloads the material "will be the place where the tort of defamation is committed."[3] Within two years of this decision, Dow Jones agreed to pay Gutnick AU$180,000 in damages and AU$400,000 in legal fees to settle the case.[4] It also issued this retraction: "*Barron's* has no reason to believe Mr. Gutnick was ever a customer of Mr. Goldberg, and has no reason to believe that Mr. Gutnick was a money laundering customer of, or had any criminal or other improper relationship with, Mr. Goldberg."[5]

"The U.S. cannot impose their laws on this country," rejoiced Gutnick in Australia. "They have to respect our law."[6] But the Australian decision also attracted the same predictably negative reaction as the French decision in the *Yahoo* case. Fierce libel laws are antiquated in the Internet age and are inconsistent with the Net's First Amendment-inspired approach to free expression. Australia has no business getting involved when a newspaper writes an article in New Jersey meant for an American audience. The Australian rule will chill speech in the United States and elsewhere, forcing newspapers around the world to bow to the most restrictive laws in the world. As a gloomy *New York Times* editorial page said, "To subject distant providers of on-line content to sanctions in countries intent on curbing free speech— or even to 190 different libel laws—is to undermine the Internet's viability."[7]

The Dow Jones–Gutnick controversy is no different than thousands of other conflicts of laws that have arisen on the Internet during the last decade. These conflicts give the lie to Frances Cairncross's 1999 prediction that the death of distance heralded by the Internet would be a "powerful force for peace" and mutual understanding among nations.[8] These conflicts of laws have not, however, had the widely predicted devastating effects on the Internet itself. Publishing and commerce are flourishing on the Internet despite the dozens of "parochial" national laws to which e-businesses are supposedly subject. And individuals continue to send e-mails, create web pages, and write blogs despite the supposed prospect of having to figure out how to comply with every law in the world.

This chapter explains why the predicted doomsday scenarios have not materialized. It begins by summarizing and extending the normative case made throughout this book for the bordered Internet. It then addresses the conflict of laws problem. The heated rhetoric about conflicts of laws masks two more salient operating principles: multinational firms want to minimize global operating costs, and libertarians want to extend the unusually tolerant values of the U.S. First Amendment across the globe. As we will see, national Internet laws are no more burdensome than the scores of conflicting national laws that multinational firms typically face, and they have no effect on the vast majority of individual Net users who, unlike global firms, lack a multinational presence. There is no denying that the bordered Internet replicates some of the familiar costs and pathologies that result when nations apply their laws to transnational communications and transactions. But like the international system itself, it also lets many different peoples coexist on the same planet while maintaining very different values and ideas of the good life. In this diversity lies a happier world than one governed by a single global law for all matters. When dreaming of a better society centered on the Internet, the many virtues of a bordered system must not be overlooked.

## Borders 2.0

This book has described three reasons why what we once called a global network is becoming a collection of nation-state networks—networks still linked by the Internet protocol, but for many purposes separate. First, peoples in different nations tend to read and speak different languages and have different backgrounds, capacities, preferences, desires, and needs. These reflect local differences in history, culture, geography, and wealth. Internet users seek out, and content providers want to provide, congenial content that reflects these differences.

Technological developments are the second reason for Internet borders. The Chinas of the world are becoming remarkably sophisticated at firewalling their countries and creating closed national networks. Internet geo-ID technologies are becoming faster and cheaper and more prevalent. These technologies enable content to be tailored to Net users by geography and permit e-firms to avoid sending content to places where it is illegal. Even the deep structure of the Internet—bandwidth distribution, increasing Internet traffic within countries and regions, and diminished traffic between countries—reinforces Internet borders.

The enforcement of national laws in cases like *Gutnick* and *Yahoo* are the third reason for Internet borders. One strong and important difference among peoples concerns their values, and people with different values disagree about the type of information they want to receive and the type of information they deem harmful. Some societies tolerate Nazi goods; others don't. Some like privacy warning labels; others don't. Some accept online gambling; others don't. Some want strong protections for intellectual property; again, others differ. These differences are reflected in different national laws, and governmental officials charged with enforcing national values must enforce these laws, as cases like *Gutnick* and *Yahoo* make clear.

The bordered Internet is widely viewed to be a dreadful development that is antithetical to the Internet's "true" purposes and undermines the Internet's promise. The issue tends to be joined most fiercely in the context of speech regulation, as the storm over the *Gutnick* and *Yahoo* cases reveal. There are many reasons for this focus, but the main one is that the Internet is a revolutionary medium of *communication*, and communication is speech. In that sense, just about every debate about Internet governance is at bottom a debate about speech governance. The most basic question about the bordered Internet, therefore, is whether speech should be regulated globally or locally.

We think that there is very little to say in favor of a single global rule for Internet speech. "Every jurisdiction controls access to some speech . . . but what that speech is differs from jurisdiction to jurisdiction," explain Lawrence Lessig and Paul Renick. "What constitutes 'obscene' speech in Tennessee is permitted in Holland; what constitutes porn in Japan is child porn in the United States; what is 'harmful to minors' in Bavaria is Disney in New York."[9] These dramatically different attitudes toward proper speech among mature democracies reflect important differences among the peoples that populate these countries—differences in culture, history, and tastes that are legitimately reflected in national and local laws.

In the United States, it is acceptable to join a political party that condones racism, and courts uphold the right of neo-Nazis to parade through predominantly Jewish towns wearing uniforms and swastikas. Other democracies, influenced by very different histories and tradition, take a different view. Israel is a democracy that rose out of the Holocaust and that persists in a nearly constant state of emergency. It bans speech that is "offensive" or causes "emotional harm," and it outlaws political parties that espouse racism or call for the destruction of the State of Israel. [10] Germany bans Nazi speech for yet a different reason, the same reason that Japan's Constitution outlaws aggressive war: it is a nation still coming to grips with the horrors it committed in the past, and it is terrified that they could happen again.[11] As we saw in chapter 1, France too bans pro-Nazi speech, as well as speech that endorses or minimizes the Holocaust. French law reflects its occupation by Nazi Germany during World War II, and its related belief that a person's right to be free from threatening and degrading speech trumps the right to voice one's political ideas, however harmful.[12]

The *Gutnick* case reveals the same underlying tension. The case arises out of deep differences between the United States and Australia on the importance of free speech, reputation, and public order. Although both countries are former British colonies influenced by the English common law tradition, they have for forty years taken vastly different approaches to free speech protections for the press. In 1964, the U.S. Supreme Court in *New York Times v. Sullivan* broke with the British common law when it interpreted the First Amendment to make it much harder for public officials to recover in libel suits against newspapers. The *Sullivan* case embraced a new "commitment to the principle that debate on public issues should be uninhibited, robust, and wide-open."[13] After *Sullivan*, it has been very hard for public figures like Gutnick to win in libel cases in the United States. The Australian High Court, however, rejects the *Sullivan* rule, reasoning that it "tilts the balance unduly in favor of free speech" and "gives inadequate protection to reputation."[14] Whereas American libel law places a high burden of proof on the alleged victim of defamatory speech, Australia places the burden of proof on the publisher and requires the publisher to reasonably believe that its statement concerning the alleged victim is true, and to give the alleged victim a chance to reply.[15] The dispute in *Gutnick* thus goes far beyond the dry rules of libel law. It reflects deeper disagreements between the United States and Australia about the processes that best secure truth, and about the relative values of robust speech versus reputation and uninhibited debate versus order.

These examples show that deeply held differences in values, even among democracies, lie behind conflicts of laws. A bordered Internet is valuable precisely because it permits people of different value systems to coexist on the same planet.

A good way to understand the case for a bordered Internet is to consider its opposite. Imagine a global law in the form of a world government or a world treaty. Set aside the insurmountable problem of creating a legitimate and reliable global executive to enforce such global norms. A more fundamental problem is that the global norms would often be unattractive, even if they could be enforced. When you choose a single rule for six billion people, odds are that several billion, or more, will be unhappy with it. Should divorce and abortion and pornography be allowed, and if so to what degree? Ought economic and environmental policy reflect the interests of poorer or wealthier nations? Similar questions arise on the Internet: Is the American approach to Nazi speech right, or the French-German-Israeli variants? Should the competing interests of the free press and private reputation be balanced Australian style or U.S. style? To what degree should gambling and pornography on the web be allowed? Should data privacy be unregulated, modestly regulated, or heavily regulated? A single answer to these and thousands of other questions would leave the world divided and discontented.

The advantage of decentralized governance is that it can better reflect differences among peoples.[16] Consider what would happen when three nations with equal populations of 100 people—A, B, and C—tried to decide whether web gambling should be allowed in their country.[17] Assume that 75 percent of the people in A, 65 percent of the people in B, and 35 percent of the people in C want to ban web gambling, with the remainder of the population in all three countries opposed to the ban. If the countries decided on a "global" rule reflecting majority preferences among the 300 people in the three territories, the result would be a global ban on web gambling with 175 people pleased and 125 displeased. But if each country can decide whether to ban web gambling for itself, A and B will ban web gambling and C will not, and in the aggregate 205 people will be pleased and 95 displeased. In this way, decentralized government can respond in a more fine-grained way to what people want and can best enhance overall welfare.

Of course, this and other arguments for a bordered Internet must confront the problem of China and other oppressive nations that do not purport to represent the interests or preferences of their people. But even the China example, as bad as it is, does not undermine the case for territorial control of the Internet. Governments did not create the technologies that China is using to keep unwanted content out. Rather, as we saw in chapter 4, the private sector created it in response to consumer demands that the Net's content be better tailored to suit individual interests—interests that, as a brute fact, cluster by geography. And as the *Yahoo* case shows, governments in democratic states are starting to demand that this technology be used to respond to entirely appropriate constituent demands to protect them not only from Nazi goods but also from hate speech, credit card theft, invasions of privacy, sexual predators, spam, and much more. Technologies of control designed to serve legitimate and desired ends can rarely be limited to those ends, and will often be co-opted for illegitimate purposes. The Internet is no exception.

The question about the optimal form of Internet governance must always be "compared to what?" While it is easy to criticize traditional territorial government and bemoan its many failures, there is no reasonable prospect of any better system of governmental organization. Even acknowledging that in places like China the laws will often not reflect the wishes of people who live there, differences among laws in the many democratic governments in the world (such as the ones at issue in *Yahoo* and *Gutnick*) are presumptively legitimate. Many elements of China's bordered Internet, moreover, *do* respond to legitimate Chinese preferences—for example, the language in which Net content is delivered, and the cheap digital goods that are helping the Chinese economy flourish.

In defending the system of decentralized national control, we are not arguing for the current number and size of territorial nation-states. Nations that are too small will lack the economic capacity to provide public goods like national defense and education. As a nation's size increases it can address these deficiencies, but at the cost of increasingly diverse values, preferences, and commitments among citizens, which makes it harder for the ever-more-distant government to promulgate and enforce rules that are viewed as legitimate by all.[18] This is one reason why many large modern democratic nations—the United States, Australia, Germany—have federal systems that make important governmental decisions at the subunit level. The European Union is an emerging territorial nation-state created (like Italy and Germany in the nineteenth century) out of smaller ones. To work it will need to retain its federalist structure, and we may now be approaching the point where its increasingly heterogeneous peoples will stall further enlargement. By contrast, many nations (including some in the EU) face devolution pressures, as distinct groups within nations clamor for greater direct control over aspects of their lives. There is a natural limit here too. In the words of UN Secretary-General Boutros Boutros-Ghali, "If every ethnic, religious or linguistic group claimed statehood, there would be no limit to fragmentation, and peace, security and well-being for all would become ever more difficult to achieve."[19]

Nation-states have always faced these competing pressures for expansion and contraction, and the Internet will surely exacerbate them in many ways. But pressures to change the size of nation-states should not overshadow the many ways that the decentralized territorial system itself promotes diversity and self-determination, even with regard to Internet communications. There is, however, another objection to decentralized control. Even if differing national laws reflect what's best for people in those countries, the argument goes, the *global* effects of national control of the Internet are ruinous for the Internet. It is to this argument that we now turn.

## Extraterritoriality

Australia's *Gutnick* decision "puts at risk the ability of Americans to speak with each other and be protected by American law when they do so," said First Amendment maven Floyd Abrams.[20] Abrams was complaining about the extraterritorial effect of the Australian decision. The Australian court effectively applied Australian laws outside Australian borders to a publication in the United States that was intended primarily for an American audience. It applied Australian law to an American company,

Dow Jones, whose political interests were not formally represented in Australia. And in so doing, the court undoubtedly caused Dow Jones to become more cautious about what it published in America, thereby contravening American free-speech values and depriving Americans and others across the globe of information.

All of this is true—but it is also inevitable and commonplace. Seventy-five years ago an international arbitral panel ruled that Canada was responsible for preventing sulfur dioxide emissions from Canada that caused agricultural damage in the United States.[21] U.S. officials, had they so desired, could have applied U.S. law to make the Canadian firm pay for the damage caused in the United States. The punishment in the U.S. of a Canadian polluter would have had the effect of raising the cost of smelting, and thus the price of metals, in Canada. But these "extraterritorial" effects of U.S. law do not call into question the United States' right and duty to protect Americans in America. If the United States does not act against the Canadian polluter, then the permissive Canadian law would have resulted in the "extraterritorial" damage in the United States. In this sense, extraterritorial effects always run in both directions when two nations try to apply their different laws to the same transnational event. These inevitable cross-border effects do not undermine the legitimacy of a nation applying its laws to redress local harms.

Consider a more recent example. In the late 1990s, Boeing and McDonnell Douglas, two American aerospace giants that did business worldwide but had their productive resources in the United States, tried to merge. The U.S. Federal Trade Commission (FTC) approved the merger, but the European Commission threatened to stop the merger because it viewed Boeing's exclusive contracts with other airlines to be harmful to European airline competition. Ultimately Boeing gave in to the commission's demands and eliminated exclusive contracting. This meant that the commission's threatened injunction raised the costs in the United States of a merger between two American companies and superceded the regulatory efforts of the FTC. But if the commission had *not* enforced the EU laws, the more permissive American laws would have caused harmful anticompetitive effects in Europe. Once again, whichever nation's law ends up applying to transnational activity will inevitably have indirect effects in another state. But these effects are perfectly legitimate by-products of the EU's action to protect Europeans from what it deemed to be the harmful local effects of offshore activity.[22]

In international law, borders are fundamental. As a general matter, nations can exercise coercive powers within their borders but not beyond.[23] But a nation can always take steps *within* its territory to stop and redress harms that come from abroad. Indeed, as we saw in chapter 5, control of local Internet intermediaries is the main way that governments control offshore Internet harms. The principle that gives a nation the right and duty to protect citizens from locally caused harms applies with equal if not greater force when the harm comes from abroad. Not surprisingly in our modern interconnected world, nations frequently apply local law to harms from abroad. In addition to the pollution and antitrust examples, nations have long applied local law to regulate unwanted television and radio broadcasts from abroad, the harmful local effects of offshore frauds, local crimes (like drug dealing) initiated elsewhere, and the like.

A government's responsibility for redressing local harms caused by a foreign source does not change because the harms are caused by an Internet communication. Cross-border harms that occur via the Internet are not any different than those outside the Net. Both demand a response from governmental authorities charged with protecting public values. When Nepali scam-artists defraud Indian investors in India, the Indian government must act, regardless of whether the fraud occurred in a magazine from Nepal or an e-mail from there. The United States wants to stop the local consumption of child pornography produced in Russia regardless of the medium— World Wide Web, magazine, or video—in which the porn appears. The French view the sale of Nazi paraphernalia as repugnant, whether it is sold on *Yahoo*'s servers or by mail-order catalogue. In short, nations have a right and a duty to protect their citizens from harm, whatever the source and whatever the medium.

These points illuminate the *Gutnick* decision. The Australian decision had effects in the United States, to be sure. But if Australia had not applied its laws to redress the harm to Gutnick in Australia, U.S. First Amendment law and speech-protective U.S. libel laws would have produced harmful and unwanted effects in Australia. This point is invariably missed by the critics of government control over the Net, who believe that the U.S. First Amendment reflects universal values and is somehow written into the architecture of the Internet. But the First Amendment does not reflect universal values; to the contrary, no other nation embraces these values, and they are certainly not written into the Internet's architecture. Enforcing the outlier First Amendment in *Gutnick* would have meant eviscerating Australian laws that reflected Australian values and concerns. But there is no reason why Australia should yield local control over its territory in order to accommodate Internet users in the United States. Nor should it absorb the costs in Australia of U.S. Internet activity simply because the Australian law might produce costs in the United States. Australia can regulate the local harm of transnational Internet activity even if doing so harms Dow Jones in the United States.

This result is not unfair to Dow Jones. Dow Jones chose to publish in Australia, and, as the court in Gutnick noted, "there is nothing unique about multinational business" that makes it exempt from local law.[24] Compliance with Australian libel laws—like compliance with Australian tax laws, Australian accounting laws, and Australian consumer protection laws—is a cost of doing business in Australia. As the Australian court noted, "If people wish to do business in, or indeed travel to, or live in, or utilize the infrastructure of different countries, they can hardly expect to be absolved from compliance with the laws of those countries."[25] Dow Jones reaps financial and other benefits from its presence in Australia. Without this presence Australian enforcement threats would be empty. Dow Jones need not remain in Australia; it can close its shop there if Australian laws become too burdensome. Its decision to continue operations in Australia after settling with Gutnick reflects the company's judgment that the benefits of doing business in Australia outweigh its costs.

Nor is the *Gutnick* decision unfair to consumers of Dow Jones news in the United States and other countries. At first glance it seems unfair if the Australian decision causes Dow Jones to stop publishing news that might have been of interest to Dow Jones readers in the United States. But again, such a result would be a consequence of Dow Jones's business decision to continue operating in Australia—a decision that weighed the financial benefits of doing business in Australia against the costs of not doing business there, including the cost of not publishing pieces globally that might run afoul of Australian libel law. Since *Barron's* chose to continue to do business in Australia, its consumers in the United States and Japan cannot legitimately expect to receive news from *Barron's* that runs afoul of Australian law. If they do not like the reduced content that results from Dow Jones's decision to remain in Australia, they can get the information from scores of other news sources that do not do business in Australia and thus have no fear of Australian libel law.[26]

The ultimate problem with criticisms of *Gutnick* is that they reject any legal outcome other than the American approach. The critics assume that wherever the Internet goes, it brings a single global cyberlaw with it, like a tortoise carrying its shell. The irony, of course, is that the tortoise shell is not a consensus global law, but rather the parochial U.S. First Amendment. Australia is a democracy that has a different conception of free speech, and tougher libel laws, than the United States. The outcome of the *Gutnick* case suggests that the "Unholy Gains" article was in fact a pack of lies that harmed Gutnick's reputation. Australians need not forego redressing this harm to one of its citizens in Australia out of deference to the U.S. Constitution.

## Multiple Laws

"It's a bad thing, not a horrible thing," said instapundit Glenn Reynolds of the *Gutnick* decision. "What moves you to a horrible thing is that because the Australian high court has done this, it will be acceptable for countries with systems of law far less congenial to free speech to do the same thing."[27] This is the result predicted by cyberscholars David Johnson and David Post, who argued in 1997 that if a territorial government could apply its laws to a Net communication, then all "Web-based activity . . . must be subject simultaneously to the laws of all territorial sovereigns."[28]

Being subject to a patchwork of conflicting laws seems like a bad, unworkable idea. The idea seems to get worse when we contemplate its effect on the decision to publish. The *Sydney Morning Herald* warned that after the *Gutnick* decision, "publishers will be tempted to produce material that is innocuous enough not to fall foul of the most draconian legal regimes."[29] In other words, publishers will be chilled by the prospect of having to comply with dozens of different laws and, racing to the bottom, will conform their content to the laws of the most restrictive nation. Glenn Reynolds warned of a "lowest common denominator approach in which Internet publishers strive not to be offensive according to anyone's standards, which is likely to mean not publishing at all, or publishing only inoffensive pap."[30]

A similar chorus of sky-is-falling rhetoric greets every judicial decision that applies local law to a Net transaction with an offshore source. And yet wsj.com and millions of other web content providers, both firms and individuals, continue to publish news and opinion online, and not only the "inoffensive pap" predicted by Reynolds.

To see why the specter of multiple laws is exaggerated, recall the main lesson from chapter 5: with few exceptions, governments can use their coercive powers only within their borders and can control offshore Internet communications *only by controlling local intermediaries, local assets, and local persons*. Australia can effectively coerce Dow Jones because Dow Jones is a multinational company with employees, facilities, contracts, and bank accounts in Australia. But the vast majority of Internet users—students, e-consumers, porn purveyors, chat room participants, web-page operators, bloggers, and over 99 percent of other Net users—have no connection to Australia or to any other country other than the one in which they live. Far from being subject to multiple laws, these persons are immune from every law but their own.

The implication of the *Gutnick* decision, then, is that small Internet content providers need not worry about complying with the laws of every nation, but large firms with a presence in many nations—content providers like CNN, Dow Jones, and *The Economist*; systems operations like Yahoo, Google, eBay, and AOL; and financial intermediaries like MasterCard, PayPal, and Citibank—must comply with local laws in the places where they do business. Australia can go after these large multinationals in Australia when the multinationals assist in violations of Australian law. But it can do nothing directly to control Internet users outside Australia who have no presence there and must instead focus on Internet intermediaries with a local presence (as we discussed in chapter 5).

This still leaves big Internet multinationals like Dow Jones to face a jumble of overlapping and contradictory laws. But there is nothing new here. McDonalds complies with different health regulations and tax laws everywhere in the world it does business. Microsoft abides by varying consumer protection laws everywhere it sells its software. Honda builds cars to meet local emissions standards in different nations. The Red Cross must learn about and follow charitable registration requirements that differ among nations. And despite the hysteria over *Gutnick*, the *Wall Street Journal* employs lawyers to monitor and comply with the different libel laws in the various countries where it publishes. In each of these cases, multinational firms incur significant costs to keep abreast of laws in different nations and to take steps to comply with these laws. These are simply the costs of doing international business.

Why should the Internet be different? The conventional answer is that Internet multinationals are different from real-space multinationals because the Internet's architecture precludes them from knowing where in the world their content goes, making it impossible to comply with all local laws or to keep prohibited content out of certain places. But the claim that companies like Dow Jones cannot reduce or eliminate risk on a geographical basis in particular states is false.

As noted above, Dow Jones can leave Australia altogether, eliminating its presence and assets there and with them any fear of Australian libel law. Having decided to stay, it could monitor or control the geographical flow of its news. Dow Jones knew it had approximately seventeen hundred Australian users, and it knew that Gutnick lived in Australia. It could have simply denied access to the Gutnick story to these seventeen hundred users. Or it could have employed one of the various geo-ID and blocking technologies that are increasingly accurate and inexpensive, and that e-firms around the world are beginning to use to avoid or manage legal risk in distant jurisdictions.[31] As we learned in chapter 4, these technologies are not perfect. But no border control technology is, and it need not be to be effective. Moreover, neither *Gutnick* nor *Yahoo* nor any other decision has placed an absolute rule of exclusion on Internet companies. Rather, firms like Dow Jones are only responsible for content that they could, through best efforts, keep out of places where it is illegal. It is true that these measures are costly But compliance with the law has never been free, and these costs are no different from other legal compliance costs in transnational commerce.

In the late 1990s, the Internet appeared to be a corporation's dream: a medium that facilitated unlimited and inexpensive access to consumers without any regulatory restrictions. *Yahoo* and *Gutnick* mark the beginning of the end of that dream. When corporate activity causes cross-border harm, nations can, and will, assert their regulatory authority. The threat of multiple regulatory exposure will not, as many have histrionically claimed, destroy the Internet. Firms will have to filter content geographically to comply with local law for only a small fraction of their communications. This will impose costs on multinational Internet firms, which will have to adjust to this cost of business just as real-space multinationals do. In light of the Internet's many efficiencies, this cost will be trivial in the long run.

The lesson of this chapter is that when communications on the Internet collide with sensitive local public policies like gambling, pornography, consumer protection, libel, and the like, there are strong reasons to prefer a decentralized approach. In these contexts, there is no legitimate basis for giving any single law a kind of global constitutional status. It does not follow from what we have said, however, that there is no place for global Internet rules. To the contrary, many aspects of the Internet need to be regulated on a global scale. As the next chapter shows, however, this is sometimes easier said than done, and even when global rules prevail, territorial governments, and especially powerful ones, have devised them to serve their interests.

# 10
ten

## Global Laws

Alexey Vladimirovich Ivanov, a twenty-something computer geek from Chelyabinsk, Russia, in the Ural Mountains, earned his living hacking the computer networks of American companies. After breaking into a firm's servers, he would contact it on behalf of "The Expert Group of Protection Against Hackers" and demand thousands of dollars in exchange for tips on how to plug its security holes. One Connecticut company that initially refused to pay received this e-mail from Ivanov:

> now imagine please Somebody hack you network (and not notify you about this), he download Atomic software with more then 300 merchants, transfer money, and after this did 'rm -rf/' [a Unix command that deletes directories] and after this you company be ruined. I don't want this, and because this i notify you about possible hack in you network, if you want you can hire me and im allways be check security in you network. What you think about this?

If a firm did not comply with his unsubtle threats, Ivanov would delete its computer files or post its customers' credit card information on the Web. Not surprisingly, most firms gave in to the extortion.[1]

When FBI officials became aware of Ivanov's scams, they sought help from the Russian police. But as Brendan Koerner explained, "The Russian interior ministry's 'Department R,' which fights cybercrime, can barely keep up with the *kontoras* in St. Petersburg and Moscow, much less police a distant outpost like Chelyabinsk."[2] So the FBI took matters into its own hands. Under the guise of a fictional American

Internet security firm called "Invita," the FBI invited Ivanov to the United States to audition for a job identifying flaws in the networks of potential Invita clients. When Ivanov arrived, undercover agents asked him to prove his ability to break into computer networks. Unbeknownst to Ivanov, the FBI was using a "sniffer" keystroke recording program to learn the usernames and passwords for his computers in Russia. After the audition, the FBI arrested Ivanov and, using his usernames and passwords, downloaded incriminating information from his computer in Russia—information later used to convict him.[3]

The Ivanov sting operation worked. But it also reveals the enormous challenges that nations face in dealing with the problem of cross-border cybercrime. The hardest problem is getting custody of the criminal, for without such custody there can be no punishment and thus no deterrence of future crimes. Ivanov used to brag to the companies that he extorted, "We're in Russia, you can't touch us, the FBI can't get us in Russia."[4] He was right. The United States has no extradition treaty with Russia, and Russia was in any event both unable and unwilling to help. Even with their luck in luring Ivanov to the United States, the FBI still needed to break into Russian computers to secure evidence of the crime. This "counterhack" violated Russian sovereignty and infuriated the Russian government, which later brought criminal charges against the FBI agent responsible for the sting operation.[5] In any event, the FBI's ability to grab incriminating data on computers abroad doesn't help much if it has no defendant.

The cybercrime problem seems to require a global solution—international laws that prohibit computer invasions and disruptions, and that establish standards for international cooperation to redress the problem. The bordered Internet does not imply that such global Internet rules have no place, any more than our bordered world implies that there is no place for international law. To the contrary, many aspects of the Net will be governed on a global scale.

This chapter's examination of global rules for the Internet reveals two general themes. The first theme complements chapter 5's focus on unilateral techniques within national borders to control conduct outside of a country's borders. Here we learn how nations that want to control Internet communications that originate abroad are sometimes driven to cooperate with other nations. These efforts aren't always successful, and contrary to the claims of the internationalists in chapter 2, Internet treaties in particular have proven elusive. The second theme is that many Internet controversies are fast transforming into disputes among nations, and classic problems of international relations. Whether the issue is online gambling, Internet domain name governance, or privacy laws—all examples discussed in this chapter—governments are fighting one another to favor themselves, using the traditional tools of international politics and international law.

## The Cybercrime Convention and the Limits of Cooperation

A "cybercrime" occurs when computers on the Internet illegally access or harm files and programs on other computers.[6] Some cybercrimes, like Ivanov's, are "access" crimes involving data theft or data tampering. Others are "disruption" crimes: viruses, worms, logic bombs, Trojan horses, denial of service attacks, and the like. A famous disruption crime was the "I love you" virus that originated on a computer in the Philippines and caused over $15 billion in losses worldwide.[7]

Cybercrimes are big business. According to the FBI and the Computer Security Institute, cybercrimes were responsible for $142 million in losses in 2004, and these figures are probably dramatically understated, because firms underreport cybercrimes for fear of adverse publicity.[8] Cybercrimes are also hard for governments to stop. They differ from many Internet activities studied in this book. As we saw in chapter 5, governments are most effective at controlling offshore Internet activity when they act through local intermediaries like ISPs and financial institutions, but most cybercrimes involve no financial intermediary. Short of examining every Internet communication, which would be costly, ISPs cannot identify and block online "criminal" activity, which does not come labeled as such. Moreover, time is of the essence with cybercrime, because the crimes can be initiated in advance of detection, pseudonymity is relatively easy to achieve, and evidence of the crime can be destroyed quickly.[9]

These difficulties are exacerbated when, as in the Russian hack and "I love you" examples, the criminals operate on a computer in another country, beyond local police's direct control. Sometimes, the government where the criminals are operating won't cooperate. Other times it would like to cooperate but lacks the financial or technological resources to do so. Legal gaps create additional problems. The creator of the "I love you" virus couldn't be prosecuted in the Philippines or extradited to the United States because creating and sending the virus globally was not a crime under Philippine law. Even if there is a legal prohibition in theory, the enforcement machinery in the source country will sometimes simply take too long, permitting evidence of the crime to be destroyed or anonymized.[10]

Crossborder cybercrime, in short, is an especially challenging problem. For a country that wants to control it, a natural answer is to look for the help of other nations—international cooperation, or a treaty. This, in fact, was what the internationalists from chapter 2 foresaw as the future—that the Internet would require the gradual replacement of national laws and governments with international regimes and international organizations. In the case of cybercrime, for example, we would expect to see a global treaty that outlawed cybercrimes worldwide and established standards for international cooperation in preventing and prosecuting such crimes.

In fact, there is such a treaty—the Council of Europe's Cybercrime Convention, which is open to signature by all nations of the world. This treaty would require nations to establish a round-the-clock "point of contact" to ensure immediate assistance for the purposes of cross-border information requests. It would provide for rapid enforcement assistance by, for example, requiring the nation where a crime originates to preserve and disclose stored computer data at the request of the nation where the crime causes damage. It would harmonize each nation's cybercrime laws to better facilitate extradition and information-sharing. Finally, it would require each nation to enact laws that enable expedited searches, seizures, and preservations of computer data in the country.

Sounds good in theory. But the fate of the Cybercrime Convention reveals the limits of treaties, and indeed of the internationalist vision discussed in chapter 2. Even in the cybercrime context where there is general consensus about the need for cooperation, it is very hard for nations to agree. For example, because nations are sensitive about sovereignty, the convention doesn't authorize unilateral cross-border searches of the type the FBI performed, even in cases of emergency or hot pursuit. Instead, it requires a nation pursuing a cybercriminal to consult with local officials before seizing, storing, and freezing data on computers located in their countries. Even with the contemplated round-the-clock consultation assistance machinery, this unwieldy step will give cybercriminals precious time to cover their tracks.[11]

These and scores of other disagreements, combined with civil libertarian complaints that the cybercrime treaty jeopardizes speech and privacy rights, slowed down the drafting and ratification of the treaty significantly.[12] Negotiation and drafting began in earnest in 1997, and the treaty was completed and opened for signature in 2001. By the fall of 2005, however, only eleven European nations and no nation outside Europe had joined it (although the U.S. Senate had approved the treaty).[13]

This lengthy process is not unusual for any treaty, and especially one that requires international cooperation in a core area of national sovereignty. But the process is too long and unwieldy to effectively regulate cybercrime, a constantly changing threat that requires immediate national responses and international cooperation. This is why nations have been relying heavily on unilateral responses, as in the Ivanov example. It is also why what international cooperation there is among nations takes place informally. For example, since 1996 the G8 countries have created a network of twenty-four-hour points of contact to address cross-border cybercrimes; negotiated numerous non-binding "best practice" guides for transnational requests for assistance and tracing Internet communications across borders; and hosted training conferences for law enforcement agencies from around the world concerning cooperation and tracing criminal and terrorist communications.[14] These and many related efforts fall short of the "hard" cooperation contemplated by the cybercrime convention, but they are far more effective than nothing.

The failure of the cybercrime convention typifies the role that treaties have played in the Internet era. With the unintended exception of international trade laws (a subject we turn to later in this chapter), the predicted rise of international treaties to govern contested Internet issues simply has not happened. The paucity of Internet treaties is remarkable. After a decade of legal conflict, aside from the stalled cybercrime treaty, not a single treaty has been drafted and ratified related to issues like defamation, gambling, speech, privacy, and the like. For the Internet, unilateral action, conflict, and ad hoc accommodation are often the best the nations of the world can do.

167

## ICANN

The Internet's future does not rest on the success or failure of the cybercrime treaty. There is, however, a "global law" without which there would be no Internet: the domain name system (DNS). As we learned in chapter 3, to be on the Net is to have a computer with an Internet Protocol address like 192.168.1.2. If you want to be found, that means having a domain name (like pseudointeractive.com or pbs.org). For the Net to work—for computers all over the world to be able to communicate with one another—the root authority must reliably correlate IP addresses with domain names and uniquely match up both with a particular computer.

Though its full potential remains untested, the root authority is very close to a truly global authority for the Internet—the ultimate intermediary on which everyone depends. That's why it has been the center of so much drama. In our last episode, chapter 3's depiction of the 1990s, we saw the United States block the efforts of the Internet Society and its allies to assert their presumed authority over the root through something called the gTLD-MoU. We also saw Jon Postel run his "test," only to find himself on the phone with Ira Magaziner.

Yet shortly after blocking the gTLD-MoU, the Clinton administration seemed paradoxically to change direction. After proving its power over the root, it appeared uninterested in actually administering Internet naming and numbering. Instead, Ira Magaziner midwived the birth of a new organization, named the "Internet Corporation for Assigned Names and Numbers," or ICANN, that would replace the United States and become the new root authority.

ICANN seemed in many ways the realization of the dreams of the engineers and others who wanted the Net to be self-governed. "The U.S. government is committed to a transition that will allow the private sector to take leadership for DNS management," said the United States in its 1998 "White Paper," which announced the ICANN plan. ICANN itself was based on a framework proposed by Jon Postel just before he died, and it reflected, according to Postel, "the consensus judgment of the global Internet community."[15] Its first chairman was Esther Dyson, the Internet visionary who had predicted in the 1990s that the Net would overrun the nation-state.[16] ICANN, said *The Econo-*

ICANN Committee Meeting (Declan McCullagh)

*mist*, is a "completely new institutional animal. It is a hybrid between an online community and a real-world governance structure" that would "regulate part of itself, across the globe, with little or no input from national governments."[17]

But ICANN was not what it seemed. The United States, while talking about things like "bottom up governance" and "the Internet community," never actually ceded control over either ICANN or the root. Legally, ICANN remained under contract to the U.S. Commerce Department. And the physical root, the computer containing the root zone file, remained under the control and ownership of the United States. The United States hadn't a clue how to run the domain name system itself, and genuinely wanted to delegate day-to-day Internet naming and numbering decisions to ICANN. And talking about "privatization" and "internationalization" temporarily distracted critics who argued that a single nation, no matter how powerful, had no right to control the root. But the United States had no real intentions to relinquish its power over such an important resource.

Milton Mueller and others have shown that ICANN's spirit of "self-regulation" was an appealing label for a process that could be more accurately described as the U.S. government brokering a behind-the-scenes deal that best suited its policy preferences.[18] As we saw in chapter 3, the United States wanted to ensure the stability of the Internet, to fend off the regulatory efforts of foreign governments and international organizations, and to maintain ultimate control. The easiest way to do that was to maintain formal control while turning over day-to-day control of the root to ICANN and the Internet Society, which had close ties to the regulation-shy American technology industry.[19] This part of the deal angered the European Union, which had been pressuring the United States to create an intergovernmental organization for Internet naming issues. But the United States effectively bought off the EU, at least for awhile, when it gave the primary role in resolving domain name trademark disputes to the Europe-based WIPO (World Intellectual Property Organization), an international organization largely beholden to intellectual property interests.[20]

ICANN has faced much criticism in its short lifetime, mainly for being unaccountable and "undemocratic." But judged by what the United States, in particular, hoped it would do, ICANN has delivered the goods. It decentralized the sale and distribution of domain names, resulting in a dramatic drop in the price of registration. It has established an effective mechanism for resolving trademark disputes that has diminished the problem of "cybersquatting" and that, more generally, has favored powerful trademark holders. And it has maintained enough stability in the naming and numbering system that people rarely worry about the Internet collapsing.

In practice, in the early 2000s, the United States remained mostly in the background, with day-to-day operations belonging to ICANN. Vint Cerf, a George Washington-like figure in Internet circles, assumed the chairmanship of ICANN, assuring the continuing influence of the original Internet Society. ICANN was subject to pressure and influence from other nation-states, powerful domestic interest groups, and a group of devoted academics.

But as time passed, the United States set aside its earlier rhetoric and made clearer claims to ultimate authority over ICANN and the root . While it once spoke of ultimately giving up all control, the Commerce Department later insisted that it had "no plans to transfer to any entity its policy authority to direct the authoritative root server."[21] The U.S. General Accounting Office even questioned whether the Commerce Department has the legal authority to transfer control of the root server to ICANN, even if it wanted to.[22] Back in 1998 the U.S. Department of Commerce promised to relinquish root authority by the fall of 2006, but in June 2005, the United States reversed course. "The United States Government intends to preserve the security and stability of the Internet's Domain Name and Addressing

System (DNS)," announced Michael D. Gallagher, a Department of Commerce official. "The United States" he announced, will "maintain its historic role in authorizing changes or modifications to the authoritative root zone file."[23]

This announcement sparked a revolt against American rule, led this time not by the Internet Society, but by the United Nations and the European Union. In the run up to the United Nations' World Summit on the Information Society in the Fall of 2005 in Tunisia, the European Union made a dramatic proposal to shift domain name governance from ICANN and the U.S. Commerce Department to a UN-affiliated intergovernmental group.[24] And the EU backed up its proposals with vague threats, reminiscent of the Internet engineers in the 1990s, to split the root.[25] The United States responded angrily to these proposals. "We will not agree to the UN taking over management of the Internet," said David Gross of the U.S. State Department. "Some countries want that. We think that's unacceptable."[26] On the eve of the Tunisia conference, the two sides averted a direct confrontation with an agreement that the United States and ICANN would remain in charge of Internet naming. But in what the EU billed as a major concession, the United States agreed to the establishment of a new Internet Governance Forum in which governments could debate and make recommendations about Internet policy issues but not exercise direct policy authority.

The Tunisia compromise is the latest round in the battle for control of the Internet's naming system—a battle in a larger war for control over the Internet. It is too early to say who will win this war. The United States still controls the physical root, and under its authority the Internet has unquestionably grown and prospered. But many nations view it as deeply unfair for the United States to set basic Internet policy for the whole world. For this book, the outcome of this battle is less important than the identity of opponents. For the struggle for ultimate control over Internet naming and numbering policy is not between governments and private cybercommunities, as many once envisioned. Rather, it is indisputably between national governments—a problem of clashing government interests and ideologies not unlike age-old disputes over global resources like oceans, air, and outer space.

## Web Gambling and the World Trade Organization

The twin-island nation of Antigua and Barbuda has a population of 68,000. The weather, a favorable government, and good connections to the United States have made it a favored destination for online casinos. At its height, the local Internet gambling industry had 119 online casinos that employed 5,000 people, or over 7 percent of the islands' population.

But this was before the Eliot Spitzer–led American crackdown that we described in chapter 5, which resulted in a significant drop in web gambling business in Antigua. Antigua may be small, but it is a nation-state nonetheless and since 1995 a full-fledged member of the World Trade Organization. In June 2003, it filed a complaint in the WTO against the United States, arguing that the various U.S. actions against offshore online gambling amounted to "an illegal barrier to trade in services." Suing the United States was perhaps a brave act, but Antigua felt it had no choice. As Antigua's WTO ambassador put it, "What we want is survival, not blood."[27]

With the WTO lawsuit, the question of online gambling became a problem of international relations and international trade law. Unhappy with U.S. policy, Antigua is trying to use global rules—trade rules—to serve its interests and the interests of its exporters: the casinos. Just as in the case of Internet governance, it shows how much what we once thought of as problems of Internet law will look to the future like problems of international relations and international trade.

In November, 2004, to the surprise of many observers, a panel of the WTO sided with Antigua, reasoning that the enforcement of U.S. gambling laws unfairly favored local U.S. casinos over international, online imports, all in defiance of basic global trade rules. In the panel's judgment, the United States failed to demonstrate that its gambling laws were something other than "arbitrary and unjustifiable discrimination between countries where like conditions prevail and/or a disguised restriction on trade."[28] Six months later, however, the appellate body of the WTO reached a different decision. It agreed with the United States that its main anti-web gambling law was valid because it was "necessary to protect public morals or to maintain public order."[29] The WTO did, however, rule illegal an American law allowing Americans to place horseracing bets with U.S.-based web gambling firms but not foreign ones.

The WTO decision transformed an ordinary national Internet regulation with cross-border effects into an issue of international trade law. In one sense this seems to fulfill the internationalist prediction that the Internet would ultimately be governed by global institutions and global laws. But at another level, the WTO decision shows how mundane Internet regulation issues have become. For the Internet dispute between the United States and Antigua is no different than garden-variety trade disputes that have been regulated by international law for over one hundred years. Once again, we see that Internet conflicts of laws lead nations to use what tools they can, including tools of international trade, to get what they want. This is a very old story indeed.

## Europe's Global Privacy Law

Quick: what's your password for the *New York Times* website? Few things are more annoying than trying to remember the scores of different usernames and passwords the Web has grown to demand. One for your bank, another for your e-mail, yet another for the retirement account you check once a year—it all becomes wearisome, quickly.

In 1999, Microsoft proposed a solution: the "dot-NET Passport" program, a digital ID system designed to make navigation among password-protected sites easy. The idea was to register the relevant personal identification information once with Microsoft, and then use a dot-NET Passport name and ID number to access scores of web pages and thus automatically convey the pertinent personal information to the site when necessary. The dot-NET Passport conveniently keeps all of your secret information for you, taking the pain out of logins and e-purchases.

The system raised obvious privacy issues. Would Microsoft keep the personal information secure? How would it use the information? Would it sell or swap it? What should Microsoft disclose? A decade ago, Internet experts argued that privacy questions like this would and should be decided by the Internet community, and that governments would be largely irrelevant to the process. As with many other issues, however, the expected collapse of national sovereignty has not occurred. Instead, there's been a shift. Many Americans will be surprised to learn that the last word on the legality of Microsoft's dot-NET Passport is not being supplied in Washington, D.C. or Silicon Valley but in Brussels. For many purposes, the European Union is today the effective sovereign of global privacy law.

The first regulator of the dot-NET Passport system, to be sure, was the U.S. Federal Trade Commission. Following complaints from U.S. consumer and privacy groups, the FTC announced in August 2002 that Microsoft had falsely represented its security protections for dot-NET Passport, and required the company to maintain a more comprehensive information security program.[30] Microsoft agreed to implement the changes, and it appeared that its legal problems with dot-NET Passport were over.

They were not. Earlier the same year, European Union investigators summoned Microsoft to Brussels. It was a familiar path for a company that had already spent years wrestling with European officials who view the company as an unlawful monopolist. This time, however, it was privacy officials from the "Article 29 Data Protection Working Party" who issued the summons. The European privacy officials wanted to know a lot more about how Microsoft was collecting user data and what it was doing with it.[31]

How could the EU purport to assert legal authority over an American company? The EU has the world's broadest and most stringent data privacy laws. A European Directive on data protection was implemented in 1998.[32] It regulates *any* "data controller," that is, anyone who "processes" data they collect. Among other things, this means that the law reaches regular people who happen to have information about their friends. In 2003, for example, a Swedish woman named Bodil Lindqvist was fined 450 Euros. Her offense: posting gossipy personal data about fellow members of her church congregation without obtaining consent.[33]

For data controllers like Microsoft and Ms. Lindqvist, the Directive imposes three relatively stringent requirements. First, they must tell consumers why they are collecting personal data and receive "unambiguous" consent. Second, data must be used only for the purposes stated during collection and not redirected to other purposes. Finally, the data collected must have a reasonable relationship to the purposes for which it is collected. To these basic requirements the Directive adds extra protection for "special information," namely, "data revealing racial or ethnic origin, political opinions, religious or philosophical beliefs, trade union membership, and . . . data concerning health or sex life." It was this latter provision that landed Ms. Lindqvist in trouble. She had revealed to the world that another church member had injured her foot and would consequently be taking some time off. As data "concerning health," it was "sensitive" under the EU law, and so Ms. Lindqvist was fined.

What makes the European Union law particularly controversial is its aggressive geographic scope. Article 4 of the European Directive applies not only to companies established in Europe but also to any company that makes use of data processing "equipment" or "means" in Europe, and to any company that may be reached consistent with international law. This is open language that has been interpreted by European officials to reach nearly any company that collects information from European citizens.[34]

It was under the authority of the 1998 Directive that the EU summoned Microsoft, and raised concerns that went beyond those of U.S. regulators—especially its concern that Microsoft was collecting more data than it needed for the purposes of its program. Microsoft had a choice: it could comply with the EU's legal demands, or it could pull out of the European market altogether, making it impossible for the EU to enforce its laws. The second option was out of the question: the European market accounts for about a third of Microsoft's sales.[35] It was a foregone conclusion, and by January 2003, Microsoft and the EU had an agreement. Microsoft would make what the European Commission called "radical" changes for the way dot-NET Passport manages user data, including more notice and more user control over how data is shared.[36]

Much more interesting was what Microsoft did next. It decided to implement its changes to dot-NET Passport not just for its European operations but *everywhere in the world.*[37] Whether you're in Miami, Auckland, Timbuktu, or somewhere in between, when you use dot-NET Passport you use a product molded by the European privacy authorities. The European Union regulated dot-NET Passport on behalf of Europeans, but the effect was to govern the whole world—at least with respect to global companies that do business in Europe.

Microsoft's decision to obey the European rule reflects a common yet important practice for large companies. We saw in the previous chapter that the Australian decision in *Gutnick* would not have a significant impact on Dow Jones's business because Dow Jones could either screen out its Australian customers or stop doing business in Australia. That was a feasible option for Dow Jones because content screening in that context is doable, and because it had a relatively small market in Australia. But Microsoft's situation is different. It has a huge market in Europe that it cannot easily give up, and the dot-NET Passport system depends for its efficacy on cross-border data mingling, making geographical screening unrealistic. In this situation—where a large and important market imposes a restrictive rule and where geographic discrimination is practically infeasible—the restrictive rule will in many cases be the dominant rule, worldwide.

There is nothing new or unusual here. The dominance of the EU rule is simply what Marc Rotenberg of the Electronic Privacy Information Center calls the "California effect" applied on a global scale.[38] When California sets new emissions standards for cars, General Motors will build cars to the Californian standard for the entire United States.[39] Its choice to do so depends, of course, on the fact that it is more expensive to create cars customized for California than just build one car for the entire country. California generally cares more about the environment than other states and for that reason gets to set standards for cars. Europe cares more about privacy than other regions and therefore sets the standard for privacy. But if Saudi Arabia or Mexico or Russia imposed privacy standards more exacting than the EU's, Microsoft wouldn't comply with the more restrictive standard globally. It would either leave those markets altogether or pay fines for privacy violations, whichever was cheaper. Unilateral global law of the sort doled out by the EU in the privacy context depends on significant market power.

So Europe's privacy laws are a fourth type of global law: Not a treaty, like the Cybercrime Convention; not enforced through the Internet's architecture, like the U.S.-dominated ICANN; and not a WTO-governed trade dispute as in the web gambling example. It is, rather, a global law that results from the unusual combination of Europe's enormous market power and its unusual concern for its citizen's privacy. For the United States, a country that did much to shed European rule centuries ago, the prospect of living under rules set by Europeans is unusual. Many Americans may like the rule coming from Europe, where privacy protection is far more generous than that provided by American laws. Of course, this means that all American users of dot-NET Passport must accept and pay for the extra privacy protection that Microsoft must provide, regardless of whether they want it. And then there is the question of whether Americans like to be governed by laws they had no part in creating—a question usually raised in other countries about American power.

# 11

eleven

## *Conclusion*
### Globalization Meets Governmental Coercion

Most contemporary assessments of globalization share two ideas. The first is a recognition that we live in an era where technology has made it easier than ever before to move capital, goods, and services across national borders and around the world. The second is a belief that globalization diminishes the relevance of borders, territory, and location, and thereby undermines the territorial nation-state's role as the central institution for governing human affairs.[1]

The Internet has widely been viewed as the essential catalyst of contemporary globalization, and it has been central to debates about what globalization means and where it will lead. "The Internet is going to be like a huge vise that takes the globalization system . . . and keeps tightening and tightening that system around everyone, in ways that will only make the world smaller and smaller and faster and faster with each passing day." That's the prediction of globalization's popularizer and prophet, Thomas Friedman, in his 1999 book *The Lexus and the Olive Tree*.[2] Friedman went farther in his 2005 sequel, *The World is Flat*, claiming to show how the Internet and related technologies have "made us all next door neighbors," and are killing geography, distance, and language.[3]

Friedman and others are right to emphasize the Internet's transformative potential. As the Internet becomes more pervasive and as more and more aspects of life become digitalized, it is indeed becoming much easier for human beings everywhere to access, learn from, share, and improve upon the impossibly varied and plentiful information

179

available on the Net. This book, in fact, was written while its peripatetic authors lived in and communicated with one another via the Net from Tokyo, Boston, Geneva, Chicago, Charlottesville, Boca Raton, and Washington, D.C., among other places—something that would have been nearly impossible a mere decade ago.

The question we have addressed in this book is not whether the technological changes of the last decade have created changes in the way human beings live or interact. The question is whether those changes have had a lasting effect on how nations, and their peoples, govern themselves. The diminishing costs of moving information on the Internet have obviously made it harder for governments to suppress communications and related activities that they dislike. The Net has allowed talented technologists, dissatisfied groups, and various types of law evaders to take advantage of the difficulty of controlling information to achieve political, social, and commercial goals.

This was also true, however, of the telegraph, the telephone, the radio, the television, and other earlier communication revolutions, all of which dramatically increased the number and speed of communications, and dramatically lowered their costs. These communication technologies produced radical changes in human organization and interaction, and required governments to develop new strategies for regulating human affairs. But they did not displace the central role of territorial government in human governance. And neither, we have argued in this book, will the Internet.

Why do theories of globalization and Internet scholarship so misunderstand and so underestimate the importance of territorial government? While the question is complex, this book has suggested a simple answer. What we have seen, time and time again, is that physical coercion by government—the hallmark of a traditional legal system—remains far more important than anyone expected. This may sound crude and ugly and even depressing. Yet at a fundamental level, it's the most important thing missing from most predictions of where globalization will lead, and the most significant gap in predictions about the future shape of the Internet.

In almost every chapter of this book, beneath the fog of modern technology, we have seen the effects of coercive governmental force on local persons, firms, and equipment. We have seen "chief Yahoo" Jerry Yang capitulate under the threats of fines and possible physical arrest in France. We have seen the Chinese government, sometimes with the help of Yahoo, seize political dissidents and put them in prison. We have seen governments around the globe threatening ISPs and search engines and credit card companies with fines, or worse, in order to coerce them into filtering out offensive Net communications. We have seen Jon Postel and the Internet's founders give up control over their creation under implied threats of government force. Even in the extreme case of music filesharing, seemingly among the hardest forms of information to control, we've seen the many hidden but important ways that government coercion affects the economics of filesharing and tilts the playing field to favor law-abiding companies like Apple.

The significance of governmental coercion can perhaps be most clearly understood by looking at what we've learned in this book about private self-governing communities as alternatives to traditional government. A major tenet of most globalization writing is that governments are of diminishing relevance compared to other forms of human organization and nonstate actors.[4] In this respect globalization writing echoes the work of legal theorists like Yale's Robert Ellickson, who argues that for many people, most of the time, law's commands are irrelevant.[5] The point is that the relevant set of rules we live by usually come from community norms, morality, the market, or, on the Internet, from the design and constraints of computer code. All of this suggests that law and government may be just one source of order among many, and perhaps not even the most important.

There's no reason to doubt that most people's lives are dominated not by law but by social norms, morality, and the market, or that the Internet is deeply influenced by its code. But the critical question is whether such sources of rules and governance can function apart from an underlying system of territorial government and physical coercion. Our book has suggested that they cannot.

The Internet was supposed to be the test case for self-governing systems that could flourish without respect to geography and territorially based coercion. It was supposed to allow like-minded people to join communities and govern themselves without respect to geography, without regard to the top-down coercive structures of territorial governmental systems, and without the usual pathologies and corruptions that characterize territorial rule. This was Barlow's vision, and it is a vision that retains a powerful hold on globalization and Internet theorists today. Friedman, for example, describes eBay as a "self-governing nation-state" constituted by its feedback system and its vigorous community norms. Meg Whitman, eBay's CEO, echoes Friedman's wonder, puffing that "People will say that 'eBay restored my faith in humanity'—contrary to the world where people are cheating and don't give people the benefit of the doubt."[6]

Our peek below the surface of eBay's self-governing facade revealed a far different story—a story of heavy reliance on the iron fist of coercive governmental power. Perpetually threatened by cheaters and fraudsters, eBay established an elaborate hand-in-glove relationship with the police and other governmental officials who can arrest, prosecute, incapacitate, and effectively deter these threats to its business model. And of course the criminal justice system is but one of the government-provided public goods on which eBay relies. Others include a reliable banking and credit environment and remedies for contract breaches. These and scores of other public goods depend on coercive governmental power—power to tax citizens to raise revenues to provide the public goods that individuals would not provide on their own, and power to deliver the public goods effectively. Without this powerful hidden-hand help of governments in the places where it does business, eBay's thriving "self-governing" community could not survive.

eBay is not the only example. Behind other successful online communities and firms, we find the quiet guarantees provided by territorial government. This was also true, for example, of ICANN, where over time a form of technocratic self-governance has emerged under the ultimate guarantees provided by the U.S. government. We have also seen how companies like Kazaa that are built to be independent of government ultimately collapse without the power to prevent abuse of its own system. In short, while we accept the importance and relevance of many forms of social influence, this book suggests an underappreciated hierarchy that makes law, and physical coercion, fundamental.

Along with faith that governments are disappearing or becoming irrelevant, another central belief in globalization theory is the inevitable homogenization of everything. Antiglobalization activist Jerry Mander, for example, warns that economic globalization will lead to "monoculture," where "every place on earth should be more or less like every other place."[7] Friedman's flat world metaphor is built on the notion that globalization is smoothing out the rough edges and frictions of different nations. As we saw earlier in the book, George Gilder had a similar idea in the 1990s, when he argued that the new communications technologies would make location irrelevant, and in the process kill the very idea of the city as a distinct place and culture.

But there's something critical missing from this story, which depicts countries and regions as essentially powerless in the face of globalization and the Internet. What's missing is the power of places—nations and regions—to protect the way they are, or want to be. We've been reminded in this book that human beings tend to cluster geographically, based on shared cultures, languages, tastes, wealth, and values. We've also seen that these different peoples in different places will often demand different types of Internet experiences and that the market will often comply. Often, however, these differences are also enforced through government coercion, as when France made Yahoo keep out Nazi goods, or when Australia made Dow Jones pay for libeling one of its citizens, or when the United States blocked Internet gambling from Antigua. This is the other side of globalization: the determined preservation of difference, the deliberate resistance to homogenizing influence. As the Internet becomes more and more bordered, as it twists and bends to meet local demands, the effects of these efforts cannot be ignored.

When globalization enthusiasts miss these points, it is usually because they are in the grips of a strange technological determinism that views the Internet as an unstoppable juggernaut that will overrun the old and outdated determinants of human organization. This leads them to say things like, "When you give people a new way to connect with other people, they will punch through any technical barrier, they will learn new languages—people are wired to want to connect to other people and they find it objectionable not to be able to do so." That's Marc Andreesen, Netscape's founder.[8] But as we have seen time and again in this book, it just isn't so. People will not always, or even usually, transcend technical barriers in order to connect to other people. Just as often, if not more so, they will conform to the technical barriers, and the technical barriers themselves will reflect local government preference.

That government-wielded force can change the very nature of the Internet itself is nowhere clearer than in China, where the brawny and self-confident People's Republic is building a nationalist Internet within its borders. As China does this, it is creating a network that is moving away from the Internet in the West, not only in its language but also in its values and deep architecture. When Friedman and so many others argue that the Internet and related technologies will inevitably open closed societies, they assume that the Internet is an exogenous and unchangeably open force. But as we have seen in this book, the openness of the network is contingent, and one of the most important things it is contingent on is governmental coercion that demands a unique architecture.

The point is even broader. It's not just that nations have the power to shape the Internet's architecture in different ways. It is that the United States, China, and Europe are using their coercive powers to establish different visions of what the Internet might be. In so doing, they will attract other nations to choose among models of control ranging from the United States's relatively free and open model to China's model of political control. The result is the beginning of a technological version of the cold war, with each side pushing its own vision of the Internet's future.

The failure to understand the many faces and facets of territorial governmental coercion is fatal to globalization theory as understood today, and central to understanding the future of the Internet. We have not argued that geographically focused governmental coercion is the only thing that matters. But we have tried to highlight the abiding significance of geography, of individuals whose attitudes and preferences differ sharply by geography, and most importantly of the national governments that use coercion to enforce national laws within their territories. In the coming decades, these factors, and the consequent struggles between nations and their national network ideologies, will do much to determine how life on the bordered Internet is lived.

# Acknowledgments

Many people have helped us with this book.

Larry Lessig, a giant among Internet thinkers, introduced us both, in different ways, to the wacky world of Internet scholarship. Larry has been a great friend and wise counselor for many years. We dedicate the book to him.

Sebastian Mallaby started as a co-author on this book at its proposal stage and contributed a great deal to many of its ideas. Sebastian was unable to continue, but we are very grateful for his support during the years it has taken us to write the book.

Dedi Felman, our wise editor, deserves special thanks for her advice, vision, enthusiasm, and patience.

We are also grateful to our various deans over the years—John Jeffries, Elena Kagan, Larry Kramer, Saul Levmore, and David Schizer—for their generous support. We also thank the law faculties at Chicago, Columbia, Harvard, Stanford, and Virginia for their advice and support.

The following people gave us excellent comments on drafts of the book or on particular chapters: Derek Bambauer, Tod Cohen, John Demers, Ben Edelman, Michael Froomkin, Orin Kerr, Jennifer 8. Lee, Doug Lichtman, Benjamin Liebman, John Manning, Rebecca McKinnon, Milton Mueller, Randy Picker, Eric Posner, Fred Schauer, Andrei Shleifer, Paul Stephan, Molly Van Houweling, Jonathan Weinberg, and Leslie Williams. In addition, we received helpful comments from participants in the "Cyberlaw Camp" held by Harvard's Berkman

Center, the University of Chicago's International Law Workshop, and workshops at the Harvard Law School and the Princeton Program in Law and Public Affairs. Bryson Bachman, Brenda Castaneda, Marc Kirkbaum, Robert Kirsch, Michael Newman, Stevan Nicholas, Chris Nosko, Jeremy Thompson, and Lee Wilson helped with outstanding research assistance. Marc and Bryson were especially vital in getting the book to press. Margaret Flynn, Kathie Kepchar, and Liane Speroni also provided important assistance.

In addition, conversations and interviews, real or through e-mail, with the following people have benefited the book immeasurably: John Perry Barlow, Martin Dodge, Ariana Eunjung Cha, Julian Dibbell, Cory Doctorow, Daniel Drezner, John Evans, William Farris, Lee Gomes, Cyril Houri, Joicho Ito, David Johnson, Marc Knobel, Andrew McLaughlin, Ira Magaziner, Elliot Maxwell, Quaid Morris, Sanjay Parekh, Eric Posner, David Post, Fred Schauer, Andrei Shleifer, Paul Stephan, Anthony Townsend, Fred Von Lohmann, Jonathan Weinberg, Nicolas Zennstrom, and Matthew Zook.

On a personal note, Goldsmith thanks his sons Jack and Will for their love, patience, and inspiration, and his wife Leslie Williams for those things and much more. Wu would like to thank his mother, Gillian Wu, for everything.

# Frequently Used Abbreviations

| | |
|---|---|
| AARP | American Association of Retired Persons |
| ACLU | American Civil Liberties Union |
| AOL | America Online (large ISP) |
| BeiDa | Beijing University |
| BMI | Broadcast Music, Inc. (one of two major music licensing organizations) |
| CDA | Communications Decency Act (1996 U.S. law that banned certain indecent communications) |
| CECC | Congressional-Executive Commission on China (U.S. Commission designed to monitor human rights and rule of law development record of China; established after the United States agreed to grant China permanent normal trade relations) |
| CN2 | Next Carrying Network (large Chinese network project from the 2000s) |
| CORE | International Council of Registrars (proposed entity that would have administered domain names, independent of any U.S. government control; now an ICANN-accredited domain name registrar) |
| DARPA | Defense Advanced Research Projects Agency (U.S. Defense department research agency that funded much of the early Internet research) |
| DMCA | Digital Millennium Copyright Act (act creating new restrictions on the circumvention of copy-protection measures, and a new system of liabilities and immunities for ISPs) |
| DSL | Digital Subscriber Line (broadband technology that transmits signals over telephone lines) |
| EFF | Electronic Frontier Foundation (non-profit founded in 1990 to defend civil liberties online) |

187

| | |
|---|---|
| ESPN | Entertainment and Sports Programming Network |
| EU | European Union |
| FTC | Federal Trade Commission |
| gTLD-MoU | Generic Top-Level Domain Memorandum of Understanding (a proposal signed in 1997 that would have eliminated U.S. government control of Internet naming and numbering) |
| HTTP | HyperText Transfer Protocol (protocol designed for transmitting information found on web pages) |
| IAHC | Internet Ad Hoc Committee (committee of prominent Internet experts formed in the 1990s to examine the governance of Internet naming and numbering) |
| IANA | Internet Assigned Numbers Authority (early authority over Internet numbering; also used as a synonym for Jon Postel) |
| ICANN | Internet Corporation for Assigned Names and Numbers (non-profit corporation, operating under contract to the U.S. Department of Commerce, that administers Internet naming and numbering) |
| IETF | Internet Engineering Task Force (standards organization that has developed most of the Internet's dominant standards) |
| IP | Internet Protocol (data-oriented protocol that specifies how data may be exchanged by any two points on a network. Today, most often joined by the TCP protocol, it is by far the dominant protocol in data networking) |
| ISI | Information Science Institute (research institute at the University of Southern California, formerly headed by Jon Postel) |
| ISP | Internet Service Provider (firm in the business of providing Internet services to home or business customers, or sometimes other ISPs) |
| ISOC | Internet Society (non-profit umbrella organization, formed in the 1990s, to oversee and coordinate various Internet standardization and administration projects) |
| LambdaMOO | Lambda Multi-user dungeon, Object-Oriented (famous example of a virtual world; LambdaMOO was run out of Xerox's Palo Alto Research Center) |
| MIT | Massachusetts Institute of Technology |
| MSN | Microsoft Network (Microsoft's ISP) |
| MUD | Multiple User Dungeon (text-based virtual world; named dungeon because early versions were usually dungeon-based games) |
| NSI | Network Solutions Inc. (corporation that was the Internet's first registrar of domain names; NSI once had a monopoly over, for example, registration of .com addresses) |
| P2P | Peer-to-Peer (decentralized network design, useful for |

| | exchanging information among large numbers of network users) |
|---|---|
| RIAA | Recording Industry of America (industry organization that lobbies for copyright protection and sues alleged copyright infringement) |
| RSS | Really Simple Syndication (protocol for distributing web content, mainly from blogs) |
| SRI | Stanford Research Institute (independent, non-profit technological research organization; not part of Stanford University, but located nearby) |
| TCP/IP protocol | Transmission Control Protocol / Internet Protocol (these two protocols, used together, are the most broadly used information transmission protocols on the Internet) |
| UN | United Nations |
| URL | Uniform Resource Locator (synonym for web address; invented for use on the World Wide Web) |
| USPS | United States Postal Service |
| WAPI | WLAN Authentication and Privacy Infrastructure (Chinese standard for secure wireless data communication) |
| Wi-Fi | Wireless Fidelity (a low-cost wireless networking technology, usually found on personal computers) |
| WIPO | World Intellectual Property Organization |

# Notes

## Preface to the Paperback Edition

1. http://blog.wired.com/27bstroke6/2006/05/googles_halfhea.html.
2. http://www.forbes.com/businessinthebeltway/2007/07/18/
   google-washington-congress-biz-wash-cx_bw_0719trade.html.
3. Ronald J. Deibert, John G. Palfrey, Rafal Rohozkinsi, and Jonathan
   Zittrain, *Access Denied: The Practice and Policy of Global Internet Filtering*
   (Cambridge, MA: MIT Press, 2008).
4. Nolan Dalla, "Unlawful Internet Gambling Enforcement Act: An
   Insider's First Views," October 1, 2006, http://www.gambling-law-us
   .com/Articles-Notes/dalla.htm.
5. http://www.telegraph.co.uk/portal/main.jhtml?xml=/portal/2007/01/30/
   ftebay30.xml
6. hppt://www.theage.com.au/news/security/online-fraud-targeted/2007/
   07/02/1183351124220.html.

## Preface

1. Julian Hawthorne, "June 1993," *The Cosmopolitan*, February 1893, 456–
   57, recounted and quoted in Carolyn Marvin, *When Old Technologies
   Were New: Thinking About Electric Communication in the Late Nineteenth
   Century* (New York: Oxford University Press, 1988), 201–2. For similar
   nineteenth-century sentiments inspired by the telegraph, see ibid., 193–
   209; see also *The Victorian Internet* (New York: Berkley Books, 1999).

## Chapter 1

1. Marc Knobel, e-mail message to Jack Goldsmith, September 9, 2004.
2. Yahoo share price as of January 3, 2000, http://bigcharts.marketwatch.

com/historical/default.asp?detect=1&symbol=YHOO&close_date=
1%2F3%2F2000&x=31&y=26 (last visited June 6, 2005).

3. "The History of Yahoo, How it All Started," http://docs.yahoo.com/
   info/misc/history.html (last visited June 3, 2005).
4. "French anti-racist group sues Yahoo," *CBS MarketWatch*, April 11,
   2000.
5. Lisa Guernsey, "Welcome to the Web. Passport, Please?" *New York
   Times*, March 15, 2001.
6. "Yahoo! serious about Nazi auctions on web," *Australian*, July 25, 2000.
7. Joelle Tessler, "Online Auction of Nazi Items Sparks Debate Issue:
   National Laws on Global Web," *San Jose Mercury News*, July 25, 2000.
8. David R. Johnson and David Post, "Law and Borders: The Rise of Law in
   Cyberspace," 48 *Stanford Law Review* (May 1996), 1372. See also
   Richard Barbrook, "HyperMedia Freedom," in *Crypto Anarchy,
   Cyberstates, and Pirate Utopias*, ed. Peter Ludlow (Cambridge, MA: MIT
   Press, 2001), 57.
9. See "Lawless," *The Economist*, 1 July 1995, 15; see also Peter H. Lewis,
   "Limiting a Medium Without Boundaries: How Do You Let the Good
   Fish Through the Net While Blocking the Bad?" *New York Times*,
   January 15, 1996.
10. Paul Krugman, "Facing the Music," *New York Times*, July 30, 2000.
11. Andrew Higgins and Azeem Azhar, "China Begins to Erect Second
    Great Wall in Cyberspace," *Guardian* (UK), 5 February 1996; see
    generally Nicholas Negroponte, *Being Digital* (New York: Random
    House, 1995).
12. Lee Dembart, "Boundaries on Nazi Sites Remain Unsettled in Internet's
    Global Village," *International Herald Tribune*, May 29, 2000, 7.
13. *La Ligue Contre le Racisme et L'Antisemitisme (L.I.C.R.A.) and L'Union des
    Etudiants Juifs de France (U.E.J.F.) v. Yahoo! Inc. and Yahoo France*, Interim
    Court Order, The County Court of Paris 6, May 22, 2000. The original
    and English translation are provided in the Appendix to the Complaint
    for Declaratory Relief in *Yahoo! Inc. v. L.I.C.R.A. and U.E.J.F.*, 169 F.
    Supp. 2d 1181 (N.D. Cal. 2001) (No. 00-21275), http://www.eff.org/
    legal/Jurisdiction_and_sovereignty/LICRA_v_Yahoo/
    20001221_yahoo_us_complaint.pdf (last visited June 3, 2005) [hereafter
    Order of May 22, 2000].
14. Janet Kornblum and Leslie Miller, "Town of Half.com is Halfway
    Home," *USA Today*, June 19, 2000.
15. Kornblum and Miller, "Town of Half.com is Halfway Home."
16. Johnson and Post, "Law and Borders," 1375.
17. Lisa Guernsey, "Are They Putting Fences Around the Net?" *San Diego
    Union-Tribune*, March 20, 2001.
18. Cyril Houri to Jack Goldsmith, personal communication, September 7,
    2004.
19. See *La Ligue Contre le Racisme et L'Antisemitisme (L.I.C.R.A.) and L'Union
    des Etudiants Juifs de France (U.E.J.F.) v. Yahoo Inc. and Yahoo France*, Interim
    Court Order, the County Court of Paris, November 20, 2000, 14. The
    original and English translation have been provided in the Appendix to the
    Complaint for Declaratory Relief at 6, *Yahoo Inc. v. L.I.C.R.A. and U.E.J.F.*,
    169 F. Supp. 2d 1181 (N.D. Cal. 2001) (No. 00-21275), http://
    www.eff.org/legal/Jurisdiction_and_sovereignty/LICRA_v_Yahoo/

20001221_yahoo_us_complaint.pdf (last visited June 3, 2005) [hereafter Order of November 20, 2000]. Cerf agreed with the other two experts that geotracking would screen out 70 percent of French users but did not go along with the 90 percent figure. The other experts arrived at the 90 percent figure by including other methods of tracking, such as self-identification. Cerf dissented from the 90 percent figure, arguing that self-identification would be ineffective because people could lie about their location, and it would likely be an invasion of privacy to force them to reveal their location and then store a cookie on their computer.

20. Ibid., 4.
21. Ibid.
22. Ibid., 6; Joel R. Reidenberg, "Yahoo and Democracy on the Internet," 42 *Jurimetrics J.* 261, 276 (2002).
23. "French Judge Orders Web Site Auction of Nazi Goods Blocked," *Chicago Tribune*, November 21, 2001.
24. "Yahoo Nazi auction ban welcomed," CNN, January 3, 2001, http://archives.cnn.com/2001/WORLD/europe/01/03/net.hate/ (last visited August 8, 2005).
25. Reidenberg, "Yahoo and Democracy on the Internet," 269. Reidenberg points out that Yahoo had a "70 percent stock ownership interest in Yahoo-France" as well as "royalty interests arising from the licensing agreement between the U.S. parent and French subsidiary." These potentially could have been seized by the French court without the agreement of any U.S. court.
26. Order of November 20, 2000, at page 20.
27. Troy Wolverton and Jeff Pelline, "Yahoo to charge auction fees, ban hate materials," *CNet News.com*, January 2, 2001, http://news.com.com/2100-1017-250452.html?legacy=cnet (last visited June 3, 2005).
28. "Yahoo Nazi auction ban welcomed."
29. Lori Enos, "Yahoo To Offer Targeted Local Advertising," *E-Commerce Times*, June 28, 2001, http://www.ecommercetimes.com/story/11621.html (last visited June 3, 2005).
30. Stefanie Olsen, "Yahoo Ads Close in on Visitors' Locale," *CNet News.com*, June 27, 2001, http://news.com.com/2100-1023-269155.html?legacy=cnet (last visited June 3, 2005).
31. "Press Release: Yahoo Introduces Yahoo China," September 24, 1999, http://docs.yahoo.com/docs/pr/release389.html (last viewed June 3, 2005).
32. Yahoo stock price as of September 3, 2002, http://bigcharts.marketwatch.com/historical/default.asp?detect=1&symbol=YHOO&close_date=9%2F3%2F2002&x=0&y=0 (last visited June 6, 2005).
33. Sumner Lemon, "Yahoo Criticized for Curtailing Freedom Online," *PC World*, August 12, 2002, http://www.pcworld.com/news/article/0,aid,103865,00.asp (last visited August 8, 2005).
34. Kenneth Roth letter to Terry Semel, "Yahoo Risks Abusing Rights in China," July 30, 2002, http://www.hrw.org/press/2002/08/yahoo-ltr073002.htm (last visited June 3, 2005).
35. Reporters Without Borders, "'Living Dangerously on the Net': Censorship and Surveillance of Internet Forums," May 12, 2003, http://www.rsf.org/article.php3?id_article=6793 (last visited June 3, 2005).
36. Peter S. Goodman, "Yahoo Says It Gave China Internet Data; Journalist Jailed By Tracing E-mail," *The Washington Post*, September 11, 2005; see

also Carrie Kirby, "Chinese Internet vs. free speech," *The San Francisco Chronicle*, September 18, 2001; Bill Savadove, "We must obey law, Yahoo! chief says after man jailed," *South China Morning Post*, September 11, 2005.

## Chapter 2

1. Julian Dibbell, "A Rape in Cyberspace: How an Evil Clown, a Haitian Trickster Spirit, Two Wizards, and a Cast of Dozens Turned a Database Into a Society," *Village Voice*, December 23, 1993, subsequently modified and published as the first chapter in Julian Dibbell, *My Tiny Life: Crime and Passion in a Virtual World* (New York: Henry Holt & Co., 1999).
2. Reviews of *My Tiny Life*, http://www.juliandibbell.com/mytinylife/tinyreviews.html (last visited June 3, 2005).
3. MUDs are also often described as "Multiple User Shared Hallucinations," or MUSHs. For a remarkably detailed description of MUDs, MUSHs, and several similar acronyms, see "Mush," *Wikipedia (The Free Encyclopedia)*, http://en.wikipedia.org/wiki/MUSH.
4. Dibbell, *My Tiny Life*, 36
5. Ibid., 37.
6. Ibid.
7. See Mitchell Kapor and John Perry Barlow, "Across the Electronic Frontier," *Electronic Frontier Foundation: Homepage*, July 10, 1990, http://www.eff.org/Misc/Publications/John_Perry_Barlow/HTML/eff.html (last visited June 3, 2005).
8. John Perry Barlow, "Electronic Frontier: Coming into the Country," *Communications of the ACM*, January 1991, http://delivery.acm.org/10.1145/110000/102876/p19-barlow.pdf?key1=102876&key2=8434458211&coll=GUIDE&dl=GUIDE&CFID=46694416&CFTOKEN=18615799) (last visited June 3, 2005).
9. John Perry Barlow, Keynote Essay for the 1994 Computerworld College Edition, "Jack In, Young Pioneer!" http://www.eff.org/Misc/Publications/John_Perry_Barlow/HTML/jack_in_young_pioneer.html (last visited June 3, 2005).
10. Ibid.
11. John Perry Barlow, "Decrypting the Puzzle Palace," *Communications of the ACM*, July 1992, http://www.eff.org/Privacy/Surveillance/?f=decrypting_puzzle_palace.article.txt (last visited June 3, 2005).
12. Kapor and Barlow, "Across the Electronic Frontier."
13. Barlow, "Jack In."
14. Communications Decency Act of 1996 (CDA), Pub. L. No. 104-104, ti.t. v, 110 Stat. 56, 133-143 (codified as amended in scattered sections of Titles 18 and 47) (invalidated in part by *ACLU v. Reno*, 521 U.S. 844 [1997]).
15. Eugene Volokh, "Freedom of Speech, Shielding Children, and Transcending Balance," 1997 *Sup. Ct. Rev.* 141, 143–44 (1997).
16. Ibid.
17. These examples are taken from the Supreme Court's decision in *ACLU v. Reno*, 521 U.S. 844, 871 (1997).
18. John Perry Barlow's "Declaration of Independence For Cyberspace," http://www.missouri.edu/~rhetnet/barlow/barlow_declaration.html (last visited August 9, 2005).

19. John Perry Barlow, "A Declaration of the Independence of Cyberspace," February 8, 1996, http://homes.eff.org/~barlow/Declaration-Final.html (last visited June 3, 2005).

20. Ibid.

21. See Mike Godwin, *Cyber Rights: Defending Free Speech in the Digital Age* (Cambridge, MA: The MIT Press, 2003), xiv.

22. Ibid., 333.

23. Ibid., 327.

24. *ACLU v. Reno*, 521 U.S. 844, 851 (1997) (Stevens, J.).

25. Ibid., 868–69.

26. Ibid., 853 (internal citation omitted).

27. Ibid., 885.

28. Ibid., 889 (O'Connor, J., joined by Rehnquist, J., concurring in the judgment in part and dissenting in part).

29. Dan Brekke and Rebecca Vesely, "CDA Struck Down," *Wired News*, June 26, 1997, http://wired-vig.wired.com/news/politics/ 0,1283,4732,00.html (last visited October 11, 2005).

30. Janet Kornblum, "CDA Reaction: No Surprise," *CNet News.com*, June 26, 1997, http://news.com.com/2100-1023-200966.html?legacy=cnet (last visited June 27, 2005).

31. Kate Hafner and Matthew Lyon, *Where Wizards Stay Up Late* (New York: Simon & Schuster, 1998). See also David D. Clark, "The Design Philosophy of the DARPA Internet Protocols," 18 *ACM SIGCOMM Computer Communication Review* No. 4, 106.

32. The IETF is not the only standards body relevant to the Internet, but it is the standards body where protocols relevant to internetworking are developed. Today, the IEEE (Institute of Electrical and Electronics Engineers) is of increasing importance and is responsible for important medium-specific protocols like Ethernet (IEEE 802.3) and the most popular wireless protocol (IEEE 802.11b), also known as Wi-Fi.

33. Paulina Borsook, "How Anarchy Works: On location with the masters of the metaverse, the Internet Engineering Task Force," *Wired*, October 1995, http://www.wired.com/wired/archive/3.10/ietf_pr. (last visited October 6, 2005).

34. Ibid.

35. See A. Michael Froomkin, "Habermas@discourse.net: Toward a Critical Theory of Cyberspace," 116 *Harv. L. Rev.* 749 (2003).

36. Borsook, "How Anarchy Works."

37. Interview with John Perry Barlow, "The Debate Over Internet Governance: A Snapshot in the Year 2000," *The Berkman Center for Internet & Society at Harvard Law School*, http://cyber.law.harvard.edu/ is99/governance/barlow.html (last visited June 6, 2005).

38. Frances Cairncross, *The Death of Distance: How the Communications Revolution is Changing Our Lives* (Cambridge, MA: Harvard Business School Publishing, 2001), 157–58.

39. Steve Case, Remarks Prepared for Delivery (via satellite) Israel '99 Business Conference, December 13, 1999.

40. Declan McCullagh, "A Data Sanctuary is Born," *Wired News*, June 4, 2000, http://www.wired.com/news/business/0,1367,36749,00.html (last visited August 9, 2005).).

41. Cairncross, *The Death of Distance*, 181.

## Chapter 3

1. Ted Bridis, "Net pioneer Postel dies after surgery," *Los Angeles Times*, October 17, 1998.
2. "Postel Disputes," *The Economist*, February 8, 1997; Michael Dillon, "Jon Postel's Legacy: A Keeper of Lists, An Internet Arbiter," *Internet World*, October 26, 1998; Roger Taylor, "Internet Founder Postel Dies," *Financial Times*, October 19, 1998.
3. Milton L. Mueller, *Ruling the Root* (Cambridge, MA: MIT Press, 2002), 161, 162.
4. Keith Moore, e-mail to Joe Baptista, "Re: new.net (was: Root Server DDoS Attack: What The Media Did Not Tell You," http://www.spinics.net/lists/ietf/msg04472.html (last visited August 3, 2005).
5. Mueller, *Ruling the Root*, 162.
6. Cf. *Barcelona.com, Inc. v. Excelentisimo Ayuntamiento De Barcelona*, 330 F.3d 617 (4th Cir. 2003).
7. David Johnson, personal conversation with Tim Wu, September 7, 2004.
8. Ira Magaziner, interview by Jack Goldsmith, September 27, 2005. The so-called White Paper issued by the Department of Commerce in 1998 also emphasized U.S. contracts as the basis for U.S. control over naming and numbering issues. See Management of Internet Names and Addresses, 63 Fed. Reg. 31741 (1998).
9. As related to Tim Wu, August 6, 2003.
10. A. Michael Froomkin, "Wrong Turn in Cyberspace: Using ICANN to Route Around the APA and the Constitution," 50 *Duke L. J.* 17, 50 (2000).
11. Ibid., 52–53; see also Andrew Hafner and Matthew Lyon, *Where Wizards Stay Up Late: The Origins of the Internet* (New York: Simon & Schuster, 1998), 252–53. The specification for the "Simple Mail Transfer Protocol," written by Jon Postel in 1982, can be found at http://www.ictf.org/rfc/rfc0821.txt.
12. Vinton G. Cerf, "I Remember IANA," included in *In Memory of Jon Postel*, Internet Society ed. (1998), http://www.isoc.org/postel/condolences.shtml#Cerf (last visited July 20, 2005).
13. Dave Crocker, "A Malaysian Journal: Changing the World Quietly," http://www.postel.org/remembrances/crocker-story.html. (last visited July 20, 2005).
14. Bob Braden, "Jon Postel," included in *In Memory of Jon Postel*, Internet Society ed. (1998), http://www.isoc.org/postel/condolences.shtml#Bob%20Braden%20(ISI.EDU) (last visited July 20, 2005).
15. Prior to 1995 anyone could register a domain for free. "Internet Timeline: 'The Little Project that Grew,'" *Toronto Star*, October 14, 1999.
16. Cerf, "I Remember IANA."
17. Bob Braden, "Jon Postel."
18. *Cooperative Agreement Between NSI and U.S. Government*, January 1, 1993, http://www.icann.org/nsi/coopagmt-01jan93.htm (last viewed July 20, 2005).
19. "$16.8 Billion Deal For Domain Name Firm," *Los Angeles Times*, March 8, 2000.

20. Dan Gillmor, "ICANN and Verisign, an Unholy Alliance," *eJournal*, February 8, 2001, http://64.233.167.104/search?q=cache:C24aEwXlsUsJ:weblog.siliconvalley.com/column/dangillmor/archives/000565.shtml+%22Verisign,+an+Unholy+Alliance%22&hl=en.
21. We are particularly indebted in this section and the next to *Ruling the Root.*
22. See Hafner and Lyon, *Where Wizards Stay Up Late*, 137–41.
23. Vint Cerf, "IETF and ISOC," *Internet Society*, July 18, 1995, http://www.isoc.org/isoc/related/ietf/ (last visited July 20, 2005).
24. Mueller, *Ruling the Root*, 95–96.
25. This e-mail and its reply are available at http://64.233.167.104/search?q=cache:va4mYGmDKggJ:dns.vrx.net/news/by_date/old/1995/Mar/cerfdeal.html+%22I+would+like+a+straightforward+answer+from+the+ISOC&hl=en.
26. Ibid.
27. Ibid.
28. Ross Wm. Rader, "One History of DNS," April 25, 2001, http://www.wowworx.com/tips/One%20History%20of%20DNS.htm.
29. Mueller, *Ruling the Root*, 143.
30. Ibid., 142–46.
31. David Crocker, "Evolving Internet Name Administration," *Internet Mail Consortium*, April 15, 1997, http://www.iahc.org/contrib/draft-iahc-crocker-summary-00.html (last visited June 5, 2005).
32. Ibid.
33. "U.S. Rejects Net Name Plan," *CNet News.com*, May 2, 1997, http://news.com.com/2100-1023-279468.html?legacy=cnet (last visited June 5, 2005).
34. See Pekka Tarjanne's keynote address, "Internet Governance: Towards Voluntary Multilateralism," from *Internet Domain Names: Information Session, Meeting of Signatories and Potential Signatories of the Generic Top Level Domain Memorandum of Understanding (gTLD-MoU)*, April 29, 1997, http://www.itu.int/newsarchive/projects/dns-meet/KeynoteAddress.html (last visited June 5, 2005).
35. International Telecommunications Union, "Press Release: 80 Organizations Sign MoU to Restructure the Internet," May 1, 1997, http://www.itu.int/newsarchive/press_releases/1997/itu-08.html (last visited June 5, 2005).
36. "80 Organizations Sign MoU to Restructure the Internet," *International Telecommunications Union*, http://www.itu.int/newsarchive/press_releases/1997/itu-08.html (last visited July 21, 2005).
37. Ibid.; see also Donald M. Heath, "Beginnings: Internet Self-Governance: A Requirement to Fulfill the Promise," *Internet Domain Names: Information Session, Meeting of Signatories and Potential Signatories of the Generic Top Level Domain Memorandum of Understanding (gTLD-MoU)*, http://www.itu.int/newsarchive/projects/dns-meet/HeathAddress.html (last visited June 5, 2005).
38. Before the Commerce Department, In re: Registration and Administration of Internet Domain Names, Docket No. 970613137-7137-01, Comments of The Internet Service Providers' Consortium, August 18, 1997. Available at the Internet Archive, http://

web.archive.org/web/19980120051641/http://www.ispc.org/policy/dns-comments.shtml.

39. Mueller, *Ruling the Root*, 165.
40. Magaziner, interview.
41. Ibid.
42. Ibid.; Elliot Maxwell, interview by Tim Wu, August 16, 2005.
43. Andrew Sernovitz, "Statement to the House Subcommittee on Basic Research," September 30, 1997, http://www.house.gov/science/sernovitz_9-30.html (last visited June 5, 2005) (written statement submitted).
44. Andrew Sernovitz's actual verbal testimony, before the subcommittee, excerpted at http://www.media-visions.com/newdom1vSe.html.
45. Andrew Sernovitz, "Statement to the House Subcommittee on Basic Research."
46. Magaziner, interview.
47. Ibid.
48. E-mail from Dave Crocker to Randy Bush, November 12, 2002, http://www.postel.org/pipermail/internet-history.mbox/internet-history.mbox.
49. Magaziner, interview.
50. Ibid.; Mueller, *Ruling the Root*, 161.
51. As recounted by Jon Weinburg to Tim Wu, July 15, 2005.
52. Ibid., 158
53. Sandra Gittlen, "CORE members face defeat," *Network World Fusion*, January 23, 1998.
54. Kenneth Cukier, "Testing Times for Net Guardians," *Communications Week International*, February 16, 1998; Magaziner, interview.
55. Postel's e-mail can be found at http://www.postel.org/pipermail/Internet-history/2002-November/000376.html (last visited June 5, 2005).
56. Rajiv Chandrasekaran, "Internet Reconfiguration Concerns Federal Officials," *Washington Post*, January 31, 1998, H1.
57. Mueller, *Ruling the Root*, 162.
58. Paul Vixie, "Requiem for Jon Postel," *Wired*, October 18, 1998, http://wired-vig.wired.com/news/print/0,1294,15679,00.html (last visited August 10, 2005).
59. Sandra Gittlen, "Taking the wrong Root? Internet veteran's DNS test raises hackles," *Network World*, February 4, 1998.
60. Public comments of David Crocker, Nov. 12, 2002, http://www.postel.org/pipermail/internet-history/2002-November/000135.html.
61. Mueller, *Ruling the Root*, 162.
62. Comments of Tom Postel, http://groups.google.com/group/net.Internet.dns.policy/browse_thread/thread/357b74036ecb6c49/d65e36fecc06c6e3#d65e36fecc06c6e3.
63. Craig Simon's message setting out his view of Jon's action, http://www.postel.org/pipermail/Internet-history/2002-November/000378.html (last visited October 5, 2005).
64. Mueller, *Ruling the Root*, 162
65. Magaziner, interview.

66. Ibid.
67. See Craig Simon, "The Technical Construction of Globalism: Internet Governance and the DNS Crisis," http://www.rkey.com/dns/dnsdraft.html (last visited August 10, 2005); see also Mueller, *Ruling the Root*, 162.
68. United States Department of Commerce, Management of Internet Names and Addresses, Docket No. 980212036-8146-02, http://www.ntia.doc.gov/ntiahome/domainname/6_5_98dns.htm.

## Chapter 4

1. The facts in this paragraph were accurate as of August 11, 2005.
2. Marry Williams Walsh, "Icelanders, Microsoft in War of Words," *Los Angeles Times*, June 29, 1998.
3. Ibid.
4. Thomas M. Edwards, "Corporate Nations: The Emergence of New Sovereignties," in *Worlds of E-Commerce: Economic, Geographical, and Social Dimensions*, ed. Thomas R. Leinbach and Stanley D. Brunn (New York: John Wiley & Sons, Inc., 2001), 298.
5. *Microsoft Worldwide*, http://www.microsoft.com/worldwide/ (last visited August 11, 2005). Edwards, "Corporate Nations," 303–4.
6. "The Coming Global Tongue," *The Economist*, December 21, 1996, 78.
7. Michael Specter, "Computer Speak; World, Wide, Web: 3 English Words," *New York Times*, April 14, 1996, 4–5.
8. Al Gore, "Remarks to the Television Academy on Telecommunications Policy," January 11, 1994, http://www.ibiblio.org/icky/speech2.html (last visited August 11, 2005).
9. "The Coming Global Tongue," 75.
10. Barbara Wallraff, "What Global Language?" *Atlantic Monthly*, November 2000.
11. David Crystal, *The Language Revolution* (Cambridge: Polity 2004), 87.
12. Internet Users By Language," Internet World Stats, http://www.internetworldstats.com/stats7.htm (last visited June 28, 2005); "Global Internet Statistics (By Language)," Global Reach, http://global-reach.biz/globstats/index.php3 (last visited June 28, 2005).
13. See, for example, Crystal, *The Language Revolution*, 91; Wallraff, "What Global Language?"
14. David Graddol, "The Future of Language," *Science*, February 27, 2004, 1329.
15. John Perry Barlow, "The Economy of Ideas," *Wired* 2.03, March 1994. Barlow himself attributed the phrase to Steward Brand. For history of the origin and uses of the phrase, see Roger Clarke, "Information Wants to Be Free", http://www.anu.edu.au/people/Roger.Clarke/II/IWtbF.html (last visited August 11, 2004).
16. J. M. Balkin, "Media Filters, the V-Chip, and the Foundations of Broadcast Regulation," 45 *Duke Law Journal* April 1996, 1143.
17. Robert H. Reid, *Architects of the Web: 1,000 Days that Built the Future of Business* (New York: John Wiley & Sons, Inc., 1997), xxiii.
18. Ibid.
19. Ibid.; see also Tim Berners-Lee and Mark Fischetti, *Weaving the Web:*

*The Original Design and Ultimate Destiny of the World Wide Web By Its Inventor* (New York: HarperCollins, 1999).

20. Michael F. Goodchild, "Towards a Location Theory of Distributed Computing and E-Commerce," in *Worlds of E-Commerce*, 78–79.

21. See George Gilder, *Telecosm: How Infinite Bandwidth will Revolutionize Our World* (New York: Free Press, 2000).

22. Bill Gates, "Bill Gates Ponders the Internet," interview by Michael J. Miller, *PC Magazine*, October 11, 1994, 79.

23. Yochi Dreazen, "Fallacies of the Tech Boom," *Wall Street Journal*, September 26, 2002.

24. Shawn Young, "Why the Glut in Fiber Lines Remains Huge," *Wall Street Journal*, May 12, 2005.

25. "City v. Country," *Forbes ASAP*, February 27, 1995, 56; see also Hal Cohen, "Invisible Cities," *Industry Standard*, October 2, 2000, http://knoke.org/PR/IndustryStandard.htm (last visited October 8, 2005).

26. "City v. Country."

27. Barney Warf, "Segueways into Cyberspace: Multiple Geographies of the Digital Divide," 6 *New Media & Society* (2004).

28. "Putting it in its Place—Geography and the Net," *The Economist*, August 11, 2001, 18.

29. A. M. Townsend,"Wired/Unwired: The Urban Geography of Digital Networks" (Ph.D. diss., Massachusetts Institute of Technology, 2003).

30. Quoted in Hal Cohen, "Invisible Cities." See also Soon-Hyung Yook, Hawoong Jeong, and Albert-Laszlo Barabasi, "Modeling the Internet's large-scale topology," *Proceedings of the National Academy of Sciences of the United States of America*, vol. 99, no. 21 (Oct. 2002), 13382.

31. Matthew A. Zook, "Old Hierarchies or New Networks of Centrality?— The Global Geography of the Internet Content Market," *American Behavioral Scientist* 44, no. 10 (June 2001); Jed Kolko, "The Death of Cities? The Death of Distance? Evidence from the Geography of Commercial Internet Usage," in *The Internet Upheaval: Raising Questions, Seeking Answers in Communications Policy* (Telecommunications Policy Research Conference), ed. Ingo Vogelsang and Benjamin M. Compaine (Cambridge, MA: MIT Press, 2000); Matthew A. Zook, "The Web of Production: The Economic Geography of Commercial Internet Content Production in the United States," *Environment and Planning A* 32, (2000): 411–26; Robert Kitchin, "Toward Geographies of Cyberspace," *Progress in Human Geography* (1998): 385, 392; Edward J. Malecki, "The Internet: A Preliminary Analysis of Its Evolving Economic Geography" (2002) http://cura.osu.edu/research/roundtables/data/Maleckipaper.PDF.; Matthew A. Zook, *The Geography of the Internet Industry: Venture Capital, Dot-Coms, and Local Knowledge* (Malden, MA: Blackwell Publishers, 2005) 25–35, 40.

32. See S. Murnion and R. G. Healy, "Modeling Distance Decay Effects in Web Server Information Flows," *Geographical Analysis* 30, no. 4 (1998): 285; Mike Thelwall, "Evidence for the Existence of Geographic Trends in University Web Site Interlinking," 58(2) *Journal of Documentation* 563 (2002).

33. Anthony Townsend, e-mail message to Jack Goldsmith, June 13, 2005.

34. Telegeography, Global Internet Geography 2005 Executive Summary

http://www.telegeography.com/ee/free_resources/gig2005_exec_sum-01.php (last visited August 12, 2005).

35. Bill Gates, Nathan Myhrvold, and Peter Rinearson, *The Road Ahead* (New York: Viking Penguin, 1995).

36. See Robert D. Hof, "What's With All the Warehouses? E-tailers See They'll Need Bricks and Mortar, Too," *Businessweek Online*, November 1, 1999, http://www.businessweek.com:/1999/99_44/b3653046.htm?scriptFramed (last visited August 12, 2005).

37. See Cade Metz, "E-Tailing:," *PC Magazine*, July 1, 2001, http://www.pcmag.com/article2/0,1759,109141,00.asp (last visited August 12, 2005).

38. Lisa Guernsey, "Welcome to the World Wide Web. Passport, Please?," *New York Times*, March 15, 2001.

39. For the best critique of such Internet essentialism, see Lawrence Lessig, *Code and Other Laws of Cyberspace* (New York: Basic Books, 1999). Cerf also ignored the importance of the asymmetrical distribution of Internet hardware, described above.

40. Based on several conversations by Jack Goldsmith with Cyril Houri.

41. On March 30, 2004, Infosplit was acquired by Quova, Inc., a then-rival geo-identification firm, for whom Houri now works.

42. David J. Lipke, "You Are Here: The Race to Bring Geography to the Borderless Web," *American Demographics*, March 2001, 65.

43. Cyril Houri suggested this analogy in conversations with Jack Goldsmith.

44. "National and State Trends in Fraud and Identity Theft, Federal Trade Commission," (2004) http://www.consumer.gov/sentinel/pubs/Top10Fraud2004.pdf (last visited August 12, 2005); Mara Der Hovanesian, "Hackers And Phishers And Frauds, Oh My!" *Business Week*, May 30, 2005.

45. See "Reaching Certain Regions and Language Speakers, Google Adwords https://adwords.google.com/support/bin/topic.py?topic=21 (last visited August 12, 2005).

46. "Putting it in its Place—Geography and the net," *The Economist*, August 11, 2001, U.S. edition.

47. Larry Barrett, "Major League Baseball Struggles to Reach Fans Online," *Baseline* http://www.baselinemag.com/print_article2/0,2533,a=147496,00.asp (last visited August 12, 2005).

48. Bob Tedeschi, E-Commerce Report, "The market is growing for software that finds Internet users' locations," *New York Times*, June 16, 2003, C1, 7.

49. "Putting it in its place."

## Chapter 5

1. "History of Sealand," http://www.sealandgov.com/history.html (last visited June 15, 2005); see also Mark Lucas, "Seven Miles Off the Suffolk Coast, The Principality of Sealand is Europe's Smallest Self-Proclaimed Independent State," *Independent*, November 27, 2004; Simson Garfinkel, "Welcome to Sealand, Now Bugger Off," *Wired*, July 2000, http://www.wired.com/wired/archive/8.07/haven.html (last visited August 15, 2005).

2. John Markoff, "Rebel Outpost on the Fringes of Cyberspace," *New York Times*, June 4, 2000; Joe Salkowski, "Sealand: Man-Made Nation Touts Privacy," *Chicago Tribune*, March 26, 2001.

3. "About HavenCo" *HavenCo.com*, http://www.havenco.com/ about_havenco/index.html (last visited June 15, 2005).

4. Roy Bates, "Rebel Sea Fortress Dreams of Being 'Data Haven,'" *Wall Street Journal*, June 26, 2000.

5. James Boyle, "Foucault in Cyberspace: Cyberspace, Sovereignty, and Hardwired Censors," 66 *U. Cin. L. Rev.* 177, 179 (1997). Boyle did not embrace this premise, but rather was summarizing the views of those who did.

6. See, e.g., 18 U.S.C.A. §2320.

7. 18 U.S.C.A. §2320(a). See also 18 U.S.C.A. §2320(e)(2)(defining the term "traffic"). According to this section of the code, "the term 'traffic' means transport, transfer, or otherwise dispose of, to another, as consideration for anything of value, or make or obtain control of with intent so to transport, transfer, or dispose of. . . ."

8. Lawrence Lessig, "Symposium: Surveying Law and Borders: The Zones of Cyberspace," 48 *Stan. L. Rev.*, 1403, 1405 (1996).

9. See Daryl J. Levinson, "Collective Sanctions," 56 *Stan. L. Rev.* 345 (2003).

10. Ibid., 365.

11. For a robust example of the 1990s view of the disintermediating effects of the Internet, see Andrew L. Shapiro, *The Control Revolution: How the Internet Is Putting Individuals in Charge and Changing the World We Know* (New York: PublicAffairs, 1999), chs. 6, 12.

12. Lawrence Lessig, *Code and Other Laws of Cyberspace* (New York: Basic Books, 1999).

13. See ibid., 207–8; see also Jack Goldsmith, "Against Cyberanarchy," 65 *U. Chic. L. Rev.* 1199 (1998); Timothy S. Wu, "Cyberspace Sovereignty? The Internet and the International System," 10 *Harv. J. L. & Tech.* 647 (1997); M. Ethan Katsh, "Software Worlds and the First Amendment: Virtual Doorkeepers in Cyberspace," 1996 *U. Chi. Legal F.* 335 (1996).

14. Edmund L. Andrews, "Germany Charges Compuserve Manager" *New York Times*, April 17, 1997.

15. John Carvel, "Prison Terms For Illegal Adoptions: Internet Babies Case Prompts Tough New Sanctions," *Guardian* (UK), March 15, 2001.

16. Matthew Schruers, "The History and Economics of ISP Liability for Third Party Content," 88 *VA. L. Rev.* 205, 227–30 (2002).

17. Michael L. Rustad and Thomas H. Koenig, "Rebooting Cybertort Law," 80 *Wash. L. Rev.* 335, 392–94 (2005); Directive 2000/31/EC of the European Parliament and of the Council, 8 June 2000 on Certain Legal Aspects of Information Society Services, in Particular Electronic Commerce in the Internal Market ("Directive on Electronic Commerce"), at http://europa.eu.int/eur-lex/pri/en/oj/dat/2000/l_178/ l_17820000717en00010016.pdf (last visited August 11, 2005).

18. See Jonathan Zittrain, "Internet Points of Control," 44 *B.C. L. Rev.* 653, 664–69 (2003); Douglas Lichtman and Eric A. Posner, "Holding Internet Service Providers Accountable," 2005 *Supreme Court Economic Review* (forthcoming 2005).

19. Ibid., 673.

20. 47 U.S.C. § 230(c)(1) (1996). See also *Zeron v. America Online*, 129 F.3d

327, 330 (4th Cir. 1997) (holding that the 1996 Communications Decency Act "creates a federal immunity to any cause of action that would make service providers liable for information originating with a third-party user of the service." *Followed by Blumenthal v. Drudge*, 992 F. Supp. 44, 50-51 (D.D.C 1998).

21. OpenNet Initiative, "Internet Filtering in Saudi Arabia in 2004," http://www.opennetinitiative.net/studies/saudi/ (last visited August 15, 2005)
22. Ibid.
23. Ibid.
24. "About Andreas," http://home.online.no/~heldal/me.html (last visited June 16, 2005).
25. David F. Gallagher, "A copyright dispute with the Church of Scientology is forcing Google to do some creative linking," *New York Times*, April 22, 2002.
26. Ibid.
27. 17 U.S.C. §512 (2000).
28. Michael Davis-Wilson, "Google DMCA Takedowns: A three-month view," http://www.chillingeffects.org/weather.cgi?WeatherID=498 (last visited August 15, 2005).
29. Ibid.
30. Jonathan Zittrain and Benjamin Edelman, "Localized Google search result exclusions," http://cyber.law.harvard.edu/filtering/google (last visited August 15, 2005).
31. Betsy Schiffman, "Online Cigarette Sales? Shocking!," *Forbes.com*, December 11, 2001. http://www.forbes.com/2001/12/11/1211tobacco.html (last visited June 16, 2005).
32. Bob Tedeschi, "Now that credit card companies won't handle online tobacco sales, many merchants are calling it quits," *New York Times*, April 4, 2005.
33. Ibid.
34. See Department of Law, New York State, Press Release, August 21, 2002, "Agreement Reached with PayPal To Bar New Yorkers from Online Gambling," http://www.oag.state.ny.us/press/2002/aug/aug21a_02.html (last visited August 15, 2005).
35. Ellen Warren and Terry Armour, "Vote-Selling Site Creator Elects to Call it 'Satire,'" *Chicago Tribune*, October 26, 2000.
36. Vote-Auction.com, http://vote-auction.net/mainframe.htm (last visited August 15, 2005); see also http://www.disinfo.com/archive/pages/dossier/id505/pg1/.
37. Janet Kornblum, "Chicago acts to end online sale of votes," *USA Today*, October 11, 2000.
38. "Domain Bank Acts to Stop Internet Vote Auction," *Business Wire*, October 19, 2000.
39. Ibid.; see also Brian Krebs and David McGuire, "Vote-Auction.com Back Online: Authorities Ponder Next Move," *Newsbytes*, November 3, 2000.
40. Henry H. Perritt, Jr., "Towards A Hybrid Regulatory Scheme for the Internet," 2001 *U.Chi. Legal F.* 215, 242 (2001).
41. Ibid.
42. Ibid.
43. Ibid., 242–43.

44. Declan McCullagh, "U.S. crime-fighters seize Websites," *CNET News.com*, February 26, 2003, http://news.zdnet.com/2100-1009_22-986225.html (last visited August 15, 2005).

45. Louis Trager, "Silicon Valley Lawmaker Says IP Law Needs Fair-Use Balance," *Washington Internet Daily*, May 31, 2002.

46. "Web Racist Sentenced," *Belfast News Letter*, April 24, 2002.

47. Gina Barton, "Overseas Internet gambling trail leads back to Wisconsin; Federal e-mail wiretaps result in convictions of state man, business partner," *Milwaukee Journal-Sentinel*, March 15, 2003.

48. Liam Reid, "The Police Sting Operation Which Led From Fort Worth to Ballymaloe, *Sunday Tribune* (Ireland), January 19, 2003; Christopher Marquis, "U.S. Says it Broke Ring That Peddled Child Pornography," *New York Times*, August 9, 2001.

49. Barry Brown, "Massive Child Pornography Investigation May Get Tangled in Procedural Red Tape, *Buffalo News*, January 19, 2003; Reid, "The Police Sting Operation."

50. Gary S. Becker, "Crime and Punishment: An Economic Approach," 76 *J. Pol. Econ.* 169 (1968).

51. See generally Richard N. Posner, *Economic Analysis of the Law* (New York: Aspen Publishers, 2003).

52. New York Attorney General's Office, Department of Law, Press Release, June 14, 2002, "Financial Giant Joins Fight Against Online Gambling."

53. Amanda Banks, "Antigua Granted WTO Hearing On US Online Gambling Ban," *Tax-News.com*, July 24, 2003, at http://www.offshore-e-com.com/asp/story/story.asp?storyname=12733.

54. Communication from info@paypro.com to Tim Wu, "Credit Card Transfer Failed—Try iGM-Pay and get 20% Extra," February 2005.

55. Ryan Lackey, "HavenCo: What Really Happened," August 3, 2003, http://www.metacolo.com/papers/dc11-havenco/dc11-havenco.pdf (last visited June 16, 2005).

56. Ibid.

57. Ibid.

58. Ibid.

59. Ibid.

## Chapter 6

1. For the original Chinese language version of this quote see http://epochtimes.com/gb/3/7/15/n343384.htm (last visited August 2, 2005).

2. "The Powerful Voice of a Mouse," *Washington Post*, December 7, 2003, p. B02.

3. "In Henan 15-Year-Old Youth Punished For Making Reactionary Argument That The Government Is Prostitute," Xinhua website, July 14, 2003, cited in He Qinglian, *"The Chinese Government's Stranglehold on the Internet,"* trans. Lee Tsienwei, http://www.cicus.org/media/He_English.pdf (last visited August 2, 2003).

4. Human Rights Watch, "Internet Dissidents, China, Liu Du," available at http://www.hrw.org/advocacy/internet/dissidents/8.htm (last visited August 2, 2005).

5. "Chinese Cyber-Dissident Told She Will Not Face Formal Indictment,"

*Agence France Presse*, December 25, 2003, cited in "People's Republic of China: Controls Tighten as Internet Activism Grows," *Amnesty International*, http://web.amnesty.org/library/pdf/ ASA170012004ENGLISH/$File/ASA1700104.pdf (last visited August 2, 2005).

6. Marguerite Reardon, "China to Trump U.S. in Broadband Subscribers," *CNet News.com*, May 4, 2005, http://news.com.com/ China+to+trump+U.S.+in+broadband+subscribers/2100-1034_ 3-5695591.html (last visited June 14, 2005).

7. Nicholas D. Kristof, "Death By a Thousand Blogs," *New York Times*, May 24, 2005; Bruce Einhorn, Ben Elgin, and Robert D. Hof, "The Giant Web race; Internet Use is Exploding in China, so U.S. Giants Like Yahoo! and eBay are Hunting Harder for Deals," *Business Week*, June 13, 2005.

8. Kristof, "Death By a Thousand Blogs."

9. Thomas L. Friedman, "Foreign Affairs; Censors Beware," *New York Times*, July 25, 2000.

10. William Farris, interview by Tim Wu, May 22, 2003.

11. William J. Clinton, The White House, Office of the Press Secretary, *"Remarks by the President to Business Leaders, and Officials and Employees of Gateway Computers,"* September 4, 1998, http:// www.clintonfoundation.org/legacy/090498-speech-by-president-to-officials-of-gateway-computers.htm (last visited August 2, 2005).

12. Remarks by President Bill Clinton on China, Paul H. Nitze School of Advanced International Studies, Washington, DC, March 8, 2000, http:/ /www.usembassy-china.org.cn/press/release/2000/clinton38.html (last visted August 2, 2005).

13. Henry Chu, "China Puts Two Well-Known Dissidents on Trial; Asia: Defendants Have Led Drive to Register Their Fledgling Democracy Party as a Counter to Communists," *Los Angeles Times*, December 18, 1998.

14. Lorien Holland, "China Detains Activist Over Opposition Party," *Agence France Presse*, June 29, 1998.

15. Chu, "China Puts Two Well-Known Dissidents on Trial."

16. "An Open Letter to Jiang Zemin from Wang Youcai's Wife," August 4, 1998, http://64.233.161.104/ search?q=cache:uxhTtlsJGckJ:www.democracy.org.hk/pastweek/ aug2_8/wang_wife.htm+An+Open+Letter+to+Jiang+Zemin+ from+Wang+Youcai%27s+Wife&hl=en.

17. Chu, "China Puts Two Well-Known Dissidents on Trial."

18. Henry Chu, "China's Thin Line Between Opinion and Subversion; Rights: Dissidents' Convictions Show that Talking about Reform and Acting on it are Treated Very Differently," *Los Angeles Times*, December 22, 1998.

19. William J. Clinton, The White House, Office of the Press Secretary, Interview of the President by CCTV, July 1, 1998, available at http:// clinton4.nara.gov/WH/New/China/19980701-5997.html (last visited August 2, 2005).

20. James Kynge, "Chinese president takes hard line on dissidents," *Financial Times*, December 19, 1998, 4.

21. China Vows to Continue Reforms but Rejects Western-style Democracy, *CNN.com*, December 18, 1998, http://www.cnn.com/WORLD/asiapcf/

9812/18/china.01/ (last visited October 11, 2005).

22. Jonathan Zittrain and Benjamin Edelman, "Empirical Studying of Filtering in China," December 2002, included in *Documentation of Internet Filtering Worldwide* (forthcoming), http://cyber.law.harvard.edu/filtering/china/ (click on "Complete list of 18,931 blocked sites, sorted alphabetically by URL") (last visited June 14, 2005).

23. Ibid.

24. Ethan Gutmann, *Losing the New China: A Story of American Commerce, Desire, and Betrayal* (San Francisco: Encounter Books, 2004), 128–29; see also Greg Walton, "China's Golden Shield: Corporations and the Development of Surveillance Technology in the People's Republic of China," *Rights & Democracy* (2001), http://www.ichrdd.ca/english/commdoc/publications/globalization/goldenShieldEng.html (last visited August 11, 2005); "Hangzhou to Build China's Largest Broadband Metropolitan-Area Network With Cisco 12000 Series Internet Routers," *Cisco Systems, Inc.*, January 17, 2002, http://newsroom.cisco.com/dlls/prod_011702.html (last visited August 2, 2005).

25. "Internet Filtering in China in 2004–2005: A Country Study," *Open Net Initiative*, http://www.opennetinitiative.net/studies/china/ (last visited August 2, 2005).

26. Farris, interview.

27. "Internet Filtering in China in 2004–2005: A Country Study," *Open Net Initiative*, http://www.opennetinitiative.net/studies/china/ (last visited August 2, 2005).

28. "China Human Rights and Rule of Law Update," United States Congressional-Executive Commission on China, June 1, 2005, http://www.cecc.gov/pages/general/newsletters/CECCnewsletter20050601.pdf (last visited August 11, 2005).

29. Mark Magnier and Joseph Menn, "As China Censors the Internet, Money Talks," *Los Angeles Times*, June 17, 2005, A1.

30. See, e.g., "'Living Dangerously on the Net': Censorship and Surveillance of Internet Forums," *Reporters Without Borders*, May 12, 2003, http://www.rsf.org/article.php3?id_article=6793 (last visited August 2, 2005).

31. Ibid.

32. Ibid.

33. Congressional-Executive Commission on China, 2003 Annual Report available at http://www.cecc.gov/pages/virtualAcad/exp/expannrept03.php (last visited August 2, 2005).

34. Ibid.

35. Howard W. French, "China Tightens Restrictions On Bloggers and Web Sites," *New York Times*, June 8, 2005, 6.

36. Times Wire Reports, "Beijing Reports Closing Illegal Internet Cafes," *Los Angeles Times*, February 14, 2005; "Violence Curbed," *Sunday Telegraph* (Australia), November 14, 2004.

37. Suqian, "The practical aspects of directing Internet opinion." *Nanfang Weekend*, May 19, 2005. Original version translation, http://www.zonaeuropa.com/20050521_2.htm.

38. Steven Pearlstein, "NATO: Bombs Aimed in Error, China's Embassy Hit Instead of Supply Building," *Washington Post*, May 9, 1999.

39. Shanthi Kalathil, "Nationalism on the Net," *Asian Wall Street Journal*,

February 22, 2002.

40. Elisabeth Rosenthal and David Sanger, "U.S. Plane in China After it Collides with Chinese Jet," *New York Times*, April 2, 2001.

41. "Beijing barks, but keeps bite in reserve," *Sunday Herald* (Glasgow, UK), April 8, 2001.

42. John Pomfret, "Anti-American Sentiment On the Upswing in China: Mood Reflects Hardening of Beijing's Position in Standoff," *Washington Post*, April 9, 2001.

43. Wang Xiangwei "Escalating Outcry Poses Threat to Japanese Trade, Investments, *South China Morning Post*, April 4, 2005.

44. Tim Johnson, "China Quietly Puts End to Anti-Japanese Unrest," *Atlanta Journal-Constitution*, May 8, 2005, at 8A.

45. Bruce Einhorn, No Sympathy from China's Cyber Elite, *Business Week*, September 17, 2001, at http://www.businessweekeurope.com/bwdaily/dnflash/sep2001/nf20010917_8982.htm (last visited October 17, 2005).

46. "China Far Outpaces India in Web Use," http://english.c114.net/newsheadline_html/200572193540-1.Html (last visited August 3, 2005).

47. Dan Ackman, "No War, But Scandal, Scandal, Scandal," *Forbes.com*, March 12, 2003, http://www.forbes.com/2003/03/12/cx_da_0312topnews.html (last visited August 3, 2005); John C. Roper, "Violations Deliberate, Ex-finance Chief Says; Blockbuster deal with Enron unit showed revenue it didn't generate," *Houston Chronicle*, May 13, 2005.

48. Thomas L. Friedman, *The Lexus and the Olive Tree* (New York: Knopf, 2000), 68.

49. "Internet Users Reaches 103 Million: Survey," *China Daily*, July 22, 2005, http://www.china.org.cn/english/BAT/135701.htm (last visited August 3, 2005).

50. Daniel Sorid, "US Tech Firms Protest China's Rules on Wi-Fi; Wireless network gear sold there must include an encryption scheme accessible to only 11 firms in that nation," *Los Angeles Times*, December 15, 2003.

51. Dapeng Zhu, "Wireless Authentication and Privacy Infrastructure Protocol (WAPI) Specification," http://www.suntzureport.com/wapi/wapi.pdf (last visited August 11, 2005).

52. Bruce Einhorn, "China's Wi-Fi Wrangle," *BusinessWeek Online*, March 15, 2005, http://www.businessweek.com/technology/content/mar2004/tc20040315_6034_tc058.htm (last visited October 12, 2005).

53. Dave Eberhart, "China Puts Gun to Head of U.S. Tech Companies," *NewsMax.com*, March. 27, 2004 available at http://www.newsmax.com/archives/articles/2004/3/27/125430.shtml (last visited August 3, 2005).

54. Rebecca MacKinnon, telephone conversation with Tim Wu, May 27, 2005.

55. Michael Rogers, "Can China build its own Silicon Valley?" *MSNBC News*, May 23, 2005, http://msnbc.msn.com/id/7915125/ (last visited June 14, 2005) (particularly second page).

56. Steven Cherry, "The Net Effect," *Spectrum Online*, http://www.spectrum.ieee.org/jun05/1219 (last visited October 12, 2005).

57. "Telegeography," http://www.telegeography.com/products/map_internet/detail-3_inset-asia.php (last visited August 3, 2005).

58. bmonday(dot)com, http://bmonday.com/archive/2005/06/13/2495.aspx (last visited August 3, 2005).
59. William Stuntz to Jack Goldsmith, August 8, 2005.
60. Peter Yu, "The Path of Sinicyberlaw," (lecture presented at *Digital Silk Road: A Look at the First Decade of China's Internet Development and Beyond*, Michigan State University, East Lansing, MI, May 23–24, 2005).

## Chapter 7

1. Arianna Eunjung Cha, "File Swapper Eluding Pursuers," *Washington Post*, December 21, 2002, A1.
2. Steve Hannaford, Industry Brief, *Music Industry*, June 28, 2003, http://www.oligopolywatch.com/2003/06/28.html (last visited August 16, 2005).
3. See Audio Home Recording Act of 1992, 17 U.S.C. § 1001 et seq.
4. The passage of these laws is discussed in Tim Wu, "Copyright's Communications Policy," 103 *Mich. L. Rev.* 278 (2004).
5. Such as MP3.com. See Tim Wu, "When Code Isn't Law," 89 *Va. L. Rev.* 679, 727 (2003).
6. Maggie A. Lange Digital Music Distribution Technologies Challenge Copyright Law: A Review of RIAA v. MP3.com and RIA v. Napster, 45 B.B.J. 14, 30 (2001).
7. Karl Taro Greenfeld, "Meet the Napster," *Time*, October 2, 2000, 60.
8. See Adam Sherwin, "Has Napster founder gone from dropout to sell-out?" *The Times* (London), March 25, 2005.
9. Harry McCracken, "He's the Lawyer Who Nailed Napster," *PCWorld.com*, Friday, January 17, 2003, http://www.pcworld.com/news/article/0,aid,108620,00.asp (last visited August 16, 2005).
10. John Perry Barlow, "The Next Economy of Ideas," *Wired* 8.10, October 2000, http://www.wired.com/wired/archive/8.10/download.html (last visited August 16, 2005).
11. For the details, see Tim Wu, "When Code Isn't Law," 89 *Va. L. Rev.* 679, 730–33 (2003).
12. Ibid., 734–36.
13. John Borland, "Kazaa strikes back at Hollywood labels," *CNet News.com*, January 27, 2003, http://news.com.com/2100-1023-982344.html (last visited August 16, 2005).
14. Chris Oakes, "Something Out of Nothing: New Venture for Kazaa Founder," *International Herald Tribune*, January 26, 2004.
15. "Post-Napster Sites Face Industry Wrath," BBC News, October 4, 2001, http://news.bbc.co.uk/1/hi/entertainment/new_media/1578616.stm (last visited August 16, 2005).
16. Todd Woody, "The Race to Kill Kazaa," *Wired*, 11.02, February 2003, http://www.wired.com/wired/archive/11.02/kazaa.html (last visited August 16, 2005).
17. *Sony Corp. of America vs. Universal City Studios, Inc.*, 464 U.S. 417 (1984).
18. Fred Von Lohmann, e-mail to Tim Wu, June 17, 2005.
19. See *MGM Studios, Inc. v. Grokster, Ltd.*, 259 F. Supp. 2d 1029, 1039 (C.D. Cal. 2003).
20. Ibid., 1046.

21. Ibid. (quoting *Sony*, 464 U.S., 431).
22. *MGM Studios Inc., v. Grokster Ltd.*, 380 F.3d 1154, 1167 (9th Cir. 2004).
23. Ibid.
24. Barlow, "Next Economy of Ideas," *Wired*, 8.10, October 2000.
25. Glynn S. Lunney, Jr., *The Death of Copyright: Digital Technologies, Private Copying, and the Digital Millennium Copyright Act*, 87 Va. L. Rev. 813 (2001)
26. "Senator Proposes Destruction of File-Swapping Computers," *Guardian* (UK), June 19, 2003.
27. Arguments Before the Comms. on Patents of the S. & H.R., Conjointly, on the Bills S. 6330 and H.R. 19,853, to Amend and Consolidate the Acts Respecting Copyright, 59th Cong. 24 (1906) (statement of John Philip Sousa), reprinted in 4 Legislative History of the 1909 Copyright Act pt. H, at 24 (E. Fulton Brylawski & Abe Goldman eds., 1976).
28. Tim Wu, "Copyright's Communications Policy," 103 *Mich. L. Rev.* 278, 303–4 (2004).
29. See Wu, "Copyright's Communications Policy," 103 *Mich. L. Rev.* 278, 313 (2004).
30. Ibid.
31. Mike Musgrove, "RIAA Plans to Sue Music Swappers, No More Warnings to Individuals," *Washington Post*, June 26, 2003.
32. Liane Cassavoy, "Music Labels Declare War on File Swappers," *PC World*, September 8, 2003, http://www.pcworld.com/news/article/0,aid,112364,00.asp (last visited August 16, 2005).
33. Jefferson Graham, "RIAA lawsuits bring consternation, chaos," *USA TODAY*, September 10, 2005.
34. RIAA Press Release, "Recording Industry Begins Suing P2P File Sharers Who Illegally Offer Copyrighted Music Online," September 8, 2003, http://www.riaa.com/news/newsletter/090803.asp (August 16, 2005).
35. Ibid.
36. Jeff Howe, "Listen, It's Isn't the Labels, It's the Law," *Washington Post*, October 5, 2003.
37. Gary Younge, "Music Giants Sue 12-Year-Old Girl For Net Theft, *Guardian* (UK), September 10, 2003.
38. John Borland, "RIAA settles with 12-year-old girl," *CNet News.com*, September 9, 2003, http://news.com.com/RIAA+settles+with+12-year-old+girl/2100-1027_3-5073717.html (last visited August 16, 2005).
39. Declan McCullagh, "P2P's little secret," *CNet News.com*, July 8, 2003, http://news.com.com/2100-1029_3-1023735.html (last visited August 16, 2005).
40. Mike Musgrove, "RIAA Plans to Sue Music Swappers," *Washington Post*, June 26, 2003, E1.
41. Brooks Boliek, "Pirates in the Cross Hairs," *Hollywood Reporter*, June 26, 2003.
42. Chris Oakes, "Something Out of Nothing: New Venture for Kazaa Founder," *International Herald Tribune*, January 26, 2004. See also Erick Schonfeld, "The True Cost of Free Music," *Business 2.0*, May 24, 2002, http://www.business2.com/b2/web/articles/0,17863,514793,00.html (last visited August 16, 2005).
43. Dan Ilett, "CA slaps spyware label on Kazaa," *CNet News.com*, November 26, 2004, http://news.com.com/CA+slaps+spyware+label+on+Kazaa/2100-1025_3-5467539.html (last visited August 16, 2005).
44. Peter Rojas "Kazaa Lite: No Spyware Aftertaste," *Wired News*, April. 18,

2002, http://www.wired.com/news/mp3/0,1285,51916,00.html (last visited August 16, 2005).

45. Sue Lowe, "Kazaa ready to unleash new network," *Sydney Morning Herald*, April 6, 2002, http://www.smh.com.au/articles/2002/04/05/1017206264997.html?oneclick=true (last visited August 16, 2005).

46. Tom Spring, "KaZaA Sneakware Stirs Inside PCs," *CNN.com*, May 7, 2002, http://archives.cnn.com/2002/TECH/internet/05/07/kazaa.software.idg/ (last visited August 17, 2005).

47. "Scam Sites—A New Threat To P2P," *Addict 3D*, April 28, 2004, http://addict3d.org/index.php?page=viewarticle&type=news&ID=1834 (last visited August 17, 2005).

48. "Kazaa Owner Complains of Copyright Infringement," *Chilling Effects*, August 11, 2003 available at http://www.chillingeffects.org/dmca512/notice.cgi?NoticeID=789 (last visited August 17, 2005).

49. Frank Ahrens, "Kazaa Offices Raided in Australia," *Washington Post*, February 7, 2004.

50. John Borland, "Apple unveils music store," *CNet News.com*, April 28, 2003, http://news.com.com/Apple+unveils+music+store/2100-1027_3-998590.html?tag=st.rn (last visited August 17, 2005).

51. "How to pay the piper," *The Economist* (U.S. ed.), May 3, 2003.

52. "Interview With Steve Jobs," CNN, April 28, 2003.

53. Ibid.

54. John Borland, Apple Unveils Music Store, *CNet News.com*, April 28, 2003, http://news.com.com/Apple+unveils+music+store/2100-1027_3-998590.html (last visited October 11, 2005).

55. "iTunes more popular than many P2P sites," *CNet News.com*, June 9, 2005, http://news.cnet.co.uk/digitalmusic/0,39029666,39189911,00.htm (last visited August 16, 2005).

56. Ibid.

57. Ibid.

58. *Metro-Goldwyn-Mayer Studios, Inc. v. Grokster, Ltd.*, 125 S. Ct. 2764 (2005).

59. Ibid., 2772.

60. Ibid., 2775.

61. Laurie J. Flynn, "Apple's Profit Quadruples, Yet Stock Falls," *New York Times*, October 12, 2005.

62. Senate Judiciary Committee, Testimony of Sam Yagan President MetaMachine, Inc. (developer of eDonkey and Overnet), September 28, 2005, http://judiciary.senate.gov/testimony.cfm?id=1624&wit_id=4689 (last visited October 16, 2005).

63. Peter Kafka, "Grokster's Bid To Go Legit," *Forbes*, September 19, 2005.

64. "Earth Station 5 Declares War Against the MPAA," *Zeropaid News*, August 19, 2003, http://www.zeropaid.com/news/3306/Earth+Station+5+Declares+War+Against+The+MPAA (last visited August 17, 2005).

65. Janelle Brown, "The Gnutella Paradox," Salon.com, September 29, 2000, http://www.salon.com/tech/feature/2000/09/29/gnutella_paradox/ (last visited August 17, 2005).

66. Debora L. Spar, *Ruling the Waves: From the Compass to the Internet, a History of Business and Politics along the Technological Frontier* (New York: Harcourt, 2001). Spar's chap. 7 predicted with astonishing accuracy the normalization of the online music industry that began to emerge in 2005.

67. Ibid., 14.
68. Ibid., 14.
69. Ibid., 20.
70. Jonathan Krim, "File-Sharing Pioneer Turns to Free Internet Calling," *Washington Post*, June 4, 2005, A1.
71. John Blau, "EBay Buys Skype for $2.6 Billion, Voice over IP could let sellers, buyers chat and offer new payment options," *PCWorld*, Monday, September 12, 2005, http://www.pcworld.com/news/article/0,aid,122516,00.asp (last visited October 11, 2005).

## Chapter 8

1. Pierre Omidyar, "One-line Bio," *Pierre's Web*, http://pierre.typepad.com/about.html (last visited June 8, 2005).
2. "Interview: Pierre Omidyar, Founder and Chairman, eBay" *Academy of Achievement: A Museum of Living History*, October 27, 2000, http://www.achievement.org/autodoc/printmember/omi0int-1 (last visited June 8, 2005).
3. Ibid.
4. Ibid.
5. Adam Cohen, *The Perfect Store: Inside eBay* (Boston: Little, Brown and Co., 2002), 8.
6. Pierre Omidyar, "Feedback Forum," http://pages.ebay.com/services/forum/feedback-foundersnote.html (last visited June 30, 2005).
7. "Q&A With eBay's Pierre Omidyar," *BusinessWeek Online*, December 3, 2001, http://www.businessweek.co.za/magazine/content/01_49/b3760605.htm (last visited June 8, 2005).
8. Cohen, *Perfect Store*, 35.
9. Ibid., 35–37.
10. "Interview: Pierre Omidyar, Founder and Chairman, eBay." (Academy of Achievement).
11. Justin Hunt, "You've Got to Be Bidding; Online Auctions," *Internet World*, December 1, 1999. Another source says 1 million in early 1998. It was 9 million in the spring of 2005.
12. "Furby: Scams and Myths," *ScamBusters.org*, http://www.scambusters.org/Scambusters27.html (last visited June 8, 2005).
13. "Short Take: eBay pulls auction of user's unborn baby," *CNet News.com*, September 7, 1999, http://news.com.com/2110-1017-230687.html?legacy=cnet (last visited June 8, 2005).
14. B. J. Roche, "Peaks and Valleys," *Boston Globe*, March 26, 2000.
15. Cohen, *Perfect Store*, 202–4.
16. *Gentry v. eBay, Inc.*, 99 Cal. App. 4th 816, 121 Cal. Rptr. 2d 703 (Cal. App. 4th Dist. 2002).
17. Internet Fraud Complaint Center, "Internet Auction Fraud," May 2001, http://www.ifccfbi.gov/strategy/AuctionFraudReport.pdf (last visited June 8, 2005).
18. "Interview: Pierre Omidyar."
19. Robert Goff, "eBay's Cop," *Forbes Best of the Web*, June 25, 2001, http://www.forbes.com/best/2001/0625/042.html (last visited October 13, 2005).

20. Carrie Kirby, "Keeping Order Online," *San Francisco Chronicle*, January 28, 2001.
21. Goff, "eBay's Cop."
22. Ibid.
23. "Testimony of Robert Chestnut, Associate General Counsel for eBay, Inc., Before the Commerce, Justice and Judiciary Subcommittee of the Senate Appropriations Committee," February 16, 2000, http://www.cdt.org/security/dos/000216senate/ebay.html (last visited October 13, 2005).
24. eBay, "Security and Resolution Center," http://pages.ebay.com/securitycenter/howcontact.html (last visited June 8, 2005).
25. "Don't Get Netted by an Internet Cowboy," *Guardian Unlimited*, April 28, 2005, http://money.guardian.co.uk/experts/legal/story/0,11106,1471602,00.html (last visited October 13, 2005).
26. Ernie Miller, "eBay to Law Enforcement—We're Here to Help," *LawMeme*, February 17, 2004, http://research.yale.edu/lawmeme/modules.php?name=News&file=article&sid=925 (last visited June 8, 2005).
27. "Q&A with eBay's Pierre Omidyar," *BusinessWeek Online*, December 3, 2001.
28. Thomas Hobbes, *Leviathan*, ch. 18 (1651).
29. eBay Square Trade, http://www.squaretrade.com/cnt/jsp/odr/learn_odr.jsp;jsessionid=kidb68iit1?vhostid=daffy&stmp=ebay&cntid=kidb68iit1 (last visited August 18, 2005).
30. eBay User Agreement, http://pages.ebay.com/help/policies/user-agreement.html (last visited August 18, 2005).
31. Ibid.
32. Cohen, *Perfect Store*, 207.
33. "Square Trade is a MEDIATION Service . . .," *CNet News.com*, April 13, 2005, http://reviews.cnet.com/5208-10168-0-10.html?forumID=104&threadID=95269&messageID=1122605&start=-250 (last visited June 8, 2005).
34. Ibid.
35. See Russell Hardin, *Collective Action* (Baltimore: Johns Hopkins University Press, 1982).
36. See Dan Farber and Phillip Frickey, *Law and Public Choice: A Critical Introduction* (Chicago: University of Chicago Press, 1991).
37. William Patry, "The Failure of the American Copyright System: Protecting the Idle Rich," 72 *Notre Dame L. Rev.* 907, 932–33 (1997).
38. "eBay Assailed Over Nazi Memorabilia," *CNet News.com*, November 30, 1999, http://news.com.com/2100-1017-233729.html?legacy=cnet (last visited June 8, 2005); Shane Hegarty, "What Am I Bid For Adolf Hitler's Dessert Spoon?" *Irish Times*, January 24, 2004.
39. "Bazee.com Re-Brands as eBay.in," *Hindu Business Line*, March 23, 2005, http://www.blonnet.com/2005/03/23/stories/2005032301860400.htm (last visited October 14, 2005).
40. "eBay to Reach Out to Small Entrepreneurs," *Hindu Business Line*, June 7, 2005.
41. Khozem Merchant, "Yahoo in Talks on Stake in Online Unit Indiatimes," *Financial Times*, February 18, 2005.

42. "CEO Held Over Student Sex Video," *BBC News World Edition*, December 17, 2004, http://news.bbc.co.uk/2/hi/south_asia/4105753.stm (last visited June 8, 2005).
43. India Information Technology Act §67 http://www.naavi.org/cyberlaws/itbill2000/ch11.html (last visited August 18, 2005).
44. S. Rajagopalan, "US Keeps Watch, eBay Says it Will Decide on its Future in India," *Hindustan Times*, December 21, 2004.
45. The claims in this paragraph were true as of August 19, 2005. The economic data came from CIA World Factbook, available at http://www.cia.gov/cia/publications/factbook/ (last visited August 20, 2005).
46. See generally "Survey, Russia," *The Economist*, May 20, 2004.
47. Stephen Holmes, "What Russia Teaches Us Now: How Weak States Threaten Freedom," *American Prospect*, July 1, 1997, http://www.prospect.org/web/page.ww?section=root&name=ViewPrint&articleId=4812 (last visited August 18, 2005). For a more optimistic view of Russian society and the Russian economy, see Andrei Shleifer, *A Normal Country : Russia after Communism* (Cambridge, MA: Harvard University Press, 2005).
48. Cohen, *Perfect Store*, 303.

## Chapter 9

1. Bill Alpert, "Unholy Gains," *Barron's*, October 30, 2000.
2. "A Jurisdictional Tangle," *The Economist*, December 10, 2002.
3. *Dow Jones v. Gutnick*, [2002] HCA 56, 2002 AUST HIGHCT LEXIS 61, 34 (High Court of Australia).
4. Norrie Ross, "Gutnick Wins Suit Against Dow Jones," *Courier Mail* (Queensland, Australia), November 13, 2004.
5. Norrie Ross, "Dow Jones Apologises to Gutnick," *Herald Sun* (Melbourne, Australia), November 13, 2004.
6. Michael Cameron, "'Sore losers' take a swipe at Aussie libel laws," *Australian*, November 18, 2004.
7. Editorial, "A Blow to Online Freedom," *New York Times*, December 11, 2002.
8. Frances Cairncross, *The Death of Distance* (Cambridge, MA: Harvard Business School Press, 1997), 259.
9. Lawrence Lessig and Paul Resnick, "Zoning Speech on the Internet: A Legal and Technical Model," 98 *Mich.L. Rev.* 395, 395 (1999).
10. Ilan Saban, "Offensiveness Analyzed: Lessons for a Comparative Analysis of Free Speech Doctrines," 2 *Chicago-Kent J. Int. & Comp. L.* 60, 64, 73, 75 (2002), available at www.Kentlaw.edu/jicl/articles/Spring2002/Spring2002.
11. Ronald J. Krotoszynski, Jr., "A Comparative Perspective on the First Amendment: Free Speech, Militant Democracy, and the Primacy of Dignity as a Preferred Constitutional Value in Germany," 78 *Tul. L. Rev.* 1549, 1554, 1597 (2004).
12. Elissa A. Okoniewski, "*Yahoo!, Inc. v. LICRA*: The French Challenge to Free Expression on the Internet," 18 *Am. U. Int'l L. Rev.* 295 (2002).
13. 376 U.S. 254, 270 (1964).

14. *Theophanous v. Herald & Weekly Times* (1994) 182 C.L.R. 104, 134–35 (Austl. H.C.); see generally Michael Chesterman, *Freedom Of Speech In Australian Law: A Delicate Plant* (Burlington, VT: Ashgate Publishing Co., 2000), 42–43, 154–55, 175–78.
15. *Lange v. Australian Broadcasting Corp.*, (1997) 189 C.L.R. 520, 574 (Austl. H.C.).
16. See generally Alberto Alesina and Enrico Spolaore, *The Size of Nations* (Cambridge, MA: MIT Press, 2005).
17. We draw this example from Michael McConnell, "Federalism: Evaluating the Founders' Design," 54 *U. Chi. L. Rev.* 1484, 1494 (1987).
18. See generally Alberto Alesina and Enrico Spolaore, *Size of Nations*.
19. Boutros Boutros-Ghali, *An Agenda for Peace: Preventative Diplomacy, Peacemaking and Peace-keeping*, June 17, 1992, http://www.globalpolicy.org/reform/initiatives/ghali/1992/0617peace.htm (last visited October 15, 2005).
20. Matthew Rose, "Australia to Hear Web Libel Suit in Landmark Case," *Wall Street Journal*, December 11, 2002.
21. Trail Smelter Case (*U.S. v. Can.*), Arbitral Tribunal, 3 U.N. Rep. Int'l Awards (1941); see also *Pakootas v. Teck Cominco Minerals, Ltd.*, 2004 U.S. Dist. LEXIS 23041 (E.D. Wa. 2004).
22. On the points made in the last two paragraphs, see generally Jack L. Goldsmith, "Against Cyberanarchy," 65 *U. Chi. L. Rev.* 1199, 1210–12 (1998).
23. The only two exceptions to this rule—the only two circumstances in which international law permits a state to use coercive force in another state—are (a) when the United Nations Security Council authorizes the use of cross-border force, or (b) when a nation acts in "self-defense" in response to an armed attack by another nation. *Charter of the United Nations, Chapter VII, Arts. 42, 51.*
24. *Dow Jones v. Gutnick*, [2002] HCA 56, 2002 AUST HIGHCT LEXIS 61, 34 (High Court of Australia), 143.
25. Ibid.
26. For further elaboration of the points in the last two paragraphs, see *Against Cyberanarchy*; and Jack L. Goldsmith, "The Internet and the Abiding Significance of Territorial Sovereignty," 5 *Ind. J. Global Leg. Stud.* 475 (1998).
27. Declan McCullagh and Evan Hansen, "Libel Without Frontiers Shakes Net, "*CNet News.com*, December 11, 2002, http://news.com.com/Libel+without+frontiers+shakes+the+Net/2100-1023_3-976988.html?tag=nl (last visited June 8, 2005).
28. David R. Johnson and David Post, "Law and Borders—The Rise of Law in Cyberspace," 48 *Stan. L. Rev.* 1367, 1374 (1996).
29. Editorial, "Defamation and the Internet," *Sydney Morning Herald*, December 12, 2002, http://www.smh.com.au/articles/2002/12/11/1039379881288.html?oneclick=true (last visited August 19, 2005).
30. Glenn Reynolds, "High Court throws a spanner in the global networks," *Australian*, December 11, 2002.
31. American Bar Association, Michael Geist, Sub-Committee Chair, Business Law Section, Cyberspace Law Sub-Section, Internet Jurisdiction Sub-Committee, *Global Internet Jurisdiction: The ABA/ICC Survey* (2004), http://www.mgblog.com/resc/Global%20Internet%20Survey.pdf (last visited August 19, 2005).

# Chapter 10

1. Brendan I. Koerner, "From Russia with Lopht," *Legal Affairs*, June 2002.
2. Ibid.
3. "Russian Roulette," *CS Online*, January 2005, http://www.csoonline.com/read/010105/russian.html (last visited August 19, 2005).
4. Koerner, "From Russia with Lopht."
5. "FBI Agent Charged With Hacking," MSNBC, August 15, 2002, http://www.msnbc.com/news/563379.asp (last visited August 19, 2005).
6. See generally Neal Kumar Katyal, "Criminal Law in Cyberspace," 149 *U. Penn. L. Rev.* 1003 (2001). Cybercrime can also occur when traditional crimes are committed using the computer (e.g. using e-mail to plan a murder). For present purposes we ignore this category.
7. Jeri Clausing "In Hearing on 'Love Bug' Lawmakers Go After Software Industry," *New York Times*, May 11, 2000.
8. Cara Garretson and Jim Duffy, "Cybercrime: The Story Behind the Stats," *Network World*, November 29, 2004.
9. See generally Jack L. Goldsmith, "The Internet and the Legitimacy of Remote Cross-Border Searches," 2001 *U. Chi Legal. F.* 103 (2001).
10. Ibid.
11. Ibid.
12. See, e.g., Dina I. Oddis, "Combating Child Pornography on the Internet: The Council of Europe's Convention on Cybercrime," 16 *Temp. Int'l & Comp. L.J.* 477 (2002).
13. A list of signatories is provided on the Council of Europe's website at http://conventions.coe.int/Treaty/Commun/ChercheSig.asp?NT=185&CM=&DF=&CL=ENG.
14. See http://www.usdoj.gov/criminal/cybercrime/g82004/g8_background.html.
15. Jonathan Weinberg, "ICANN and the Problem of Legitimacy," 50 *Duke L. J.* 187, 209 (2000).
16. Esther Dyson, *Release 2.0: A Design for Living in the Digital Age* (New York: Broadway, 1997), 105,106.
17. "The Consensus Machine," *The Economist*, June 8, 2000.
18. Milton Mueller, "ICANN and Internet Governance: Sorting through the Debris of 'Self-Regulation,'" 1 *Info, the Journal of Policy, Regulation and Strategy for Telecommunications, Information and Media* No. 6, 497, 504 (1999).
19. Milton Mueller, *Ruling the Root* (Cambridge, MA: MIT Press, 2002), 198.
20. Ibid.
21. Ibid., 197.
22. Ibid.
23. "U.S. Principles on the Internet's Domain Name and Addressing System," http://www.ntia.doc.gov/ntiahome/domainname/USDNSprinciples_06302005.htm (last visited August 19, 2005).
24. Tom Wright, "EU and U.S. clash over control of the Net," *International Herald Tribune*, September 30, 2005.
25. Richard Wray, "EU Says Internet Could Fall Apart," *The Guardian*, October 12, 2005.

26. Bradley Clapper, "U.S. Insists on Keeping Control of the Web," *Business Week*, September 29, 2005.

27. Warren Giles, "U.S. Online Internet Gambling Plan May Be Challenged by Antigua," *Bloomberg News*, March 25, 2003.

28. United States—Measures Affecting the Cross-Border Supply of Gambling and Betting Services WT/DS285/R (04-2687), 10 Nov. 2004, para. 6.607.

29. Ibid., WT/DS285/R (05-1426), 7 April 2005, para. 327.

30. Federal Trade Commission, "Microsoft Settles FTC Charges Alleging False Security and Privacy Promises, August 8, 2002, http://www.ftc.gov/opa/2002/08/microsoft.htm (last visited June 8, 2005).

31. Article 29 Data Protection Working Party, "Working Document on On-line Authentication Services," adopted January 29, 2003, http://europa.eu.int/comm/justice_home/fsj/privacy/docs/wpdocs/2003/wp68_en.pdf (last visited June 9, 2005).

32. Council Directive 95/46/EC, 1995 O.J. (L 281) 31, http://www.cdt.org/privacy/eudirective/EU_Directive_.html (last visited July 24, 2005).

33. The Court of Justice of the European Communities, Press and Information Division, "Press Release No. 96/03: Judgment of the Court in Case C-101/01 Bodil Lindqvist," Nov. 6, 2003, http://www.curia.eu.int/en/actu/communiques/cp03/aff/cp0396en.htm (last visited June 9, 2005).

34. Article 29 Data Protection Working Party, "Privacy on the Internet—An Integrated EU Approach to On-line Data Protection," at 28, November 21, 2000 (applying the substantive law of a Member State under Article 4 in the context of cookies on hard drives in a Member State), http://europa.eu.int/comm/justice_home/fsj/privacy/docs/wpdocs/2000/wp37en.pdf (last visited August 19, 2005).

35. Richard Wilner, "Euro-Trashed—Gates Ordered to Split Windows, Media Player," *New York Post*, December 23, 2004.

36. Lisa Lucca and Tom Miles, "Microsoft Fixes Passport to Meet EU Privacy Rules," *Globe and Mail* (UK), January 31, 2003.

37. Matt Loney, "Microsoft Agrees to Passport Changes," *CNet News.com*, January 30, 2003, http://news.com.com/2100-1001-982790.html (last visited August 19, 2005); Francesco Guerrerra, "EU Forces Microsoft to Change Passport Program," *Financial Times*, January 31, 2003.

38. Kristi Heim, "Europe's Tough Privacy Rules Spill Over to U.S.," *San Jose Mercury News*, August 30, 2002, http://www.ehto.org/states/usa/toughprivacyrules.htm (last visited July 24, 2005).

39. Jeff Plungis, "How California Beat Detroit: Big 3 Lose Emissions Fight by Lacking Alternative Plan," *Detroit News*, July 14, 2002.

## Conclusion

1. Not all globalization writers share this view. A prominent exception, from whom we have learned much, is Daniel Drezner. See Daniel Drezner, *Who Rules? The Regulation of Globalization* (manuscript, 2005).

2. Thomas L. Friedman, *The Lexus and the Olive Tree: Understanding Globalization* (New York: Farrar, Straus & Giroux, 1999), 141.

3. Thomas L. Friedman, *The World is Flat: A Brief History of the Twenty-First Century* (New York: Farrar, Straus & Giroux, 2005), 8, 10, 176.

4. See Drezner, *Who Rules?*, chapters 1–2.
5. Robert Ellickson, *Order without Law: How Neighbors Settle Disputes* (1994; repr., Cambridge, MA: Harvard University Press, 2005).
6. Friedman, *World is Flat*, 454–55.
7. Jerry Mander, "The Homogenization of Global Consciousness: Media, Telecommunications and Culture," (2001), http://www.lapismagazine.org/manderprint.html.
8. As quoted in Friedman, *World is Flat*, 63.

# Index

Note: Page numbers in *italics* indicate photographs and illustrations.